REPROJECTING THE CITY
URBAN SPACE AND DISSIDENT SEXUALITIES IN
RECENT LATIN AMERICAN CINEMA

LEGENDA

LEGENDA is the Modern Humanities Research Association's book imprint for new research in the Humanities. Founded in 1995 by Malcolm Bowie and others within the University of Oxford, Legenda has always been a collaborative publishing enterprise, directly governed by scholars. The Modern Humanities Research Association (MHRA) joined this collaboration in 1998, became half-owner in 2004, in partnership with Maney Publishing and then Routledge, and has since 2016 been sole owner. Titles range from medieval texts to contemporary cinema and form a widely comparative view of the modern humanities, including works on Arabic, Catalan, English, French, German, Greek, Italian, Portuguese, Russian, Spanish, and Yiddish literature. Editorial boards and committees of more than 60 leading academic specialists work in collaboration with bodies such as the Society for French Studies, the British Comparative Literature Association and the Association of Hispanists of Great Britain & Ireland.

The MHRA encourages and promotes advanced study and research in the field of the modern humanities, especially modern European languages and literature, including English, and also cinema. It aims to break down the barriers between scholars working in different disciplines and to maintain the unity of humanistic scholarship. The Association fulfils this purpose through the publication of journals, bibliographies, monographs, critical editions, and the MHRA Style Guide, and by making grants in support of research. Membership is open to all who work in the Humanities, whether independent or in a University post, and the participation of younger colleagues entering the field is especially welcomed.

STUDIES IN HISPANIC AND LUSOPHONE CULTURES

Studies in Hispanic and Lusophone Cultures are selected and edited by the Association of Hispanists of Great Britain & Ireland. The series seeks to publish the best new research in all areas of the literature, thought, history, culture, film, and languages of Spain, Spanish America, and the Portuguese-speaking world.

The Association of Hispanists of Great Britain & Ireland is a professional association which represents a very diverse discipline, in terms of both geographical coverage and objects of study. Its website showcases new work by members, and publicises jobs, conferences and grants in the field.

Editorial Committee
Chair: Professor Trevor Dadson (Queen Mary, University of London)
Professor Catherine Davies (University of Nottingham)
Professor Andrew Ginger (University of Bristol)
Professor Hilary Owen (University of Manchester)
Professor Christopher Perriam (University of Manchester)
Professor Alison Sinclair (Clare College, Cambridge)
Professor Philip Swanson (University of Sheffield)

Managing Editor
Dr Graham Nelson
41 Wellington Square, Oxford OX1 2JF, UK

www.legendabooks.com/series/shlc

STUDIES IN HISPANIC AND LUSOPHONE CULTURES

Reprojecting the City

Urban Space and Dissident Sexualities in Recent Latin American Cinema

BENEDICT HOFF

LEGENDA

Studies in Hispanic and Lusophone Culture 13
Modern Humanities Research Association
2016

Published by Legenda
an imprint of the Modern Humanities Research Association
Salisbury House, Station Road, Cambridge CB1 2LA

ISBN 978-1-909662-46-9

First published 2016

Copy-Editor: Charlotte Brown

CONTENTS

❖

For my parents, and for George

ACKNOWLEDGEMENTS

The doctoral research on which this book is based would not have been possible without the financial support of the School of Modern Languages, Cultures and Area Studies at the University of Liverpool. I must also thank the Association of Hispanists of Great Britain and Ireland for partially funding the publication of this book following my success in their 2014 publishing competition.

During my research trip to Brazil and Argentina, staff at the following libraries and archives were extremely helpful in helping me source relevant material: the Cinemateca at the Museu de Arte Moderna, Rio de Janeiro; the FUNARTE Centro de Documentação, Rio de Janeiro; the UFF university library, Niterói; the Biblioteca Nacional, Buenos Aires and the Instituto Nacional de Cine y Artes Audiovisuales, Buenos Aires. Thanks also go to the staff and students at the Instituto de Arte e Comunicação at the Universidade Federal Fluminense for making my time as a visiting doctoral student so enjoyable and for providing such useful feedback on my initial pieces of written work. I must also thank Rob and Richard at O Veleiro guesthouse in Rio for their hospitality, friendship and support during my various visits to Rio and the unique insight they have given me into life in Brazil's 'marvelous city'.

Without the unwavering support and inspiration provided by my former PhD supervisors, Dr Lisa Shaw and Professor Richard Phillips, this project surely would not have been completed. I thank Richard for introducing me to the fascinating field of cultural geography and Lisa for her insight, attention to detail, patience and infectious enthusiasm. The project has also benefitted from the advice and suggestions of João Luiz Vieira, Alison Smith, Claire Taylor, Lúcia Sá, Rob Williams and George Taxidis, whom I also thank for their contributions. A special mention must also go to Charlotte Gleghorn who has been a constant presence throughout my academic career, both as a friend and colleague who has consistently encouraged and inspired me along the way. I would also like to acknowledge the inspiration provided by my former school teacher, Chris Hurley, who originally ignited my interest in Hispanic cultures.

Early versions of some of the material in this book have been published in journals and edited volumes, as follows. Parts of Chapter 2 were published in Portuguese in the journal *Contracampo* 19 (2008) and small sections of Chapter 5 were published in English in *Stars and Stardom in Brazilian Cinema* (London: Berghahn, 2016). I am grateful to the publishers for their permission to reproduce this material here. A big thank-you also to Karim, Janaina, Irit and in particular Kirsten at Studio Karim Aïnouz for obtaining on my behalf the book's wonderful cover image taken from Madame Satã [set film title in italics].

Finally, thanks must go to my friends and family, in particular my parents and my partner George, for always having faith in my abilities and providing support and affirmation when it has been most needed — these pages are dedicated to you.

A NOTE ON TRANSLATIONS
AND FILM REFERENCES

Translations relating to foreign language books, articles and journals are my own except otherwise stated. Translations relating to film dialogues and voiceovers relate to the translation provided on the DVD release, except where this translation is defective and I provide my own. Due to the large number of films I make passing reference too in my analysis, only the titles of the book's five focus films have been translated. In terms of country of origin, only the main country of production has been cited within the in-text references. Other production partners can be found for the relevant film within the filmography; this provides a list of all the films cited in this book. Definite and indefinite titles in Portuguese, Spanish, English and French have been ignored in the alphabetical ordering of films. All the dates and countries of production have been standardized using the data published on the Internet Movie Database.

LIST OF ILLUSTRATIONS

INTRODUCTION

'A Beautiful Sinister Fairyland'?

It is a hot afternoon in Santa Cruz, Bolivia's most populous city. Jessica, a young mestizo girl begins the long walk home from school to the poor working-class suburbs where she resides. On the way a large advertising billboard catches her attention. Staring down at her is an attractive, blond, blue-eyed boy (naked, of course, save his underpants) framed by two equally attractive, blonde, blue-eyed girls who drape themselves deferentially over the muscular demigod in their midst. 'Buy our underwear,' suggests the persuasive look in the models' eyes, 'and you too might be afforded the success with the opposite sex we so enjoy'. The advertisement is particularly resonant for Jessica because she too, like the girls in the advertisement, is also on a mission to 'get her man' at a *quinceañera* [sweet fifteen] party to be held later that evening. Before she leaves, however, her father is quick to remind her of the consequences of such overt demonstrations of female sexuality in her own particular social milieu and threatens to kill her if she were to end up pregnant and sully the family's honour. His warnings will fall on deaf ears.

Meanwhile, on the other side of town, a group of rich teenage boys prepare for a night out. They are going 'slumming', a practice which consists of gate-crashing these *quinceañera* parties and bedding the young female attendees who are easily seduced by their easy charm and false promises of a better life. This is where Jessica will meet the smooth-talking Fabián to whom she will lose her virginity and fall pregnant. While their brief communion has the potential to change the course of Jessica's life forever, for Fabián it is utterly forgettable and he soon leaves the party to join his friends on another popular ritual — cruising the streets in their SUV and intimidating the city's sex workers. The pair of cross-dressing male sex workers who tout for business at the same busy traffic intersection where Jessica earlier encountered the underwear advertisement are an easy target. As the vehicle speeds towards them a box is produced by one of the gang who proudly hands each of his friends a rotten egg. The tinted windows are then lowered and the vehicle slows sufficiently to ensure the boys a good aim, before the sex workers are duly pelted with the offending articles. The sex workers scream after the vehicle but the boys are too busy congratulating themselves on their mission to hear. 'Vermin', hisses one of the boys, 'they shouldn't even be allowed to breathe'. The vehicle then speeds into the night and on towards the local brothel where one of the younger boys is subsequently taken to lose his virginity.

These are not scenes from real life but are taken from Rodrigo Bellott's *Dependencia sexual* [*Sexual Dependency*] (2003), a Bolivian-US coproduction charting

FIG. 0.1. Culture clash: Jessica examines the RiGO BoSD advertisement in
Dependencia sexual (Rodrigo Bellott, 2003: Wellspring Media)

the disparate (sexual) lives of four teenagers living on opposite sides of the equator
and for which the underwear advertisement serves as a binding motif.[1] I begin
with it here because it highlights some of those 'standard issue' representations that
have come to inform our (western) imagination of Latin American cities and the
sexual life within them.[2] These cities are spaces where the legacies of colonialism
collide with the realities of twenty-first-century global capitalism to produce
highly fractured cityscapes of violence and gaping social inequality where, beneath
a particularly rampant form of sexual proclivity, lurks a triple menace of machismo,
misogyny and homophobia. E. A. Lacey alluded to this (perceived) erotic edginess
in an essay for the Gay Sunshine Press entitled 'Latin America: Myths and Realities'
(first published in 1978) in which he proclaimed somewhat sensationally that:

> Latin America was seen as being — with that exasperating quality of paradox
> that inevitably creeps into our perception of the alien and the unfamiliar —
> both magical and menacing, a beautiful, sinister fairyland where the usual rules
> of logic were suspended and anything good or bad might happen, and usually
> did. (Lacey 1991: 481)

Dependencia sexual's vision is perhaps rather less sanguine and the innovative use
of split screen, employed throughout almost the entirety of the film, brings the
experience of city living and urban sexual life in Bolivia into stark relief with
that of metropolitan USA. In Santa Cruz, sexual oppression (and its negotiation)
can, in particular, be read as a more general allegory of (under)development in
Bolivia. It is not that discrimination does not exist in the USA envisaged by
Bellott, but the film seems to imply that the American characters unlike their
Bolivian counterparts have, through the highly institutionalized form of identity
politics of the university campus, developed the emancipatory tools with which
to negotiate this discrimination. A female student named Adina, for example, like
Jessica, similarly had to endure the misogynistic impulses of her father when she
was growing up, and the appearance of Jessica in the left-hand screen at several

points in the fourth story directly aligns the two girls' experiences. In turn, a gay character named Jeremiah, like the cross-dressing sex workers, similarly incurs the wrath of (supposedly) heterosexual, sexually insecure young men who subject him to a torrent of homophobic abuse in the gymnasium locker room. It is difficult to imagine Jessica, however, joining a women's theatre group or being given the opportunity to study women's literature and develop the sort of militant (black) feminist consciousness we associate with Adina. Nor is it likely that the two male sex workers would have the luxury of exchanging an evening's work on the streets in order to attend one of the 'sexuality workshops' that Jeremiah leads at the university's LGBTQ (Lesbian, Gay, Bisexual, Transgender and Queer) society to develop confidence and self-esteem around their gender identity and profession.

From this perspective, the split screen which so characterizes *Dependencia sexual* alludes not only to the 'fractured' nature of Latin American cities, but to a broader set of oppositions through which their relationship with the rest of the world has been envisaged. Most obviously oppositions between centre and periphery, but, concomitantly, between 'us and them', rich and poor, modern and traditional, included and excluded, empowered and marginalized, the west and the rest. From this perspective, the dividing line between the two screens can be said to represent a division between what are often perceived, as Richard Parker puts it, to be 'two distinct moral universes, north and south of the equator' (1999: 1). Each corresponds to two apparently very different sexual cultures:[3] one which is predominantly white, Anglo-Saxon, 'civilized' and 'tolerant', but where 'development' has been achieved with the inevitable loss of a certain degree of libidinal vitality; and the other, which is predominantly mestizo, Latino, inherently 'uncivilized', but whose under-development allows it to retain something inherently 'primal', rendering it both 'sinister' and 'beautiful', to evoke the rather tawdry allure of Lacey's phraseology.

Reprojecting the City destabilizes this dividing line, disrupts such oppositions and renders them less presumably indestructible, showing how the image of Latin American cities has been reprojected in recent cinematic representation and asking how this reprojection disturbs and unsettles these broader, global geographies of sexuality and the assumptions and values around which they have been constructed.

FIG. 0.2. 'Beautiful sinister fairyland'? Cross-dressing sex-workers pelted with rotten eggs in *Dependencia sexual* (Rodrigo Bellott, 2003: Wellspring Media)

In particular, it asks what new light this filmic depiction of urban dissident sexualities can shed on the processes of capitalism, globalization and urban development in the region, which all too often are conceived of in negative, reductionist terms. How, for example, does the representation of metropolitan sexualities decentre and deconstruct the idea of a homogeneous globalized urban gay culture? How does this representation relocate the centres of regulation with regards to bodies and same-sex desire and disturb our understanding of global cultural flows in terms of their direction and mediation? Does the representation of more disruptive practices such as S/M speak of their capacity to subvert and redefine the dominant power relations underpinning the modern industrial city?[4] Does the queer body stand here for 'liberation', or 'the liberation of capital to achieve its aims'?[5] Are the metropolitan margins envisaged simply as having been 'left behind' or are they constructed as alternative sexualized spaces of resistance and empowerment? And how does the representation of dissident sexual cultures in these spaces force us to re-evaluate our perception of exactly where and when the globalization of sexuality began?

Cinema, Dissident Sexualities and the City

But why cinema and why dissident sexualities? What can they tell us about Latin American cities, their development and their relationship with the wider world that the 'real' stuff of human geography and urban studies cannot? Films, after all, are 'mere' representations which at their best inform, at their worst distract, but which are always inferior to the supposedly unedited reality with which social scientists have traditionally concerned themselves. In turn, dissident sexualities and their associated subcultures are merely curious, but nevertheless inconsequential, by-products of the urban process of little interest to 'serious' researchers. Or so conventional wisdom has had us believe. Thankfully a full-scale revision of these attitudes has been underway for some time now. The work of scholars such as David Clarke, Stuart Aitken, Mark Shiel and Chris Lukinbeal, amongst others, has elevated film geography to an important emerging specialism within cultural geography which itself has asserted itself as one of the most vibrant subfields of human geography and, amidst a more general 'spatial turn' within the academe, a vital inter-disciplinary bridge between the social sciences and the humanities.[6] The likes of David Bell, Gill Valentine, Michael Brown, Jon Binnie, Richard Phillips and Kath Browne, in turn, continue to unearth the centrality of sexuality, both in its heteronormative and dissident forms, to the production of space.[7] There has, however, been only limited cross-pollination between these two trends, with essays on cinematic urbanism marked by a certain western/heterocentrism, whilst research into space and (dissident) sexualities within cultural geography has tended towards the mapping of literary geographies, often in relation to the cities of the global north. *Reprojecting the City* thus takes contemporary currents in a new, exciting direction not only by adopting a Latin American, majority-world focus, but by firmly locating itself at the intersection of film studies, gender/queer studies and urban studies.[8]

And there is an inherent logic to this, since these three phenomena have always been natural bedfellows. Ever since the Lumière brothers' first ever celluloid depiction of urban life as it unfolded outside a factory in Lyon (*La sortie des usines*, 1895), cities have provided immense inspiration for filmmakers, their plethora of physical and social spaces, diverse populations and the pluralities and contradictions these inevitably produce, all providing fertile subject matter. As cinema developed as a profit-making industry, filmmakers also became increasingly reliant on the city as a primary source of spectatorship for their films, whilst the cinema theatres themselves, with the rise of more privatized forms of entertainment such as radio, television and computer games, played an important role in the maintenance and/or reinvigoration of city centres as (profitable) spaces of leisure and entertainment. Film-going was, as James Donald writes in the context of 1960s America, 'a way of "going out" that blended seamlessly with this new culture of "staying in"' (2010: 323).

Indeed, as Donald goes on to note, cinema has also played a fundamental role in consolidating urban suburbs, with the need to expand the basis for profit ensuring the spread of cinemas throughout the city so that as much of the population as possible was in striking distance of a theatre, a model which has been repeated throughout much of the industrialized world (2010: 323). As such, the suburbs, albeit in a highly commodified and generic form, have become centres of entertainment in themselves, subsuming another function of the city traditionally the domain of 'downtown'. In this sense, it is not just the genesis of the shopping mall which has contributed to the rapid decentring of our urban landscapes, but also the cinema complexes which are almost always now contained within them.[9] Like branded clothing, pop music, MP3 players and food and drink items, the films projected onto the big screen are also products through which civic identity and our individual and collective relationships with the rest of the world are increasingly negotiated.

On a formal level too, parallels between the city and the cinema cannot be underestimated. Of all cultural forms, cinema undoubtedly has developed the shrewdest ability to express the nuances of urban life, with cinematography, *mise-en-scène*, location filming, lighting and editing coalescing to express the pace and spatial complexity of cities in a manner to which the written word and static painted or photographic images can only allude. Our respective experiences of cinema and the city also bear striking similarities. Distraction and anonymity are both sensations we have come to associate with urban life *and* film viewing. The city's sense of speed and our rapid-fire experience of a rollercoaster of different emotions — fear, anticipation, elation, dread and so on — when traversing its spaces have also become stock features of the cinema-going experience which we now require and expect when visiting our local multiplex. From one perspective this endless assault on the human senses is perhaps having the overall effect of producing ever more 'blasé' city inhabitants as Georg Simmel argued in 1903, and by extension, we might argue, cinema goers too.[10] And yet from another, our fascination with the city and our hunger for its experience, whether that be in 'reality' or in front of the cinema screen, shows no sign of abating. Indeed, we might suggest that, as our urban fabric becomes ever more dislocated, the material relationship between the city and this most fragmented form of story-telling is set to grow ever more intricate.

Latin America itself has a rich history of critical urban cinema. The release of Luís Buñuel's acclaimed *Los olvidados* in 1950 was a watershed moment in this respect, its powerfully unsentimental portrayal of childhood misfortune in a Mexico City slum providing audiences both in Mexico and abroad with a stark counterpoint to the rather exoticized version of 'Latin Americana' they had previously been fed on the silver screen. In Brazil following a brief flirtation with an American-style studio system (which ended abruptly in 1954 with the collapse of the São Paulo-based Vera Cruz studios) *cinema novo* [new cinema] directors such as Nelson Pereira dos Santos were beginning their own social realist cinematic inquiry into urban Brazil, of which Dos Santos's *Rio, 40 Graus* (1955) and *Rio, Zona Norte* (1957) serve as two pertinent examples. The stark depictions of Buenos Aires's underbelly portrayed in Lautaro Murúa's *Alias Gardelito* (1961) and Leonardo Favio's *Crónica de un niño solo* (1965), in turn, signalled the mood of change present at the time in Argentina, where calls for an alternative critical, realist national cinema would later coalesce into the formation of the Grupo Cine Liberación by directors such as Fernando Solanas and Octavio Getino, responsible for the seminal *La hora de los hornos* (1970).

More recently, critical cinematic mediations of the urban condition have typically corresponded to the region's much maligned experience of neoliberalism and insertion into a globalized economy. In this respect, Alejandro González Iñárritu's *Amores perros* (Mexico, 2000), Fernando Meirelles's *Cidade de Deus* (Brazil, 2002) or Fabián Bielinski's *Nueve reinas* (Argentina, 2000) immediately come to mind as three of the most highly-acclaimed and/or commercially successful Latin American films made in the first decade of the twenty-first century, though less internationally-renowned productions such as Verónica Chen's *Vagón fumador* (Argentina, 2001) or Adrián Caetano and Bruno Stagnaro's *Pizza, birra, faso* (Argentina, 1998) also provide highly apposite accounts of the contradictions inherent in Latin American city living. Such representations, have, in turn, prompted a new wave of academic inquiry into cinematic and other cultural mediations of the city, of which Joanna Page's *Crisis and Capitalism in Contemporary Argentine Cinema* (2009), Jens Andermann and Álvaro Fernández Bravo's *New Argentine Cinema: Reality Effects* (2013), Lúcia Sá's *Life in the Megalopolis: Mexico City and São Paulo* (2004), David William Foster's *Mexico City in Contemporary Mexican Cinema* (2002) and Lúcia Nagib's *Brazil on Screen: Cinema Novo, New Cinema, Utopia* (2007) all serve as pertinent examples. These trends form part of a wider phenomenon in which visions of city living from the 'margins' are beginning to intrude upon the global spatial imagination, reprojecting and redefining our hitherto western-centric, and often limiting, understandings of urban life. The genesis of the megalopolis coupled with the increasing transnational reach of flourishing film and television industries which now extend beyond their traditional markets means we are just as likely to encounter images of Lagos, Mexico City, Mumbai, Rio de Janeiro, Hong Kong, Beijing, São Paulo and Shanghai as we are London, Paris, Berlin, New York and Los Angeles.

But what of sexuality, in particular its dissident forms? What relationship does this occupy in relation to cinema and the city? At this point it might be useful to return momentarily to *Dependencia sexual*, a film that can be situated within this contemporary body of urban cinema and which arguably takes its cues from González Iñárritu's rather better-known and critically/commercially

FIG. 0.3. Putting Latin American cities on the map: Mexico City in *Amores perros* (Alejandro González Iñárritu, 2000: Optimum Releasing)

successful *Amores perros*. Like *Amores perros*, Bellott's film is similarly fragmented into distinct, but overlapping narrative segments, protagonized by characters from highly contrasting social backgrounds whose worlds periodically collide. The fictional RiGO BoSD underwear advertisement which forms the central binding motif for these seemingly disparate stories, similarly recalls the Enchant perfume advertisement that asserts such a presence in the lives of the Mexico City inhabitants González Iñárritu's film seeks to depict.[11] Indeed, Tyler, the American underwear model in Bellott's film, like Enchant model Valeria, also appears in the film as one of the principal protagonists. But whilst, in these respects, *Dependencia sexual*, despite its innovative use of split screen, might ultimately be deemed as being somewhat derivative, the advertisement itself is used to differing effect. In *Amores perros*, Valeria's image, both as it is manufactured by Enchant for consumption by the characters of the diegetic world and how it is later presented to us, the viewer, after her horrific accident, is mobilized as a cipher for the destructive nature of consumer society in a general sense, which is positioned as a contributing factor to the syndromes of crime and violence with which Mexico City is afflicted. Here, the pleasure derived from consumerism seemingly has less to do with the state of owning a given product, or enriching a collection of pre-existing items, rather those 'incandescent and glorious moments' of sale and purchase (Sarlo 2001: 21).[12] It is significant in this respect that, Octavio, for example, does not steal the car in which he plans to escape Mexico City with Ramiro's wife, but purchases it with money earned in the city's parallel criminal economy, specifically that of dog fighting. Similarly, Ramiro does not shoplift the Sony Walkman he proudly gives to his wife in one scene, but rather purchases it with the proceeds of an armed raid on a local pharmacy that he was involved in.

Dependencia sexual's inquiry into the repercussions of the advertising image present within its own story differs in the sense that it is articulated specifically in relation to the sexualized nature of this image, which according to the film's press pack, is concerned with 'a political economy of beauty — a beauty which is still only white, skinny, blonde and blue-eyed' (Bellott 2003) and which Tyler so aptly embodies. In contrast to *Amores perros*, however, membership of the world envisaged by RiGO BoSD appears to be less contingent on the purchasing of material goods (although some of the characters do buy into the brand) and more related to participation in the sexual act itself, of which there are multiple images through the course of the film's narrative. Each of these acts, however, wholeheartedly fails to prove what it sets out to do, and here the film proposes this world as little more than a simulacrum whose ideals, for the characters concerned, are largely unattainable. And yet, of course, this unattainability is, in many respects, the key to successful advertising. As Henri Lefebvre writes: 'the body as represented by images of advertising [...] serves to fragment desire and doom it to anxious frustration, to the non-satisfaction of local needs' (1991: 310). This frustration, in turn, stimulates a constant craving in the consumer for more. In *Dependencia sexual*, with the full relevance of the film's title perhaps now a little clearer, the consequences are far reaching — a damaging sense of personal malaise and self-loathing amongst its protagonists, manifested through repeated episodes of homophobic, misogynistic and racial abuse.

The above discussion is important because it reveals sexuality as the third (but often ignored) party in this cinema-city relationship, one that is tangentially located between the concepts concerned. For if, as Michel Foucault proposed in his seminal work *The History of Sexuality, Volume 1* (1978), we might conceive of sexuality not as an essential, pre-given characteristic of the self but rather a 'technology of power' that has been 'produced' and 'deployed' since the nineteenth century, then we must also recognize the importance of the city in this process. The original 'need' for sexuality, can, in the first instance, arguably be traced back to the development of cities as major centres of industry, for it was here where the human body now required its closest supervision in order to maintain industrial productivity and ensure the continued expansion of labour power. This came in the form of what Foucault terms 'bio-power', a set of diverse techniques and strategies elaborated in order to achieve 'the subjugation of bodies and the control of populations', of which the deployment of sexuality itself, he argues, would become one of the most important (1978: 140).[13] It would, in turn, be within cities where sexualities would be produced and from where sexual discourses would ultimately be disseminated. As Richard Phillips and Diane Watt write in *Decentring Sexualities: Politics and Representations Beyond the Metropolis*, Foucault's account contains a 'hidden geography' corresponding to the religious, legal, medical and political institutions who oversaw these processes (and continue to do so) and which are generally located in metropolitan urban centres (2000: 1). Dissident sexualities and cultures have also historically thrived within cities, not only due to the anonymity of cities and the corresponding ability they afford for evading surveillance but also by way of their liberatory potential, for it is here, as Phillips and Watt subsequently note, where the emancipatory movements which shadow those institutions that discursively constitute and regulate sexualities are also broadly located (2000: 1).

And it is amidst this issue of visibility where cinema, in turn, reinserts itself into the equation. One of the central foundations on which Foucault's *History of Sexuality* was written was the idea that the 'deployment' of sexuality was, contrary to popular belief, concerned less with the repression of sex but more with a modern compulsion to speak incessantly about it:

> For many years, we have all been living in the realm of Prince Mangogul: under the spell of an immense curiosity about sex, bent on questioning it, with an insatiable desire to hear it speak and be spoken about, quick to invent all sorts of magical rings that might force it to abandon its indiscretion. (Foucault 1978: 77)

If this is the case then, as Linda Williams argues in *Hardcore: Power, Pleasure and the Frenzy of the Visible* in reference to Foucault's invocation of Diderot's 1748 fable *Les Bijoux indiscrets* cited above, amidst this modern compulsion to find 'the magic that will speak sex', the motion picture, has surely been the most recent manifestation of such 'magic' (Williams 1989: 2). This is because cinema, in addition to its deft ability to capture the complexities of urban life, also constitutes — and much more so than painting or even photography — a particularly apposite method of representing the human body and the cadences of its movement through space either as an individual entity or in interaction with other bodies. Films essentially 'tell' through 'showing' which, as Williams continues, means that we are now able to satisfy our curiosity about sex directly, to locate ourselves as 'invisible voyeurs positioned to view the sex "act" itself rather than only hearing about it' (1989: 3). In this sense, she conjectures, it has become possible to satisfy, and further incite, 'the desire not only for pleasure' but also 'the pleasure of knowing pleasure' (1989: 3).

Whilst Williams's discussion is articulated in the specific context of pornography, the 'speaking sex phenomenon' has not only been fundamental to the circulation and entrenchment of hegemonic sexual discourses (pornography, she argues, despite its seemingly 'deviant' status is, in actual fact, characteristically defined by the 'typical' or 'normal' behaviour associated with heterosexual male sexuality), but also their critical, non-heteronormative counter-discourses too. These have recognized the need to address the longstanding silence and/or negativity surrounding same-sex desire and to announce this desire not only as existent but also as valid and legitimate. It comes as no surprise, then, that within the more general context of sexual liberation in the USA, as David William Foster notes, the public display of homoerotic gestures, acts, rituals and practices became, in the 1970s, central to the conquest of gay rights in order to confirm 'not only the erotic liaison between individuals but the centrality those liaisons have in their lives' (2003: 82). Cinema again (in both its conventional and pornographic forms), for the reasons stated in the previous paragraph, would become synonymous with this 'display imperative', as he puts it (2003: 82).

Many such films released in the last thirty years or so in Latin America have evidenced their own 'display imperative', even if this cannot always be neatly aligned with the identity issues or 'coming out' narratives often associated with a self-consciously 'lesbian', 'gay' or 'queer' brand of cinema. Some pertinent examples would be *O beijo da mulher aranha* (Brazil, 1986), *Doña Herlinda y su hijo* (Mexico, 1985), *Fresa y chocolate* (Cuba, 1993), *En el paraíso no existe el dolor* (Mexico, 1995), *No se*

FIG. 0.4. The 'display imperative' evident in *El cielo dividido*
(Julián Hernández, 2006: Strand Releasing)

lo digas a nadie (Peru, 1998) and *La virgen de los sicarios* (Colombia, 2000, see Chapter 3). David William Foster's *Queer Issues in Contemporary Latin American Cinema* (2003) leads the sizeable bibliography for these films which no doubt will merit further academic attention for many years to come. However, a critical lacuna has emerged relating to films produced in the first two decades of the twenty-first century such as *Madame Satã* (Brazil, 2002, see Chapter 5), *Dependencia sexual* (Bolivia/USA, 2003, see Introduction and Postscript), *Amarelo manga* (Brazil, 2002, see Chapter 4), *Tan de repente* (Argentina, 2002), *Un año sin amor* (Argentina, 2005, see Chapter 2), *El cielo dividido* (Mexico, 2006, see Chapter 2), *Contracorriente* (Peru, 2009), *La león* (Argentina, 2007) and *Eu não quero voltar sozinho* (Brazil, 2010). Gustavo Subero's excellent *Queer Masculinities in Latin American Cinema: Male Bodies and Narrative Representations* (2014) moves towards bridging this critical lacuna as well as taking forward the discussion into new territory through his insightful analysis of Brazilian pornographic films. *Reprojecting the City* builds on this bibliography in the specific context of the celluloid city, through the analysis of five key films produced since the year 2000 whose representations are intimately bound up with the city.[14]

By locating itself at the intersection of cinema, dissident sexualities and the city, this book assumes, then, not a mutual exclusivity on the part of these three concepts but an intimate interaction between them. (Re)positioned in dialectical relation with one another they coalesce within my analysis at a conceptual 'sweet-spot', emerging as bi-directional lenses through which to observe, and shed light on, the other. And by examining how urban space produces dissident sexualities in Latin American cinema and how, in turn, dissident sexualities (re)produce the celluloid landscape, I propose that the dividing line between these 'two moral universes' represented by *Dependencia sexual*'s split screen might begin to be dissolved, thus destabilizing broader oppositions which structure the global spatial imagination.

In this sense, my analysis tends to shift backwards and forwards, always attentive to the potential interplay between centre and periphery, the local and the global. My discussion is particularly concerned with problematizing the sometimes atomized conceptions of 'Latin American' sexualities within the social sciences and cultural studies. Here supposedly 'modern-', 'western-' influenced models of organizing sexual desire around a politics of identity are often attributed to a white, predominantly male, educated, urban middle-class elite, whilst those residing in the metropolitan margins and in rural areas are seen as having to 'make do' with their own, traditional distinctively 'Latin American' (read less progressive) model.

As the films themselves clearly show, such delineations have always been a great deal messier. Latin America is a region defined by syncretism and hybridity where centre and periphery, local and global, far from existing as discrete categories, constantly infiltrate and redefine each other. Certainly the 'west' has never had a monopoly on ideas about 'gay identity' and some men and women in Latin America were organizing their sexual desire around a lived identity long before the Stonewall riots of 1969, the point at which we are often led to believe that 'it all began'. In this respect my analysis moves beyond the well-trodden narratives of subalternity and dependency and seeks to relocate the so-called 'periphery' to the centre of things. Here Latin American cinematic cities emerge, I argue, not merely as spaces of prejudice, discrimination, exclusion and violence, but also as ones of hope, empowerment and productive possibility, firmly imbricated in the global (re)production of sexualities and sexual discourses.

Approach, Structure and Progression

In terms of its approach, the book strives for a flexible and nuanced reading of the films which cuts through the frequently polarized debates currently occurring within the academe in this domain. Combining contextual information about sexuality and the urban process in the cities concerned with close readings of the films, the analyses are informed by a sophisticated, syncretic theoretical framework which synthesizes ideas from a range of disciplines including queer theory, gender studies, urban studies, postcolonial theory, postmodern theory and cultural geography. Whilst I argue the (imagined) geography implicit in Foucault's writings to be somewhat problematic, I regard his discussions on the body and power as useful and important. In this respect, overall what dominates through the book is a queer Foucauldian perspective in the sense that it sees sexuality as a form of power and knowledge which has been discursively produced, and deployed, as he puts it, in order to multiply and diversify techniques of social control. From this perspective the concept of 'liberation' must be viewed with a degree of suspicion in that according to this relational concept of power, it can never wholly assume a position of exteriority with regards to hegemonic power structures. As I argue in Chapter 1, this perspective does not preclude the idea of self-empowerment, it is just that it sees this self-empowerment in terms of resistance rather than liberation per se. And, as the title of the book suggests, it is here where the 'dissident' nature of the sexualities represented in the films resides.

Chapter 1 outlines the scope of the book as a specifically critical intervention, mapping the theoretical and contextual terrain on which the remaining chapters are built. It will be particularly useful for students and researchers of film studies and cultural geography who are unfamiliar with Latin American cultures, as well as Latin Americanists interested in film geography and issues relating to space, gender and sexuality. Returning to *Dependencia sexual*, Chapter 1 begins by exploring the historical roots of this bifurcated vision of sexuality embodied by the split screen, how it has come to be replicated within the social sciences and cultural studies and why it is problematic. In teasing out the spatial dimensions of sexuality and its relationship to capitalism and urban life, I acknowledge that the impulse to speak back to homogenizing narratives of 'gay liberation' is understandable given the very different way in which capitalist modernity has played out in Latin American cities. However, I argue that 'speaking back' has often verged on the fetishization of difference, which overlooks the inherent transnationality of Latin American sexualities (both in their normative and dissident forms) thereby creating a false 'other'. Whilst in this respect I highlight the shortcomings of dependency theory and postcolonial perspectives on the Latin American urban condition in its privileging of narratives of domination, I also remain cognizant of the limits of the sometimes overly-optimistic counter-responses from postmodern thinkers who may overestimate the potential for agency and localized transformative practice on the margins. It is here where I propose an analytical approach that cuts through these polarized opposing positions and make my case for the highly syncretic but ultimately queer methodology used in my analysis of the films which follows.

Chapters 2 and 3 progress this discussion in the context of contemporary film, looking at how the cinematic representation of Buenos Aires and Medellín reproject, in very different ways, this imagined geography of dissident sexuality, and, in turn, our perception of Latin American metropolitan centres more generally and what this designation (metropolitan) implies. Buenos Aires, in particular, has often been quoted as a city that has been particularly susceptible to trends originating elsewhere, what Alan Sinfield might term 'a localized version of the metropolis'. Focusing on Anahí Berneri's *Un año sin amor* [*A Year Without Love*] Chapter 2 examines how in the film tensions between spaces of globalized homonormative gay culture and those of the more underground yet similarly internationalized and commodified S/M scene challenge the idea of Buenos Aires merely as a 'receiver city' (and the notion of co-optation and slavish replication this implies) and instead locate it as part of a highly decentred supra-territorial space. I also consider how the HIV virus is represented here as an alternative metaphor for globalization which fractures the supposedly umbilical relationship between capitalism and gay identity and redefines who exactly is 'included' and 'excluded' from the spaces of mainstream gay culture.

Chapter 3 then moves on to Barbet Schroeder's *La virgen de los sicarios* [*Our Lady of the Assassins*], considering how this relationship is played out in the context of a different kind of globalized city (Medellín) where urban modernity is envisaged largely as deriving from the underground economy of the drug cartels. Particularly important here are the processes of urban socio-spatial realignment imaged in the film, whereby organized crime and illegal transnational flows of capital appear to collapse the once peripheral *comunas* into the centre, dehermeticizing previously distinct social groupings and accompanying cultural models. By showing how 'modern' metropolitan models of dissident sexuality and associated spaces are reclaimed by those once on the periphery, I argue that the film provides, as does Berneri's production, an important intervention in terms of redefining both the 'global city' and the 'global gay'.

Chapters 4 and 5 examine how the 'metropolitan' — both on the level of the spatial and the sexual — has been reimagined through marginal filmic perspectives from within the gaps and fissures that characterize this now highly dislocated urban fabric. Drawing on Phillips and Watt's ideas in *Decentring Sexualities*, I look at how films construct these gaps and fissures as 'in-between' spaces of both power and danger. Here, removed from the regulation of the centre, hegemonic sexualities may be least stable and most open to challenge. Sexual minorities themselves, though, may be less able to speak for and defend themselves due to their distance from the emancipatory institutions also located at this centre. Chapter 4 deploys this conjecture in relation to the depiction of Recife Antigo, the old dilapidated centre of the north-eastern Brazilian city of Recife, presented in *Amarelo manga* [*Mango Yellow*]. I foreground the contradictions of this space, constructed in the film as one of sexual proclivity and perversion but in which 'liberation' serves as an irrelevant luxury on a laundry list of more basic needs. In turn, I read misogyny, domestic violence and homophobia in the film not as 'natural' expressions of 'traditional' north-eastern masculinity but rather as shifting gender roles prompted by modern economic restructuring and informalization of labour markets in the North East.

Chapter 5 takes forward this idea that supposedly 'marginal' spaces are, in fact, deeply implicated in both national and global modes of economic and cultural production and consumption, in the context of the 1920s and 1930s Lapa (Rio de Janeiro) depicted by *Madame Satã* [*Madame Satan*]. I look at what the film's representation of this bohemian demi-monde has to say about early manifestations of globalization and the productive potential of such in-between spaces, where even before the growth of supra-territorial space, marginalized groups in Lapa, Harlem and Montmartre were bypassing the regulation of the centre and establishing their own trans-local dialogues. I then come back to the discussion of Chapter 1, showing how the protagonist's experience of homosexual identity and community challenges the notion of 'global queering' as an entirely contemporary phenomenon driven by the global north. The film is an apt one with which to finish in that it speaks loudly of sexual cultures beyond the west who have their own histories and their own futures and who shape, not just absorb, wider, global trends.

In the Postscript, 'Queer Afterthoughts', I resume the framing discussion of *Dependencia sexual* where this book begins, revealing the twist in Bellott's tale. The split screen, I argue, is symbolic of the *dualities* inherent in contemporary city living and the experience of urban sexual subcultures north and south of the equator rather than the divisions to which, as I argued in the Introduction, the film initially seems to allude. Finally, I restate my case for queer theory, arguing for its continued relevance both to cultural studies and contemporary sexuality politics.

A Note on Bibliography and Choice of Films

In a final matter for consideration, it would seem important to explain briefly my choice of films examined in the chapters which follow and what kind of decisions informed these choices. Nationality inevitably played a role, in so far as Brazil, Argentina and, to a lesser extent, Colombia, are the Latin American countries with which I am most familiar and possess the firmest grounding regarding their respective histories, cultures and cinematic production, hence the presence of films from these countries. The date of production was another significant consideration. As the book title states, I am chiefly examining *recent* examples of Latin American cinema which, in this context, means the period 2000–2006. This reflects my desire to avoid replicating the already sizeable bibliography relating to queer-marked Latin American films produced in the twentieth century and to respond to the critical lacuna that has emerged amongst a more recent body of films produced in the opening two decades of the twenty-first century. Unsurprisingly, the most important influencing factor in my choice of films, however, concerns the strong presence asserted both by the city and dissident sexualities within the respective narrative worlds of the films and the potential each offers for rigorous investigation of the interplay *between* these two concepts, which, of course, forms the foundation of this book.

The chapters that follow therefore do not claim to provide an exhaustive, *geographically balanced* account of the cinema-city relationship in the Latin American context. Indeed, although the book makes reference to over ninety films from Latin America and beyond for context and breadth, readers will notice that the main corpus is relatively small by film studies standards. This somewhat conservative focus reflects my concern that adequate space be given in which to situate each film within its particular local/national context. All too often books attempting region-wide studies try to cover as many films from as many countries in a bid for broader commercial appeal. The risk, however, is producing little more than a whistle-stop tour of Latin American cinema from which the term 'Latin America' itself emerges as a homogenizing concept that annihilates difference and overlooks the local and the specific.

Chapters 2–5 can therefore best be considered each as four separate but interlinked interventions mapping four diverse cinematic geographies which together might contribute to a much broader interdisciplinary process of critically reprojecting our understanding of urban space and dissident sexualities in the majority world.

My discussion also does not claim to account for *all* the multiple expressions of sex in (urban) space that have been envisaged in recent Latin American cinema. The reader will notice, in particular, the absence of films dealing with female same-sex desire and lesbian relationships in my discussion. This I acknowledge as a potential weakness that runs the risk of replicating a more general trend within the academe which has traditionally privileged the discussion of male same-sex desire. In the context of this book, however, this absence reflects the still limited number of Latin American productions dealing expressly with lesbian relationships where the city exerts a strong enough presence within the films' narrative worlds to be included in a study of this nature. A notable exception is Diego Lermán's *Tan de repente* (Argentina, 2002) which focusses on a road-trip of sexual self-discovery undertaken by three young women from Buenos Aires. Arguably, however, the representations contained within the film are premised on non-metropolitan understandings of female sexuality and for this reason the film will serve as the starting point for forthcoming research relating to cinematic spaces of sexuality beyond the metropolis, rather than being included here.

Finally, since the primary research for this book was undertaken, a number of important books have been published which are of direct relevance to my own discussion in the chapters which follow. These include Gustavo Subero's titles *Queer Masculinities in Latin American Cinema: Male Bodies and Narrative Representations* (2014) and *Representations of HIV/AIDS in Contemporary Hispano-American and Caribbean Culture: Cuerpos suiSIDAs* (2014), Juana Suárez's *Critical Essays on Colombian Cinema and Culture: Cinembargo Colombia* (2012), Tatiana Heise's *Remaking Brazil: Contested National Identities in Contemporary Brazilian Cinema* (2012) and Bruno Carvalho's *Porous City: A Cultural History of Rio de Janeiro* (2013). Whilst it has not been practical to revise substantially primary research in light of these new texts, I have endeavoured to take account of this material and incorporate references to it where possible.

Notes to the Introduction

1. For further discussion of this film in a translation context please see my article 'Uma experiência com a linguagem do cinema: objectivos, efeitos e consequências (*Dependencia sexual* de Rodrigo Bellott (Bolivia/USA, 2003)' (Hoff 2009).
2. Reflecting the decentred perspective that characterizes this book, I desist from capitalizing 'western' when used in reference to occidental cultures, western media, western identity politics, and so on, in order to de-emphasize the unity of the so-called 'West' and deprivilege the term, even though it is often convenient in argument to point to it as such.
3. 'Sexual cultures' are defined here as a system of sexual meanings and practices that emerges from historically-specific social and psychological conditions.
4. I use S/M in this book as opposed to S&M since the latter implies the existence of two separate (albeit complimentary) practices, whereas the former indicates reciprocity and 'symbiotic inter-dependency' (Polhemus & Randall (1994), in Sullivan 2003: 152) which is how I understand S/M in the context of the film discussed in Chapter 2.
5. I borrow here Quiroga's phraseology (2000: 12).
6. See, for example, Lukinbeal (2005), Shiel & Fitzmaurice (2001), Aitken (2006) and Clarke (1997).
7. See, for example, Bell & Valentine (1995), Brown (2000), Binnie (2004), Phillips & others (2000) and Browne & others (2007).
8. I borrow the term 'majority world' from Doreen Massey who uses it (see, for example, Massey, 2007) as a way of moving beyond the terms 'non-western' and 'developing'. These (often inadvertently) define 'other places' in relation to 'our world' and therefore concomitantly position the latter at the centre of things, despite its limited relevance for the majority of the world's population.
9. See, for example, Sarlo (2001).
10. See Simmel (in Bridge & Watson 2010).
11. In May 2001, as an 'artistic experiment', Bellott launched the RiGO BoSD underwear advertising campaign, comprising the RiGO BoSD website and, for a month during principal photography, a 10 × 4 metre-high billboard on Banzer Avenue in downtown Santa Cruz (Bellott 2003). According to the director, within a month, the website became 'one of the most visited

websites in Upstate New York' and Bolivian manufacturers of American clothing apparently began 'enquiring about the manufacturing rights' (2003: 3).

12. Here Sarlo argues that because consumer items lose value from the moment they come into our hands, we have become 'collectors in reverse', who instead of collecting things themselves, 'collect[s] the acts of acquiring things' (2001: 21).

13. According to Foucault, from the seventeenth century, 'power over life' subsequently evolved in two basic forms. The first, he writes, was concerned with an 'anatomo-politics of the human body', a disciplinary procedure which sought to optimize its capabilities, extort its forces, increase its usefulness and docility and consolidate its integration into systems of efficient and economic controls, resulting in what he terms the notion of 'the body as a machine' (1978: 139). The second, which evolved later, relates to 'a bio-politics of the population', a series of interventions and regulatory controls which supervised the 'species body', that is, the human body as the basis of biological processes: birth rate, mortality, life expectancy, the level of health and so on, and all the conditions that may cause these to vary (1978: 139). The deployment of sexuality would become, he writes, one of the most important of these 'arrangements'.

14. These five films include *Dependencia sexual*, whose discussion in the Introduction, Chapter 1 and the Postscript is used to frame my analysis of the other four films in Chapters 2 to 5.

CHAPTER 1

Mapping/Negotiating the Terrain: Towards a Queer Urban Geography of Latin American Cinema

Sexuality, Space and the Geographical Imagination

In her book *For Space*, Doreen Massey argues that space and how it is conceived has been fundamental to the way in which the minority world has traditionally viewed itself as being at the centre of things — all seeing, all conquering — while the rest of the world lies passively 'in wait'. The historical recounting of the Spanish conquest of the Americas is one such example, she argues. These 'voyages of discovery' typically imagined space as 'an expanse we travel across', she writes: '[Hernan] Cortés voyaged across space, found Tenochtitlán, and took it' (2005: 4). The conception of space as something that can be crossed and conquered has various repercussions, she continues. Implicitly it equates space with land and sea and makes space 'seem like a surface; continuous and given' and, in this sense, she argues, it 'differentiates' (2005: 4). 'Hernán, active maker of history, journeys across this surface and finds Tenochtitlán upon it', whilst other places, peoples, cultures are relegated merely to the status of phenomena 'on' this surface (2005: 4). It is not an innocent manoeuvre, she argues, since it means they are deprived of their own histories. Immobilized, 'they lie there, on space, in place [and] await Cortés (or our, or global capital's) arrival', she concludes (2005: 4).

Historically, sexuality has fulfilled an important function in structuring this spatial imagination. Anne McClintock points out that the Americas, along with Africa and Asia long figured as a 'porno-tropics' for the European imagination: 'a fantastic magic lantern of the mind onto which Europe projected its forbidden sexual desires and fears' (1993: 22). She writes that the colonial conquest was typically envisaged here in terms of an invitation — from an enticing, pre-modern, virgin land embodied by the figure of the supplicant indigenous female — to the civilizing masculinity of Spanish and Portuguese imperial mastery. She refers here to the union depicted in Jan van der Straet's drawing 'América' [*c.* 1575] to illustrate her point though there are numerous other examples in Latin American culture: the relationship between Portuguese colonialist Martim and the Tabajara indigenous woman from which José de Alencar's novel *Iracema* (1865) takes its name, comes to mind here.

Of course this 'encounter' was not merely symbolic: if 'taking' the Americas was concerned with territorial expansion and exercising the symbolic powers of the Spanish and Portuguese crowns, then the literal sexual conquest of local populations would be intimately bound up with this process. Here, as Ilán Stavans writes in his illuminating essay 'The Latin Phallus', the 'phallus, as well as gunpowder, was a crucial weapon used to subdue' (1996: 145). And we need look no further, he argues, than the sexual lexicon of contemporary Spanish (and Portuguese too, I would contend) for clues to this violent eroticism. *Cacete* (Portuguese) [cudgel], *pistola* (Portuguese/Spanish) [gun], *lanza* [lance], *rifle* [rifle], *ametralladora* (Spanish) [machine gun] are amongst the plethora of weaponry-associated nouns used to refer to the male member, for example, whilst some of those relating to the vagina — *racha* [crack/fissure], *fenda* (Portuguese) [slit/tear], *hueco* [hole] or *raja* [crack/slit] (Spanish) for example — distinctly evoke the image of wounding or injury. The verbs used to describe the sexual act itself correspondingly carry similar connotations of battle or combat, with *descargar* (Spanish) or *descarregar* (Portuguese) [to discharge] sometimes used to refer to ejaculation, whilst a woman might *rendirse* (Spanish) or *dar-se* (Portuguese), namely 'surrender', to a man's sexual advances. For Stavans, this linguistic spectre of violence and the gender messages encoded within it, are symptomatic of the fact that the 'primal scene' of the clash with colonial power is still 'unhealed rape' in contemporary Latin America (1996: 145). Machismo, as a cultural style, he argues, is something that 'endlessly rehearses this humiliating episode [of conquest] in the history of the Americas' (1996: 145). The verb *chingar* [to fuck/screw] (prevalent in Mexican slang), in particular, serves for Stavans as the absolute verbal embodiment of all that is 'ambiguous' and 'excessive' about macho sexuality: '*Chingar* is what a macho does to a woman, what the Iberian soldiers did to the native Indian population, what corrupt politicians do to their electorate' (1996: 151).

Read from Stavans's perspective then, the representations of gender and sexuality we encounter within the two opening stories of *Dependencia sexual* are arguably less concerned with some sort of timeless Latin American 'essence', but rather with behavioural codes which emanate, at least in part, from foreign (and specifically European) shores. This, in turn, begins to open up a more nuanced consideration of the RiGO BoSD advertisement. The North American image we encounter here, contemplated by the adolescent Jessica against the backdrop of Bolivia's most populous city, alludes to the fact that the discursive production and material enactment of gender and sexuality has never taken place in isolation but has always been caught up in the transnational flow of ideas, cultures and ideologies. As Benigno Sanchéz-Eppler and Cindy Patton write, sexuality (and by extension, gender too I would suggest) is 'intimately and immediately felt but publically described and internationally mediated' (2000: 2).

(Unfufilled?) Histories of Sexuality in Latin America

This transnational, polycentric understanding of sexuality may seem common sense amidst the current tendencies towards post-structuralism. However, it is surprising how contemporary accounts of sexuality subscribe to a western-centric view of things. Michel Foucault's *History of Sexuality, Volume 1* (1978), for example, in its refutation of the 'repressive hypothesis' did fulfil the literal promise of his book, but the history he provided, as Peter A. Jackson points out, was rather sweeping in its conception of broad global regions (in Phillips 2006: 7). In this respect he distinguished between societies in which erotic art (*ars erotica*) produced the 'truth' about sex — Rome, Japan, India and the Arabo-Moslem societies — and those where this production has been the domain of legal, medical, educational and other types of confession (*Sciencia sexualis*), namely 'our civilization' or 'the West' (2006: 7). In addition to this somewhat problematic division of the world into 'discrete moral universes', to borrow Richard Parker's phraseology (1999: 1), Foucault's account cross-hatches this rudimentary imagined geography with an equally questionable tension between centre and periphery. 'The nineteenth century witnessed a generalization of the deployment of sexuality', he writes, 'starting from a hegemonic centre' with 'eventually the entire social body provided with a sexual body' (1978: 127). The words 'from' and 'eventually' are telling, implying a developmental understanding of sexuality whereby the production of sexual discourses occurs from a fixed point (i.e. metropolitan Europe) through a gradual process of diffusion over space and time. His words also contain a latent sense of inevitability, implying that those lying on the periphery of this radius of influence — the metropolitan margins, provincial towns and villages and former or current overseas colonies, for example — would take longer to be 'reached' by these discourses but reached they would be. Resistance, it seems, was futile.

The diffusion of a globalized form of gay identity and culture embodied in what Dennis Altman terms the 'Global Gay' (1996), is frequently spoken about with the same sense of inevitability and often subscribes to a similar geographical imagination of things.[1] The opening sequence of John Scagliotti's documentary *Dangerous Lives: Coming Out in the Developing World* (2003) is, in this respect, telling. Overlaid with images of gay pride marches, footage from the hit British television series *Queer As Folk* (1999/2000) and a proud lesbian couple cradling what we presume to be their newborn baby, a voiceover reads:

> Homosexuality has been part of our world since the time of the ancients. But in the mid-twentieth century, homosexuals in Western societies created something new: a public identity and a visible culture. In the last decade of the twentieth century, this heightened visibility began spreading throughout the developing world. In the West very few people knew about this historic upheaval until fifty-two men on a Nile riverboat in Cairo were arrested for crimes of debauchery.

The voiceover then moves towards the discussion of Cairo's status in the 1990s as the Middle East's 'gayest' city, declaring that what was happening there 'had its antecedents in San Francisco's Castro, New York's Greenwich Village, Amsterdam's

Warmoesstraat and the Marais in Paris', places which it posits as 'gay meccas' in the post-war period. From this viewpoint, then, the production of globalized gay identity and culture begins at a Euro-American centre, and through a process of 'global queering', as Altman terms it (1996), spreads stealthily across the planet reaching even the most 'peripheral' and 'unlikely' destinations — in this case Egypt. Here the emergence of a dissident urban sexual subculture constructed around the notion of gay identity is not viewed as something that has occurred organically in this land of the 'ancients', merely a copy of an original cultural model produced in the 'West' which sets the tone and leads the way for the 'Rest'.

Latin Americanists have always been somewhat suspicious of such narratives, since the dissemination and reception of both normative and counter-hegemonic sexual discourses in the region have always been partial, uneven and incomplete. In the nineteenth century ideas emanating from the European medical establishment announcing homosexuality 'as one of the first forms of sexuality' (Foucault 1978: 43) were indeed highly influential. Here sodomy, a sinful, deviant sexual act which previously anybody was capable of committing, increasingly became viewed as a 'condition', something that was 'innate' and thus the realm of a specific individual with an accompanying identity.[2] Whereas 'the sodomite had been a temporary aberration', writes Foucault, 'the homosexual was now a species [...] nothing that went into his total composition was unaffected by his sexuality' (1978: 43). As José Quiroga notes, in the postcolonial era the taxonomization of sectors, behaviours and practices with which these ideas were concerned would play a fundamental role in consolidating and regulating the 'shape' of newly independent 'national bodies' in the region (2000: 13): 'If modernization entailed taxonomy and the goal of the nation was modernity then it follows that those practices that were "pre-modern" remnants of an atavistic past and threatened a presumably "pure" national body would be seen unfavourably' (2000: 13).[3]

This process, he continues, would, however, occur rather differently in Latin America when compared to Europe. In Latin America, announcing the homosexual meant 'pointing at the "invert" or passive partner while the active partner remained "somewhat" invisible, the remnant of a non-hygienic past' (Quiroga 2000: 13). Although he does not elaborate on which period of the region's past he is referring to, the visibility and/or denigration directed towards the passive partner in penetrative male same-sex relations and the relative invisibility, condoning or even prestige enjoyed by the active partner does indeed appear to have a long history. As evidenced in Pete Sigal's edited volume *Infamous Desire: Male Homosexuality in Colonial Latin America* (2003), many colonial observers such as Cieza de León, chronicler of the conquest in Peru, consistently drew attention in their writings to the widespread practice of (ritualized) sodomy in indigenous societies in which transvestism was cited as being a central element (2003: 2). Cieza's account was, to a large extent, politically motivated and brought with it 'much ideological baggage from Europe' (2003: 2). For not only did it serve to feminize symbolically the native population and bolster within the colonial imagination a sensation of invincibility and domination, but it also contributed to the sense of justification for imperial expansion into the Americas itself.[4] This reflected the distinctly developmental discourse relating to sexual deviancy present within conquest ideology, writes Sigal, whereby it was argued that sodomy was most extensive in the least civilized societies, a marker of backwardness and degeneracy. The imposition of European civilization would destroy such activity, it was argued, just one way in which colonialism was regarded as a force for betterment (2003: 122).

In fact, as Richard Trexler suggests in *Sex and Conquest: Gendered Violence, Political Order and the European Conquest of the Americas* (1995), in many pre-Conquest societies passivity amongst males was loathed, with effeminate boys and men often the subject of humiliation (1995: 67). For him, the mythical figure of the 'berdach' served less as an indicator of tolerance with regards to non-normative gender identities and sexual behaviours as opposed to the expression of specifically gendered forms of power relations. In a society where masculinity was prized, the transvestiting and/or raping of another boy or man by a noble was a means of limiting the former's ability to wield power. The attainment of prestige, and the assertion of superiority, could, in turn, be achieved by forcing another noble to hand over his transvestited boys thus increasing the number of dependent males directly answerable to him (1995: 74). The behaviour of the conquistadores was not altogether dissimilar, and with the widely acknowledged rape of Indian women that took place, it is likely that male rape also featured as part of their 'violent eroticism'. Here the symbolic feminization of indigenous cultures evident in colonial literature would incorporate a physical aspect, with the act of anal penetration serving as 'proof' of the inherent effeminacy, weakness and degeneracy of those men in charge of indigenous Indian society whilst simultaneously confirming the masculinity of the conquistadores and the legitimacy of their 'civilizing' mission.

Stavans again traces the 'excessive masculinity' often associated with Latin(o) American men back to the region's history of conquest claiming them to be 'machos, dominating figures, rulers, conquistadores' but also 'closeted homosexuals' (1996: 148). According to his account, 'the lawless path of male eroticism' embodied in the colonial experience dictates that 'sooner or later the macho's glorious masculinity will be shared in bed with another man' (1996: 148). According to this logic and returning to *Dependencia sexual*, it is quite conceivable that Joaquín and his friends might have procured the services of the transvestite sex workers they verbally and physically abuse, without this erotic interaction necessarily impinging on their status as heterosexual men within the peer group. Indeed, in a more extreme scenario this abuse might not have been limited merely to the throwing of rotten eggs, but rather have taken the form of *non-consensual* intercourse with the said prostitutes, viewed by the sex workers not as an aberration but as a legitimate form of heteronormative masculine assertion.

Although in the realm of the social sciences the likes of Roger Lancaster (1992) and Ana Maria Alonso and Maria Koreck (1988) partially support the idea that male honour and prestige can be enhanced through penetrating another man, other critics such as Steven O. Murray find this highly problematic and more 'a *maricón* fantasy than a plausible empirical explanation' (1995: 52). Nevertheless, even if Murray is right, the above discussion of Latin America's indigenous past and its subsequent (sexual) conquest is nevertheless useful in shedding light on the roots of this 'traditional' gender-identified model whereby male homosexuality is determined by role as opposed to sexual object choice and which has served as one of the primary themes in work on homosexuality in the region (see, for example, Lancaster (1992, Nicaragua), Salessi (1995, Argentina), Carrier (1995, Mexico), Schifter (1998, Costa Rica), Fry (1982, Brazil), Parker (1999, Brazil) and Almaguer (1998, Latino North America)). It also explains why, after the supposed introduction of western medical sexual discourses in the nineteenth century, 'naming the homosexual' might have meant pointing at the 'invert' or the passive partner, whilst the active partner, if not exalted, lauded or admired by his contemporaries, as Lancaster, Alonso and Koreck imply, then has at least continued to remain 'somewhat invisible', as many of the socio-anthropological studies referenced above indeed suggest.

Capitalism, Gay identity and Urban Space

Foucault's history of sexuality, then, remains partially unfulfilled in Latin American contexts it would seem. Taking this forward, we also might venture that the logics underpinning more contemporary accounts of 'global queering', as Altman (1996) puts it, in turn, begin to short circuit. Within the realm of academic theory, the correlation between capitalist development, the resultant genesis of the modern metropolis and the emergence of gay identity and associated spaces, is certainly now well rehearsed. Indeed by 1983, John D'Emilio's seminal article 'Capitalism and Gay Identity' had already put to bed the notion of the 'eternal homosexual' (1983: 101), or 'the idea that gayness was always there, waiting to be uncovered' (Sinfield 2000: 21). According to D'Emilio (but see also Knopp 1992) the consolidation of a system of free labour in the mid-1800s and the advent of the factory system, whereby production was split into public and private forms, separating the home from the workplace and production from reproduction, created a separate 'domestic sphere' relating to the home. For men, this would become a refuge from and independent of the 'cruel' economic world of work, given over to the nurturing of happiness and emotional wellbeing. For women, engaged in unwaged domestic labour and now dependent on male wages for their economic survival, the experience of home was rather different — not as something distinct from the workplace (there was no separation) but as a space marked by the absence (at least during working hours) of men.

As Larry Knopp argues, these new experiences of separate, gendered public and private spaces (characterized, of course, by very unequal power relationships) had the consequence of creating new forms of subjectivity in people's lives and (now quoting Zarestsky 1976) the modern notion of a 'personal' or 'private life' (1992: 658). For women, he continues, generally relegated to the private, domestic sphere, this was defined by creating relationships of working co-operation with other women, building women-centred networks and other supportive cultural institutions (1992: 659). Whilst these afforded the possibility of same-sex erotic encounters, Knopp makes the point that lesbianism could only exist if it did not fundamentally threaten the unequal power relationship between men and women; as an exclusive alternative to women's sexual bonds with men, it simply was not economically feasible for most women. The situation, however, was quite different for men who were afforded greater possibilities for constructing a personal life *outside* the family unit (or, more radically, rejecting it completely) due to their relative physical detachment from the family home, engagement in waged labour and the resultant ability to exist independently of its structures. In this sense, a 'gay lifestyle' (at least as we understand it today), was for men, in theory at least, considerably more feasible. These differences aside, however, both these gendered experiences highlight, according to Knopp:

> [The] profound contradiction between industrial capital's need for disciplined and conformist gender-divided labour forces and its creation at the same time of real and imagined spaces of 'personal life' that enabled women and men (albeit in very different ways and to different extents) to explore personal identities based on nonconformist gender roles and sexual practices. (Knopp 1992: 660)

Ultimately, however, as Knopp notes in previous work on gay involvement in gentrification in New Orleans (1990, 1995), it would be the eventual *decline* of manufacturing employment in many North American cities that would consolidate such spaces as firm territorial and economic bases through which to assert political power and foster a material sense of community. On the one hand, he argues, the concomitant rise in white-collar administrative, managerial and service-sector jobs drew a disproportionate number of gay people into the previously industrialized city centres where these sectors were now based. On the other hand, confronted with the relative heterosexism and homophobia supposedly virulent in (suburban) 'family' neighbourhoods and the latent availability of inexpensive housing stock ready for renovation in these often depressed downtown areas, gay people were simultaneously given the opportunity not only to reside in such areas but also to invest in their regeneration. Here they began to take their own alternative codings of space 'out of the closet' and into the public sphere, resulting in 'the proliferation of visible [...] lesbian and gay commercial, residential and leisure spaces' (1995: 158). As such, 'the gentrified gay neighbourhood', became, he writes, 'a defining characteristic of both the "new" inner-city and the "new" gay identity' (1992: 665).

More recently these materialist accounts have, in turn, become cross-hatched by debates examining the impact of globalization and the growth of supra-territorial space on the production of globalized forms of dissident sexuality, identity and culture discussed briefly above. For Altman, as well as other critics such as Bob Cant (1997) and John Champagne (1999), 'global queering' again appears overwhelmingly to be driven by the expansion of the free market and consumer society with American cultural references, in particular, supposedly defining 'contemporary gay and lesbian meanings for most of the world' (1996: 2). And, for all these above critics, transnational commodities are cited as the primary carriers through which these cultural references are disseminated. For Champagne, these take the form of 'rainbow flag pins and stickers, circuit party fashion, depilatories for men, sex toys and pornography' amongst others (1999: 146), whilst Altman stresses the importance of books, films, magazines and fashion (1996), though music too arguably merits acknowledgement.

The logic of capitalist modernity, in particular its more recent neoliberal, globalized forms, however, has been played out rather differently in Latin American

FIG. I.I. The internationalized commercial gay scene depicted in *El cielo dividido*
(Julián Hernández, 2006: Strand Releasing)

contexts. As Nestor García Canclini writes in *Hybrid Cultures: Strategies for Entering
and Leaving Modernity* (1995), 'the most-reiterated hypothesis in the literature on
Latin American modernity may be summarized as follows: we have had an exu-
berant modernism with a deficient modernization' (1995: 41). What García Canclini is referring to here is the perceived disparity between the utopian ideals of
modernism as a cultural project centred on the renewal of symbolic practices (art,
literature, architecture and so on) in an experimental or critical sense, and what
modernization as a socio-economic process has actually delivered in its (re)con-
struction of modernity (1995: 11).

It was not, for instance, until the 1940s that mass industrialization and urbanization
actually occurred in Latin America. Until the onset of the debt crisis in the 1970s,
most Latin American countries did indeed achieve impressive records of economic
growth in these years due to ISI (import-substitution industrialization), based on
the development of a strong manufacturing sector, stimulated by aggressive national
investment and the imposition of high tariff walls to discourage manufactured
imports (Hershberg & Rosen 2006: 5). These years saw, in turn, the genesis of a
sizeable working class who were able to organize themselves strategically in order
to secure greater equality in wealth distribution, income and political participation
(2006: 5).

However, whilst Eric Hershberg and Fred Rosen argue that 'ISI afforded note-
worthy opportunities for upward mobility and [...] the sustenance of social solid-
arities', they also recognize that 'these achievements were woefully partial' (2006:
4). Exclusion, they write, was particularly widespread in the countryside where
agrarian reform remained an elusive promise with the traditional dominant olig-
archies resisting any efforts to modernize land-tenure regimes (2006: 5). With cities

therefore serving as the focal point for industrialization, the 1950s and 1960s, in turn, saw the mass exodus of these rural populations to the region's metropolitan areas, which struggled to integrate these new populations into their burgeoning urban fabrics. It was, in that period, write Kees Koonings and Dirk Krujit, when 'de facto second-class citizenship' began to acquire the distinctly urban face it is often associated with today (2007: 8).

Although this lack of integration was seen as a mere 'delay' in modernization that would be overcome (ISI was ideologically bound up with ideas of national integration), the shift from protectionism towards free-trade neoliberalization in the 1980s, propelled increasingly in the 1990s by globalization and the advent of (globalized) service-based economies (see, for example, Sassen 2001) has only served to exacerbate further this phenomenon of social splintering. As such, much of the urban population in Latin America and other regions of the majority world find themselves increasingly 'separated, spatially, socially and culturally' from the (lower and upper) middle-class city of law enforcement, public services and formal employment (Portes in Koonings & Krujit, 2006: 7) and instead belonging to a permanent informal sector engaged in a parallel economy often of criminal proportions (see, for example, Castells 2000).

Thus whilst, as Ella Shohat and Robert Stam argue, minority-world 'modernization' theories have blamed majority-world underdevelopment on cultural traditions and assumed that it 'need only follow in the footsteps of the West to achieve economic "take off"' (1994: 17), the brief account provided above shows this to be somewhat misguided. As Koonings and Krujit conclude pessimistically:

> Two decades of neo-liberal reforms, formal democratization and globalizing urban modernity, however, have produced nothing but disillusion for the 50–70 percent of urban denizens estimated to live on the wrong side of the breach of poverty, insecurity and exclusion. (Koonings & Krujit 2006: 1)

With this in mind, the assumption that minority-world logics relating to the production of sexually dissident identities, cultures and spaces (and which correlate this process with (neoliberal, globalized) capitalist development) will automatically be fulfilled in majority-world contexts must also therefore be called into question.

FIG. 1.2. The split screen in *Dependencia sexual* embodies the 'fractured' nature of Latin American urban life (Rodrigo Bellott, 2003: Wellspring Media)

In the minority world, as D'Emilio writes, capitalism 'has gradually undermined the material basis of the nuclear family by taking away the economic functions that cemented the ties between family members' (1983: 108). However, in areas of the majority world such as Latin America, lack of stable employment opportunities, the still limited reach of the welfare state and the resultant precarity of existence this engenders for much of the population means that for many, the family (in conjunction with wider social networks) continues to fulfil a highly important role as an economic support structure for offspring long after the age at which many young people in countries such as the UK would have left home.

On a purely practical level, this necessarily inhibits the construction of an erotic life regardless of one's sexuality. However, it is especially true of those attracted to members of their own sex where the repercussions of being discovered in a same-sex erotic liaison may be more far-reaching. In this respect, Quiroga makes the point that whilst the issuing of masks to participants of the first ever gay pride march in Buenos Aires in 1993 may have conflicted with the discourse of unproblematized visibility peddled by North American identity politics, in doing so it raised the very important point that declaring one's sexuality 'whatever the cost' becomes rather more problematic in contexts where this involves relinquishing something as basic as the food on one's plate or the roof over one's head (2000: 2). He continues that even for those who held their sexuality as a kind of 'open secret', whereby their families had come, albeit tacitly, to accept their partners, the mask was still of significance, for the social fabric such families depended on would have been destroyed 'had the very notion of homosexuality as *identity* been put on the dinner table' (2000: 2). 'To expect men and women to choose family exile as the price of a homosexual identity', he continues, 'was certainly too much to ask in such a tightly knit context of relations' (2000: 2).

Of course, this is not to say that a 'gay identity' cannot be adopted and lived strategically in more protected, tolerant and temporary contexts whether they pertain to the virtual spaces of online networking sites, for example, or the material spaces of the gay world such as bars, clubs, saunas or motels. Richard Parker's research in particular has shone light on the highly contingent nature of gay identity for many Brazilian men from various socio-economic backgrounds (Parker 1999) and his ideas are relevant to the way this identity plays out in other Latin American countries too. However, as will be discussed in Chapter 2 in relation to *Un año sin amor*, accessing such material spaces is still nevertheless often contingent on financial solvency, as is the ability to buy into the consumer culture around which the likes of Altman, Cant and Champagne argue gay identity is constructed. This ability, as the previous discussion demonstrates, is for many social sectors highly compromised. Even the virtual gay world which, in theory, can be accessed relatively cheaply by low-income groups through local internet cafes may be similarly off-limits for those men or women worried about who may be looking over their shoulder or monitoring their browsing activity remotely.

Thus whilst it is possible to theorize a Latin American gay identity — as Gustavo Subero does in the introduction to *Queer Masculinities in Latin American Cinema: Male Bodies and Narrative Representations* (2014) on the basis that 'most of the countries

[...] have undergone the same cultural and social processes with regards to issues of same-sex desire' (2014a: 4) — the proliferation of the global metropolitan gay model has not been as presumably indestructible as western critics such as Altman would have us believe. Rather, the evidence seems to suggest that it has been restricted to those sectors of the population most able to participate in the market, buy into consumer culture, take part in the political process and access educational and social institutions. The sexual culture that consequently emerges is one inflected not only according to highly dichotomized (racialized) class differences but also an accompanying geography structured around metropolitan centres and non-metropolitan urban and rural margins.

In 1982, for example, Peter Fry noted that whilst the 'so-called "homosexual", "entendido" or "gay"' could be found within certain sectors of the middle classes in the large Brazilian metropolises, the 'traditional model' nevertheless remained 'dominant in poor and working-class neighbourhoods of the Amazon region and also in the north and northeast regions of Brazil in rural areas and among the poor in the large conurbations' (1982: 82). Nearly twenty years later, David Higgs in the specific context of Rio de Janeiro, would argue that co-resident gay couples were still 'virtually unknown' in the *favelas* and the city remained in a '1950s holding pattern where discreet, mostly white, prosperous gays could survive on the margins of bourgeois propriety by avoiding any challenge to the heterosexist ascendency' (1999: 162).

In Colombia (specifically the city of Cali) the organization of same-sex desire according to active/passive binaries is noted again by Urrea Giraldo and others as being prevalent in poorer areas of the cities (particularly the eastern sector, populated mainly by blacks). They also make the point that within organizations representing sexual minorities these appeared almost exclusively as the domain of middle-class, self-assumedly gay, white or mestizo men with almost a complete lack of young black men due to their 'socio-spatial' exclusion (2006). In the Bolivian context, Paulson notes a similar phenomenon in relation to the establishment of a gay centre in the city of Santa Cruz in the 1990s in which only a small portion of men who had sex with men participated in project activities, 'such that this chapter of gay genesis left out many men who were too poor, too rich, too white, too indigenous, too masculine, too feminine' (2006: 14).

Whilst David William Foster's account of 'contested space and homoeroticism' in Buenos Aires is generally more positive in outlook, it suggests that the city's reputation as a locus of gay visibility and activism in the post-dictatorship era can similarly be aligned with 'urban privilege', whilst 'Argentine machismo' and the dictates of compulsory heterosexuality these imply continue, within the national imagination at least, to be the domain of the urban margins and 'mythical countryside' as embodied by the figure of the Gaucho, the suburban *compadrito* and the Peronista/unionized labourer (1998: 87). On a more general level, according to Foster, 'the homogenization among [queer] demographic concentrations in the United States has yet to become the norm in Latin America' (1998: 84).

Beyond Dependency and Subalternity

Perhaps unsurprisingly given this seemingly ambivalent position assumed by gay culture and identity politics in the region, in the specific arena of cultural production, certain cultural critics have been reluctant to read representations of same-sex desire as they appear in poetry, literature or film as pertaining to some sort of 'international/homoerotic/queer canon', as Foster puts it (2003: xviii). Daniel Balderston and José Quiroga, for example, are particularly critical of two anthologies entitled *Now the Volcano: Anthology of Latin America Gay Literature* (1979) and *My Deep Dark Pain is Love: A Collection of Latin American Gay Fiction* (1983) published by the San Francisco-based Gay Sunshine Press. Bringing together, under the banner of 'Latin American Gay Literature', excerpts from the work of Salvador Novo (Brazil), Adolfo Caminha (Brazil), Luis Cernuda (Mexico), Reinaldo Arenas (Cuba), Luis Zapata (Mexico), Jorge Marchant Lozano (Chile) and Tulio Carella (Argentina) amongst others, editor Winston Leyland and translator E. A. Lacey are accused of being 'bent' on creating the illusion of an 'imagined community' in which these writers apparently 'speak to each other' when, in reality, it is only within the space enabled by the said volumes that any such dialogue actually exists (Balderston & Quiroga 2003: 102). According to Balderston and Quiroga, many of the later 'internationalist gestures' of the USA gay and lesbian movement can be seen in these 'consumer objects', which spawned, they claim:

> A belief in the 'universality' of the gay experience, spilling off into a process by means of which identity categories create new pan-national subjects (gay male writers), deracinated from their context and always in a position of literary and political subservience to their First World 'brethren'. (Balderston & Quiroga 2003: 87)

Foster himself avoids these pitfalls, stating that the essays contained within his volume 'are not specifically interested in lesbigay lives, at least those lived on the level of lesbian or gay or bisexual or any other non- or anti-patriarchal identity'. Instead, he writes that the films are read 'as texts firmly grounded in specific issues of Latin American national societies and a continental (although primarily urban) understanding of sexuality' (2003: xviii). 'These are Latin American cultural productions', he states, 'and I wish them to be understood primarily as such' (2003: xviii). And yet this perspective brings with it its own limitations. In this respect (putting to one side the fact that of the fourteen films analyzed in his study eight are coproductions with non-Latin American countries, three contain dialogue in French, English and Bambara respectively, four are directed by non-Latin American directors and two feature non-Latin American actors in their lead roles) in the realm of sexuality, Foster's insistence on a Latin American 'continental understanding of sexuality' is problematic not least because it succumbs (somewhat involuntarily) to the very process of 'othering' we presume the said critic would be keen to avoid.

As Stephanie Dennison and Song Hwee Lim warn in the introduction to *Remapping World Cinema* (2006) 'where there is Orientalism there is also Occidentalism' (2006: 4). On one level, occidentalism can be said to overestimate the hegemony of the minority world, seeing it, to borrow Shohat and Stam's phraseology, 'as an all-powerful mover and shaker' (1994: 17). This is something for which dependency theory more generally has been criticized. It tends to imagine a 'hierarchical global system controlled by metropolitan capitalist countries and their multinational corporations' in which 'First World' prosperity is achieved at the expense of 'Third World' poverty and a whole host of other social ills (1994: 17). This seems to be the point that Bellott's aptly named *Dependencia sexual* is trying to make, the RiGO BoSD advertisement apparently symbolizing a North American-managed 'economy of beauty' from which the negative by-products of its ruthless pursuit of profit, namely 'marginalization and abuse', are presented as being particularly virulent in the brand's more distant markets, in this case Bolivia.

Yet as Manuel Castells (2000), J. K. Gibson-Graham (1996) and others have argued, capitalism has been as uneven and diverse in the minority world as anywhere else and its neoliberal forms similarly exclusionary and prone to exacerbating pre-existing social cleavages. In this respect, one of García Canclini's opening propositions in *Hybrid Cultures* is that the traditional view of a 'repressed and postponed' Latin American modernity, that is but a 'belated and deficient echo', is erroneously premised on 'measuring our modernity with [overly] optimized images of how that process happened in the countries of the centre' (1995: 44). This logic can be extended to Latin American dissident sexual cultures, whose perception, to borrow García Canclini's phraseology, merely as 'belated and deficient echo[es]' of those in the minority world, similarly subscribes to the misguided presumption that here they are already homogeneous, fully-formed entities with which all sexual dissidents identify and include themselves. In this respect, Phillips and others' aforementioned edited volume *Decentring Sexualities* constitutes an important intervention. Focusing on 'core countries' but not 'core positions within those countries', or rather on 'liminal' or 'in-between' spaces on the margins of sexual geography such as the suburbs, small towns or rural areas, the essays contained within highlight that there are many men and women who 'disidentify' with identity politics or the commercial gay scene and for whom a gay bar or LGBT centre may be equally as 'foreign' to them as it would be to a Bolivian, Colombian or any other Latin American national. In this respect, Jarod Hayes argues, 'it is important for us to render less presumably indestructible homosexuality (and heterosexuality for that matter) as we know it in the west' (in Binnie 2004: 84).

On another level, occidentalism, as Dennison and Lim write, has had the concomitant effect of 'confining non-Western cultures only to ghettos' (2006: 4) or, as Shohat and Stam argue, to 'a homogeneous block, passively accepting the economic and ideological imprint of the First World' (1994: 18). *Dependencia sexual*, for example, assumes that the world's most successful fashion labels (in this case RiGO BoSD) are located in the global 'north', presumably because a comparable product in South America is either inferior or unable to compete with its American or European counterparts. In fact, it is quite feasible that the advertised underwear could have come, for example, from Brazil, another 'dominant' global player in the fashion industry, and home to brands such as Osklen or Melissa which can be found in shops from São Paulo to Santa Cruz, New York to New Delhi.[5] Similarly, whilst Bellott attributes the disturbing representations contained within his film to a 'media-centred culture' that is similarly associated with the global north, this ignores the fact, as Shohat and Stam argue, that 'media imperialism' is currently being subjected to 'powerful reverse currents' (1994: 31) whereby audiovisual products of Brazil's RedeGlobo or Mexico's Televisa, for example, compete with North American fare across Latin(o) America and further afield in countries such as Russia or Portugal.

Postcolonial theory, something which the presspack to *Dependencia sexual* cites explicitly as having influenced the film (Bellott 2003), has been similarly criticized for its 'metrocentrism'. In this respect, Aihwa Ong argues it to be a 'metropolitan theory of third-world subalternity [which] tend[s] to collapse all non-Western countries into the same model of analysis in which primacy is given to racial, class and national dominations stemming from the European colonial era' (1999: 32). Privileging a narrative of 'domination' is particularly problematic in the sense that it implies victimhood whilst denying possible agency and resistance on the part of the individual. This is an issue which has been raised in relation to Gayatri Chakravorty Spivak's famous essay 'Can The Subaltern Speak?' (1988). Here, Spivak, engaging with the discourse of *sati* [widow sacrifice] in which the Hindu patriarchal code converged with colonial accounts of Indian culture to eradicate any suggestion of a woman's voice, proposes that 'no scene of speaking' can arise for the subaltern woman and no discursive space can emerge from which she can form an 'utterance'. 'For the "true" subaltern group, whose identity is its difference, there is no unrepresentable subaltern subject that can know and speak itself', she writes (1988: 285). Critics such as Benita Parry take issue with this model of the 'silent subaltern' because it assigns 'an absolute power to the hegemonic discourse in constituting and disarticulating the native' whilst showing a 'deliberated deafness to the native voice where it is to be heard' (1987: 34–35). Parry argues, for instance, that Spivak's reading of Jean Rhys's *Wide Sargasso Sea* (1966) is deficient because it ignores the 'traces and testimony of women's voices on those sites where women inscribe themselves as healers, ascetics, singers of sacred songs, artisans and artists' (1987: 35).

Such criticism might similarly be directed at Scagliotti's documentary, *Coming Out in the Developing World*. Despite the initial optimism attributed by the opening sequence to the arrival of 'heightened [gay] visibility' in the majority world, the film ultimately seems more concerned with focusing on the cost of such visibility for queer citizens living in countries where cultural norms and local laws have yet to 'catch up' with the values of globalized gay culture concurrently in circulation. Taking the arrest of fifty-two men on a Nile riverboat in Cairo for 'crimes of debauchery' in 1991 as its point of departure, the film then takes the viewer on a predictably bleak whistle-stop tour of the 'developing world', providing a range of suitably harrowing accounts of human rights' abuses against LGBTQ citizens in countries as far afield as Pakistan, Namibia and Honduras. This is not to belittle the ordeals which are recounted by the documentary's participants — some of them are indeed shocking and the documentary in this respect fulfils an important expository and educative role. What *is* problematic, however, is that virtually all these participants turn out to be emigrants speaking from the USA or Canada, with the narrator stating: 'For those few who glimpsed the possibility of living an honest gay life only to have it taken away, there was no turning back [...] exile in the West was the only option'. This may well be true, but one cannot help but wonder what became of those who did not have the privilege of that 'option', with the discussion of gay and lesbian activism and sexuality politics in the countries in question disappointingly brief. Rather, the very fact that the final words in the documentary, 'I will fight for my rights', are then followed by a postscript informing us that the speaker of the words emigrated to Western Canada in 2003, seems to suggest that gay 'liberation' in fact begins and ends in North America. In this sense, the 'ordinary' queer citizens of Pakistan, Namibia and Honduras are deprived of a voice in this film, spoken for by their more fortunate, and in many cases, more wealthy, brethren residing in countries on the other side of the world. In turn, the more 'discreet' and 'elliptical' paths to liberation that those 'left behind' might be forging go wholly unmentioned. As Phillips reminds us, these may be less easily recognizable than those associated with gay and lesbian politics and thus provide more conceptual and empirical challenges but nevertheless they are no less productive or legitimate (Phillips 2006: 19).

What emerges from this discussion is that merely dismissing supposedly 'western-driven' phenomena as either inherently defective in a majority-world context (democracy, human rights and capitalism) and/or detrimental to economic and social wellbeing (neoliberalism and globalization) *at the expense* of any consideration of agency and localized transformative practices, only serves to further deprive these societies, as Massey puts it, 'of their own trajectories, their own histories and the potential for their own, perhaps different, futures' (2005: 5).[6] Within the geographical imagination, in turn, the centre-periphery dichotomy is not challenged but rather remains ever more firmly entrenched both on the level of the global and the local, 'obliterating the multiplicities [and] contemporaneous heterogeneities of space' (2005: 5). This rings particularly true for imagined geographies of dissident sexuality whereby the large metropolises of the minority world, London, New York, Los Angeles and other (perceived) centres of global capital, are regarded as the harbingers of the 'modern' metropolitan gay model which is then replicated (always deficiently) amongst the moneyed elites pertaining to 'local versions of the metropolis' (Sinfield 2000: 21) such as São Paulo, Bangkok, Cape Town, Buenos Aires and so on. Poorer (and often darker) queer citizens residing in the urban margins and rural spaces merely have to 'make do' with their own 'traditional' model, according to which non-metropolitan urban sexualities and rural sexualities are rather problematically elided.

Such an imagining of things obfuscates more reflexive and nuanced readings of the above phenomena, particularly globalization and neoliberalism. As Binnie reminds us, it has long been a touchstone of contemporary cultural studies that globalization wields 'diverse, spatially uneven effects' (even if, he continues, this is often overlooked in studies of sexual geographies) (2004: 36). In this respect, and to redirect our discussion more concretely back to the city, García Canclini argues in *Imaginarios urbanos* [*Urban Imaginaries*] (1997) that traditional models of conceptualizing space are being made increasingly redundant. He writes that 'megalopolises' such as Mexico City, for example, now contain at least four cities, superimposed onto one another: the historical-territorial city (the historic centre), the industrial city (marked by expansion into the urban periphery), the informational-communicational city (the domain of financial and informational networks) and a fourth city composed of diverse but coexisting temporalities: 'un montaje efervescente de culturas de distintas épocas' [an effervescent montage of cultures from different [historical] periods] (1997: 89). This contradictory and chaotic 'video clip' city, as García Canclini terms it, is symbolic of what he perceives to be the ungraspable nature of a city which is no longer experienced as a totality by its inhabitants who 'transita, conoce, experimenta pequeños enclaves' [traverse, get to know, experience [it as] tiny enclaves] (1997: 82).

And yet rather than capitulating to the idea of a fractured city characterized *solely* by gaping social chasms exacerbated by imposed segregation, surveillance of populations and the disintegration of democratic uses of public space, as imaged in Teresa Caldeira's *City of Walls: Crime, Segregation and Citizenship in São Paulo* (2000), García Canclini suggests that globalization's transformation of contemporary cities into communication hubs offers the possibility to bridge these chasms and 'recomponer esta totalidad' [reassemble this totality]. Televisa's daily deployment of a helicopter to map Mexico City's traffic jams and the transposition of these images onto the television screen is one such example which he provides. It is, he argues, an extremely effective 'simulacra' [simulation], one which, 'nos permite orientarnos en el tránsito y ayuda a desarrollar imaginarios sobre aquello que desconocemos' [allows us to orientate ourselves in traffic and helps us develop our imagination of those places we don't know] (1997: 83). For García Canclini, communications technology and the renewed participatory possibilities it affords has created 'nuevos actores sociales' [new social actors] who 'parecen saber mas que el intendente de la ciudad, más que los políticos, mas que los movimientos populares, porque cada uno de estos actores tradicionales parece ocuparse de pequeños fragmentos' [seem to know more than the mayor of the city, more than politicians, more than popular movements, because each of these traditional actors inhabit and oversee tiny fragments of space] (1997: 81). His view is echoed by José Joaquín Brunner who speaks of a 'new class' of 'receiver-consumers' who 'process, interpret, appropriate and live this mass of produced and transmitted signs [of a decentred and deterritorialized culture] in their own way, individually or, at times, collectively' (2002: 22–23). These accounts would appear to reflect the 'optimism' with which some postmodern thinkers such as Jean-François Lyotard have viewed the now highly dislocated communicative structure of post-industrial society. For Lyotard, the collapse of 'grand narratives' in the wake of the new relationship between science and technology has given way to what he terms 'little narratives'. Irreducibly local in nature and eschewing the unifying pretence of modern reason in favour of a heterogeneous field of exploration and possibility, these 'little narratives' embody new forms of knowledge, 'no longer transmitted *en bloc,* once and for all' but 'served', he writes, 'à la carte' (1984: 48).

Yet many Latin American thinkers remain deeply suspicious of this postmodern celebration of new communication technologies and the potential they might offer for new conditions of knowledge and existence. In the Colombian context, for example, Jesús Martín Barbero opines that 'some of the most perverse expressions and instrumentalizations of the crisis of coexistence are, precisely in the communications domain' (2002: 42). For him, the media has deliberately instilled a

FIG. 1.3. Bridging the gap: Medellín's new cable car system integrates the *comunas* with the city's downtown area (© Quinn Kampschroer/Pixabay 2016)

latent sense of distrust within Colombians, forcing them to retreat to the secure, privatized space of the home, allowing television 'to absorb the communication which is impossible in public squares and in the street theatre of politics' (2002: 42). In this sense, he argues:

> In this divided and torn country, television has become not only the sacrificial lamb responsible for the violence and demoralization that accosts us, but is also the one strange and only place where Colombians vicariously and perversely arrange to meet. (Barbero 2002: 42)

Sarlo's account in *Scenes from Postmodern Life* betrays similar ambivalence. She writes, 'on the roofs of houses, on the muddy slopes occupied by slums, along village alleyways and on deteriorating apartment blocks, television antennae extend imaginary lines, making for a new cultural cartography' (2001: 88). This pertains not to the school, public library, political committee or neighbourhood club, the traditional domains of social interaction, but rather to spaces 'more in tune with media culture': shopping malls, nightclubs, video games arcades and so on (2001: 92). She is quick to point out that schools could perhaps benefit and increase their efficiency by making new use of the skills their pupils have learned in these domains, 'skills such as the feeling for speed acquired by playing video games; the ability to take things in and respond when faced with a set of superimposed messages; or they could make new use of the content, both familiar and exotic provided by the media'

(2001: 99). Yet ultimately, she questions to what extent these 'skills' really equip students with the intellectual capacities that are required in the worlds of work, technology and politics. For her, media culture may indeed have undermined 'old powers', but they nevertheless lack 'the will or ability to lay the foundations upon which to construct new, autonomous powers' (2001: 92).

Towards a Queer Urban Geography of Latin American Cinema

The terrain of these debates is, then, complex and confusing, characterized by divergent and often contradictory discursive trajectories along which it is easy to lose oneself or reach a dead-end. This book negotiates a cautious path between these opposing perspectives, with the process of 'reprojecting the city' as a critical intervention, incorporating various dimensions. Broadly speaking, as previously stated, this means challenging the predominance of minority-world accounts of cinematic urbanism by relocating 'the city' to the majority-world context of Latin America. Incorporating dissident sexualities into the cinema-city relationship, in turn, not only corrects the heterocentrism of these accounts, but precisely through their relocation simultaneously speaks back to the homogenizing, globalizing discourses often associated with North American and European sexuality politics, and with lesbian and gay studies. In this instance, 'speaking back' means disrupting the view of capitalist modernity, in particular its neoliberal, globalized forms, as a universal, homogenous experience according to which the production of dissident sexualities and cultures will follow the same universal logic no matter where one resides in the world. On one level, this implies drawing attention to the unequal power relations inherent in a hierarchical global system which produces the wealth of the minority world at the expense of the poverty of the majority world and thus in effect prohibits, rather than encourages, the production of 'modern' metropolitan models of sexuality in these countries. And yet, in this sense, whilst betraying a postcolonial perspective, my analysis nevertheless refuses to capitulate to a solely 'subaltern' discourse which sees the minority world as an 'all powerful mover and shaker' and which simultaneously relegates the sexual citizens of the majority world to victimhood and passive acceptance. Rather, 'reprojecting the city' is concerned with disrupting centre-periphery dichotomies, proposing the urban margins as potential spaces of productive possibility capable of infiltrating and critically transforming the 'centre', ultimately rendering such oppositions untenable. Whilst this dual process of (de/re)centering — remaining wary of 'grand narratives', but embracing the fragmentary and 'little narratives' as Lyotard terms them — may appear unambiguously 'postmodern' in its intent, my analysis is nevertheless cognizant of the limits of 'productive possibility' and consistently suspicious of terms such as 'freedom' and 'liberation'. In this sense, what ultimately predominates here might most readily be described as a queer Foucauldian perspective. David Halperin provides the following (oft-quoted) definition of 'queer' at its most basic and fundamental level:

> Queer is by definition *whatever* is at odds with the normal, the legitimate, the dominant. *There is nothing in particular to which it necessarily refers.* It is an identity without an essence. 'Queer' then, demarcates not a positivity but a positionality *vis-à-vis* the normative. [Queer] describes a horizon of possibility whose precise

extent and heterogeneous scope cannot in principle be delimited in advance. (Halperin 1995: 62)

Subero deploys this quotation in the opening chapter of *Queer Masculinities in Latin American Cinema*, arguing a queer perspective to be useful for the Anglo reader in that it offers 'a broader scope to understand manifestations of same-sex sexuality within a wider context beyond either heteronormativism or the politics of homosexuality as experienced in the west' (2014: 19). But is this *all* queer theory is about? If it is to reassert itself as being more than just a vague analytical tool of aesthetic criticism or a useful lens through which to view the 'indefinable' then arguably it requires a little more elucidation. Halperin's definition above is certainly a good starting point in this respect. Like other poststructuralist accounts of subjectivity and social relations 'queer' here remains inherently 'open' and rejects totalizing and universalizing discourses on the grounds that they leave little room for difference, complexity and ambiguity, one of the main criticisms aimed at the unitary notion of identity espoused by the lesbian and gay lobby during the 1970s. And yet by refusing the notion of objective, universal truths, 'queer' necessarily negates the idea of a 'true (sexual) self' constructed around an 'innate' sexuality. Foucault, often regarded as 'the granddaddy' of queer theory suggested instead that sexuality should be seen as a form of power and knowledge which has been discursively produced and deployed, to borrow his phraseology, in order to multiply and diversify techniques of social control. Power dwells not in repressing sexual drives but in producing different sexualities that are categorized and rated according to what is deemed acceptable and not acceptable within dominant social mores. Those individuals who identify with and practise these sexualities can then be approved or normalized on the one hand, or marginalized, disciplined or treated on the other. In this respect Halperin makes the point that Foucault pours cold water on the idea of 'sexual freedom': for whilst it may have liberated our sexuality it has not liberated us *from* our sexuality (1995: 20). Rather, it is but another form of domination, producing the illusion of personal freedom whilst ensuring that the exercise of that freedom is contingent on submission to pre-prescribed and (intrinsically limiting) models of understanding and organizing our desires.

Foucault's apparent rejection of a liberationist agenda has prompted his detractors to ask, somewhat disparagingly, exactly what kind of politics and/or ethics queer theory (for which the philosopher's ideas still remain a cornerstone) is trying to promote. Halperin, in his seminal defence of the late philosopher and historian *Saint Foucault: Towards a Gay Hagiography* (1995), provides a convincing response to this question. He makes the point that Foucault was very much in favour of individual self-empowerment, it is just that he saw this empowerment in terms of resistance rather than liberation per se. If social domination is effected by the production and deployment of apparatuses of power and knowledge then it has the potential to be simultaneously reversed by uncovering, making visible and denaturalizing the (often ingeniously disguised) mechanisms at play in this production and deployment. And it is in this reversing, observes Halperin, that the 'object' position often ascribed to those who are the focus of expert discourse might simultaneously be flipped (if only momentarily) into a 'subject' positionality (1995: 56).

This process can be seen in a practical sense at the heart of Foucault's political undertakings. Halperin, in this respect, draws attention to Foucault's founding of the Groupe D'Information sur les Prisons (GIP) in the early 1970s. Here his intervention was not concerned with drafting proposals for the reform of the French prison system but rather with recording and gathering information and democratizing the distribution of this information amongst inmates so that they were in a better position to articulate their own needs and advance their own political projects (1995: 55). This facilitated 'the emergence of new circuits of knowledge and power', circuits that might generate different distributions of authority and thereby alter the overall strategic situation in which the governors and the governed found themselves (1995: 56). But it is perhaps Foucault's ideas surrounding the transgressive potential of practices such as S/M which offer the most salient examples of what might count as explicitly queer praxis, argues Halperin. S/M's subversive element lies in its eroticization of society's disciplinary technologies which become the subject of ritual re-enactment. Here power differentials — and the roles and boundaries they imply — are toyed with, subverted and transgressed, 'playing the world backwards' to quote Foucault (1967: 124). Within these games, strategic power relations are demoted from their role in perpetuating personal or political subjugation and are instead subordinated to the overall purpose of creating human pleasure (in Halperin, 1995: 86).

In both cases, power is viewed as not inherently repressive and centred in one particular individual or group, rather diffuse and productive, flowing through networks of interconnected relations. And 'where there is power', suggests Foucault, 'there is resistance' (1978: 95–96). This resistance may ultimately reveal itself as 'a handle or support for power' but it may also emerge as its 'adversary' (1978: 95–96). It is this relational understanding of power which largely informs my analysis of the films which follows, since it allows points of dissonance and resistance to be identified more easily within cinematic urban landscapes which at first glance might easily be written off as inherently oppressive spaces (the Santa Cruz we encounter in *Dependencia sexual* is one such example). Foregrounding the transgressive potential of the body in these spaces is key here because it, in turn, brings into view those more subtle and often fleeting acts of dissonance, which 'behind the scenes' nevertheless continue to infiltrate, disrupt and destabilize the patriarchal foundations underpinning the modern industrialized city. As a critical intervention *Reprojecting the City*, therefore, is also concerned with reclaiming and making the case for queer theory at a time when it increasingly comes under fire, either from academics who believe its recent applications lack rigour or from those involved in sexuality politics who argue that it holds little relevance to the lives of the people it purports to speak for. My analysis, I hope, will challenge both these perceptions.

A Relational Understanding of Space and Place

Like 'queer', 'space' has also become a buzzword in cultural studies of late, but one which is often poorly defined, particularly in terms of how it relates to 'place'. It seems pertinent to provide some elucidation here before proceeding to analysis of the films. Viewed through a postmodern lens, urban space in the contemporary era might, in its crudest form, most readily be conceived of in terms of the 'fragment', coexistent with a multiplicity of other fragments which together transmogrify into the highly decentred place of the contemporary city. It is a moderately visual and thus graspable conception of space and place, and, in this sense, useful when dealing with cinematic representations of the city, which give primacy to making urban space 'perceivable' to the viewer but in a necessarily fragmented way due to the manner in which film texts are constructed through editing. At the same time, however, the implication that each 'fragment' corresponds to a 'portion' of geographic space not only tends to replicate the notion of 'space as surface' but its concurrent connotations of fracture and rupture simultaneously imply disconnection and separation. This is problematic in the sense that it mitigates against the sort of inter-relational conception of space and place required when, for example, discussing 'power networks' or a 'multiplicity of points of resistance'.[7]

In this respect, Doreen Massey's conception of space-time provides a constructive counterpoint to this view of 'space as [fragmented] surface'. This conception still subscribes to the notion of relativity, 'space as the product of interrelations, as constituted through interactions' (2005: 5), but endows it with a temporal aspect, 'space as the sphere of a multiplicity of trajectories [...] a simultaneity of stories so far' (2005:130). In this way, places are conceived of not as 'portions' of geographic space but in terms of 'spatio-temporal *events* [...] weavings together of trajectories of 'stories so far' or *moments within power-geometries*' (2005: 130). To travel through space is not to travel across a surface but to travel 'across trajectories' (2005: 130). In turn, to travel between places is to move between collections of trajectories and to 'reinsert' oneself into those to which one relates. Through this account place is disassociated from fixed location. This is perhaps more easily imagined in an urban context, (multicultural) cities such as London, for example, as constituted through their inhabitants and a vast patchwork of cultures with overlapping histories and multiple connections/interfaces to and with other parts of the world. Yet as Massey points out, some of our strongest evocations of 'place' are bound up with notions of nature and wilderness. In this context, how can we conceive of place as an 'event'? Massey uses the example of Skiddaw, a mountain in the Lake District, which despite its apparent 'timelessness' has, she points out, its own long and turbulent history, a history which has a geography too. She writes:

> For *when* the rocks of Skiddaw were laid down, about 500 million years ago, they were not 'here' at all. That sea was in the southern hemisphere, about a third of the way south from the equator towards the south pole. (Rude shock this, for Skiddaw is a mountain which, in English imaginations, is inextricably of the 'The North'). (Massey 2005: 133)

Massey's account is relevant here because it allows us to 'face up to the challenges of space', as she puts it, to reject the notion of space as a container 'for always-already constituted identities' and instead to recognize its 'coeval multiplicities [...] its radical contemporaneity [and] its constitutive complexity' (2005: 8). From this perspective, space is an interactional space, in which there are always connections to be made — it is 'a space of missing links and loose ends' (2005: 12). And when space is 'open', as Massey writes, the 'future is open' too (2005: 11). Space as a simultaneity of 'stories so far' discounts the possibility of 'one' world which waits in 'the same historic queue', as western accounts of capitalist modernity would have us believe. Instead it allows us to acknowledge the existence of other peoples, travelling along their own specific trajectories, making their own histories and their own futures and — to insert this into the realm of sexuality — with their own distinct interpretations and specific means of achieving sexual 'liberation' or 'freedom'. This coincides with one of the fundamental poststructuralist cornerstones to have influenced queer theory, that is, the prioritization of the local and the specific over universalisms and ahistoricisms of 'grand' narratives.

In this respect, the appearance of the term 'Latin American' in the title of this book might appear somewhat contradictory and certainly one should acknowledge that a 'regional' study of this nature runs the risk of reproducing the same binary geographical imagination it wishes to destabilize. Nevertheless, 'national' frameworks cannot be necessarily held up as being any more representative of the fullness of human experience. For precisely one of Massey's aims in drawing attention to 'the relational constructedness of things' and conceiving of 'place' as an 'event' is to problematize the concept of the national and the claims to unitary identity and culture it implies. Certainly, if everything is, and always was, 'thrown together', as Massey's account suggests, identities, cultures and even the ground on which we stand, cannot be thought to embody any notion of authenticity or pre-given coherence. Rather, what makes something 'distinct' and 'specific' is almost invariably in flux and comes from 'elsewhere', as her account of Skiddaw, this supposedly emblematic 'symbol of the North' [of England], aptly demonstrates.

Thus in the context of this book, the term 'Latin America' is not deployed as a homogenizing concept which obliterates difference and collapses it into a nebulous, globalized 'stew'. Rather its deployment acknowledges the diversity that exists between specifically *localized* dissident sexualities and urban spaces as they are imagined in cinematic mediations of Buenos Aires, Medellín, Recife and Rio de Janeiro. This does not imply that the 'national' should necessarily be ignored, indeed care is taken to situate each of the four films firmly within their own diverse national (cinematic) cultures. However, my analysis acknowledges that localized productions of sexuality and urban space may equally take place in dialogue with wider cultural or economic flows which cannot be neatly aligned with any one particular nation state. In this sense, it does not presume the local and the global to be monolithic, mutually exclusive formations, but rather, as Massey suggests, mutually dependent categories.

Pleasure (and Wisdom) in 'Not Knowing'

One of the pleasures of cinema (and the same can be said for other forms of cultural production such as art and literature) is that the stories it tells, in contrast to the frequently polarized debates occurring in the academe, tend not to assume inflexible subjective positions nor seek to provide coherent, fully-legible accounts of highly complex issues which often defy totalizing explanations. They allow the mind to wander, to produce its own meanings and interpretations: there is never a 'wrong' answer. This is particularly true of the films discussed in this book which lend themselves readily to the sort of queer methodology which I mobilize in my analysis, one which arguably precludes the formation of a singularized, definitive hypothesis. Their account of the relationship between urban space and dissident sexualities is plural, multifaceted, ambivalent and frequently contradictory. In this sense, it is true to say that the reader of this book who searches for 'answers' will often be frustrated. And yet arguably, in order to avoid what David Bell and Gill Valentine describe as doing 'violence to the multiple expressions of "sex" in "space"' (1995: 2), we need to assume such multiple subjective positions and consider the cinema-city-sexuality relationship from multiple points of view through a range of approaches and perspectives. These might necessarily disqualify any concrete and graspable 'conclusion'. There is, however, I would argue, great pleasure (and wisdom) in this 'not knowing'.

Notes to Chapter 1

1. Altman defines the 'Global Gay' as a figure pertaining to a 'definable group of self-identified homosexuals [....] who see themselves as part of a global community, whose commonalities override but do not deny those of race and nationality' (1997: 424).

2. The boundaries of the term sodomy have varied from place to place, and it has been used both as an umbrella term to refer to 'crimes against nature' (non-procreative sex that might take place between two men or women, or between a woman and a man) or, more specifically, as a way of indexing specifically anal sexual relations between two men.

3. Substantive historical research on this process is scarce but James Green's *Beyond Carnival: Male Homosexuality in Twentieth Century Brazil* (1999) and Jorge Salessi's *Médicos, maleantes y maricas: Higiene, criminología y homosexualidad en la construcción de la nación Argentina, Buenos Aires, 1871–1914* [*Doctors, Villains and Queers: Hygiene, Criminology and Homosexuality in the Construction of the Argentine Nation, Buenos Aires, 1871–1914*] (1995) provide enlightening accounts of its occurrence in the Brazilian and Argentinian contexts, respectively, and suggest the presence of a similar phenomenon in other Latin American countries in one form or another at the time.

4. In this respect Richard Trexler suggests that 'it is a widespread characteristic of patriarchal conceptions of political order that power in politics is said to belong to males or those perceived to be male, while dependency is said to be the fate of the female' (2003: 70).

5. Brazil's textile and clothing sector exported $1.4 billion in 2010, up 20 per cent from 2009 figures (Bevins 2011).

6. Subero argues in this respect that whilst homosexuality in Latin America has been traditionally linked to foreign experiences of same-sex desire, gay subjects in the region have borrowed or reappropriated the Anglo-European gay experience as their own, reworking it in a way that has seen the emergence of a type of gay identity that corresponds uniquely to Latin American territory (2014: 8).

7. The idea of space 'as an arena within which objects interact under the watchful eye of the scientist' (McDowell & Sharpe 1999: 257) has, in recent years, been largely replaced with an (inter)relational conception of space bound up with Marxist theories of 'historical materialism' which emphasize the symbiosis existent between the spatial organization of society and the functioning of capitalism (McDowell & Sharpe 1999: 259). Put another way, space has increasingly been viewed as being 'folded into' social relations (see, for example, Harvey 1990), what Soja has variously referred to as the 'socio-spatial dialectic' (see, for example, Soja 1980).

CHAPTER 2

Buenos Aires: *Un año sin amor*

Decentring the 'Global Gay': S/M, the HIV-Positive Body and Transnational Space

Untying the 'Global Gay'

Chapter 1 discussed materialist academic perspectives used to examine the relationship between capitalism, the city and gay identity and how these have fed into more recent debates examining the impact of globalization and the growth of supra-territorial space on the production of globalized forms of dissident sexuality. On a general level, this chapter builds on this discussion to consider how such themes have been mediated in a Latin American cinematic context. For if, as Altman, Cant and Champagne all suggest, 'global queering' is driven by the expansion of a globalized free market and consumer society, then transnational commodities, of which films serve as quintessential examples, must be regarded as important vehicles through which associated cultural references are disseminated. Although Foster, rightly or wrongly, argues that the films included in his study defy inclusion within an international gay, lesbian or queer film canon, the same certainly cannot be said of more recent productions in which the spaces of globalized gay culture form an explicit backdrop to their narratives. By way of a prologue, I wish briefly to reflect on one such film — Julián Hernández's *El cielo dividido* [*Broken Sky*] (Mexico, 2006) — as it raises some important questions which will be later explored in the discussion of *Un año sin amor* which follows.[1]

Recounting the love triangle that unfolds between three male university students in Mexico City, this highly stylized production with aesthetic nods to the films of Pedro Almódovar or Wong Kar Wai but more readily corresponding to an ambiguous brand of internationally queer cinema crossing the genres of 'art-house' and soft-porn, arguably embodies what Champagne terms as a 'fictive gay sensibility' (1999: 146).[2] This he defines as a 'distinct political, artistic and social identity' characterized by a 'shared consumer taste, a predilection for certain forms of art, décor, clothing, food and drink' (in Field 1995: 145). In this respect, within the film, national referents in terms of location and *mise-en-scène* are lacking, with

FIG. 2.1. 'Global Gay': The protagonist of *El cielo dividido* depicted next to the brandings of local business sponsors in the end credits (Julián Hernández, 2006: Strand Releasing)

Mexico City's iconic architectural landmarks ignored in favour of what Marc Augé might term the 'non-places' of the Zona Rosa (bars, clubs, restaurants, saunas and so on) which lie at the centre of Mexico City gay life, or so the film would have us believe.[3] Within these spaces cultural references are distinctly transnational in nature, internationally renowned Sol is apparently the beer of choice, drunk by impeccably styled young men gyrating to techno and house music, the place names emblazoned upon their impossibly tight t-shirts such as 'Holland', leaving the viewer in no doubt as to their cosmopolitan credentials. Specifically Mexican national issues are, in turn, subordinated to the (supposedly) internationally-legible theme of young gay love, which is negotiated in a highly stylized form by way of a diverse colour palette, a predominance of long drawn-out scenes and a preference for silence or music in place of dialogue. Here, the 'display imperative' previously discussed in the context of Linda Williams's *Hardcore* is clearly on show, the erotic interactions of the queer body celebrated and brought to the fore through lingering long-takes which are always reluctant to cut away. In this respect, whilst the film's concern with the 'corporal' is developed at the expense of its narrative elements which, arguably, come off as rather inconsequential, the film's representation of the sexual act — unapologetic, explicit and yet simultaneously tender and erotic — arguably marks a welcome departure from the stereotypes of sordidness and anonymity typically associated with gay sex in Mexican cinema.

As optimistic as *El cielo dividido*'s portrayal of a more open gay culture may be (in notable contrast, for example, to the more sombre representations of (repressed) same-sex desire present in earlier Mexican films such as Arturo Ripstein's *El lugar sin límites*, 1978), the protagonists' daily regime of house music and haute couture can hardly be upheld as representative of the realities experienced by the majority of Mexico's young queer citizens. Press reception of the film was accordingly somewhat ambivalent. According to Carlos Bonfil, for example, writing in the

Mexican newspaper *La Jornada*, the 'edén de tolerancia' [eden of tolerance] imaged in the film, seemingly free from homophobia, discrimination and, we might add, poverty and social exclusion too, 'contrasta con la realidad' [is at odds with reality] (Bonfil 2007). In this respect, he continues, whilst the director has previously claimed a debt in his work to the films and novels of Pier Paolo Pasolini, no such claim can be upheld in the case of *El cielo dividido*. For whilst the characters of Pasolini's novel *Una vita violenta* [*A Violent Life*], (originally published in 1959), for example, were certainly unapologetic in their attitude towards their sexuality, this attitude was premised precisely on their status as marginalized social pariahs as opposed to members of the sort of (imagined) gay community solaced in social acceptance that we see in *El cielo dividido*. For Bonfil, what was once transgressive in Hernández's films thus appears in *El cielo dividido* merely as a bland and 'reiterative' form of homoeroticism communicated through a succession of 'Benetton-style' kisses (2007).

In this respect, he implies, the film falls victim to the very 'bourgeois stupidity' that Pasolini so virulently condemned in his famous essay 'Abiura dalla trilogia della vita' [Disavowal of the Trilogy of Life] (1975), where he argued that the fight for democratic expression and sexual liberation had become supplanted by the powers of consumerism and the false illusion of tolerance this conceded. Certainly *El cielo dividido* makes no secret of its indebtedness to the commercial Mexican gay scene, the end credits proudly paying homage to local gay business sponsors such as the Fun-Fit Gym and Furor Products, whilst reminding us that the film was shot on location in the popular gay bars of La Estación and Cabaré-Tito VIP, all against the backdrop of black and white film stills showing the film's protagonists in various states of erotic embrace.

The above discussion is important in that it highlights the essential ambivalence surrounding Altman's figure of the 'Global Gay' who appears so aptly embodied here by the protagonists of *El cielo dividido*. On one level, the film's representation of a highly commodified gay culture affirms the relationship between capitalism and gay identity discussed in Chapter 1. And yet the way in which membership of these commercial spaces and the consumption/mobilization of associated brands of music, fashion and alcohol is positioned as a *sine qua non* for this identity makes it difficult to regard gay consumer culture, at least as it is imagined here, as being in any way affirmative or liberatory. In this respect, Champagne argues for the need to be cognizant of the fact that whilst capitalism is one of the preconditions of a modern gay identity, 'it also works to "manage" that identity in its own interests and often in opposition to those of real human beings' (1999: 150). From this perspective, then, the desire of many sexual dissidents to embrace a 'Global Gay' identity, might more readily be understood as little more than a trivialized form of 'false consciousness', at least this is the view Binnie infers from Altman's account which, he argues, sees 'global queering' as a form of western imperialism (Binnie 2004: 59).

On another level, the fact that the protagonists of *El cielo dividido* uniformly possess the ability to buy into this culture (whether or not we regard such an act as 'affirmative' or 'liberatory') simultaneously reproduces the myth that gay men and women somehow constitute an economically privileged class. As discussed in Chapter 1 gay and lesbians may occupy a certain relationship to capitalism but this is simultaneously 'fractured' by class, race, gender and other factors, something particularly relevant to Latin American countries, argued to be sites of long-standing social cleavages which only seem to have been exacerbated by global capitalism, in particular its neoliberal forms. This 'fracturing', in turn, has served as an explanation for the apparently limited presence of the metropolitan gay model in Latin American countries, often correlated, particularly in the social sciences, with white, middle-class men residing in the affluent areas of the region's major metropolitan centres (see Chapter 1). Whilst they may possess the economic means to indulge what Field terms the 'mythical gay sensibility' centred around a 'shared consumer taste and a predilection for certain forms of art, décor, clothing, food, drink and international travel' (in Champagne 1999: 145), as recent political economic perspectives have revealed, not everybody is invited to the party.

The 'Global Gay' consequently emerges from these accounts as a highly ambivalent figure who appears either as an unwitting accomplice in global capitalism's ruthless pursuit of profit or as a doppelgänger to a marginalized and excluded 'other', relegated to the status of passive victimhood. On a broad level, then, this chapter attempts to beat an alternative path through this theoretical tug of war surrounding the 'Global Gay', seeking to untie this figure from what is a dual conceptual bind. Turning to Anahí Berneri's *Un año sin amor*, my discussion considers how this film both supports and unsettles these economic perspectives on queer globalization. I argue that whilst the Buenos Aires of the mid-1990s, a period which constituted the apogee of Argentinean neoliberal reform, appears in the film as highly conducive to the emergence of globalized gay culture, access to and free circulation of its associated spaces is certainly highly selective and by no means universal. I then go on to consider to what extent the ambits associated with the practice of sadomasochism in the film function for the protagonist as an 'alternative' space in which to confront the crisis of identity engendered by his illness; and how they mitigate his resultant sensation of corporal alienation. Engaging with Michael Brown's ideas of 'closet space' and his mobilization of David Harvey's notion of the 'spatial [economic] fix', my analysis shifts back and forth revealing the spaces of S/M, like those pertaining to the commercial gay scene, to be similarly commodified and exclusionary and yet, at the same time, potentially threatening (in contrast to 'homonormative' gay culture) to heterosexualized gender relations underpinning the industrial city. As Knopp argues, the relationship between capitalism and sexual citizens is not about a solely 'unidirectional casuality' according to which gay identity and relations emerge in urban space *only in function* to capitalism. Rather, as Knopp argues, capitalism and capital accumulation might actually serve to encourage lesbigay consciousness and/or politics (1995: 155). His position is echoed by José Quiroga, for whom gays and lesbians may be 'cultural constructions of capitalism' but also represent modes of defiance 'that use its tools in order to undermine its repressive paradigms' (2000: 12).

Un año sin amor: Going Global

Of all the Latin American national film industries, that of Argentina can perhaps be regarded as the most prolific purveyor of films definable under the banner of a self-consciously 'Queer' or 'Lesbigay' branded cinema. Edgardo Cozarinsky's *Ronda nocturna* (2005), Veronika Chen's *Vagón fumador* (2000), Diego Lerman's *Tan de repente* (2003), Lucía Puenzo's *XXY* (2007) and *El niño pez* (2009), and Santiago Otheguy's *La león* (2007) constitute some notable examples, whose greater or lesser degree of success on the international festival circuit has firmly placed Argentina on the global lesbian and gay cultural map. Certainly *Un año sin amor* also takes its place amongst these other notable productions and perhaps marks more familiar territory for international audiences than the Colombian film *La virgen de los sicarios* (2000), inflected as we will see in the following chapter with issues of a more nationally-specific nature.

Set in Buenos Aires in 1996, *Un año sin amor* unfolds according to the journal of protagonist, Pablo Peréz (played by Juan Minujín), an aspiring *porteño* writer suffering from HIV.[4] Shifting constantly between the space of his imagination as it is indulged on the screen of his word-processor and that of the material world from which he feels increasingly estranged, the film chronicles the development of his illness and subsequent search for human connection (and romance?) in the city's underground queer S/M scene. The story was originally written as a semi-auto-biographical novel by the real-life Pablo Peréz, who collaborated with Berneri in writing the screenplay, and accordingly in the film the journal of the fictional Pablo is eventually published. It is a pin-prick of hope amidst what is an otherwise sombre, and at times desperate story, which as Diego Batalle notes, eschews much of the humour and sarcasm of its written source in its quest for narrative distance (2005).

Such a sense of malaise and detachment has become characteristic of many recent examples of Argentinian independent cinema, which as Gonzalo Aguilar notes, departs substantially from its antecedents, particularly in terms of the relationship it shares with its audience (2006: 26). In contrast to Adolfo Aristarain's *Tiempo de revancha* (1981), Luis Puenzo's *La historia oficial* (1985) or more recently Carlos Sorín's *Bombón el perro* (2004), by way of example, the current tendency, Aguilar writes, leans more towards open endings, a lack of allegories, ambiguous, self-absorbed 'zombie' characters, erratic narration, an absence of national identifiers, and a rejection of identity and political demands. He surmises that 'todas estas decisiones que [...] hacen la opacidad de las historias, que en vez de entregarnos todo dirijido, abren el juego de la interpretación' [all these decisions [...] endow the stories with an opaqueness, which instead of handing us everything on a plate, opens up a game of interpretation] (2000: 26).

In *Un año sin amor* we encounter a multi-faceted protagonist who refuses to pander to the demands of his family who, like his potentially exigent audience, oscillate between equal measures of sympathy and frustration. The film's 'conclusion', if we can call it that, is also suitably vague, producing more questions than answers — a narrative rendering, one might say, of Pablo's own lingering sense of incompleteness. And in terms of its setting, visual references to Buenos Aires are surprisingly scant, the film's cinematic landscape (in contrast, as we will see, to that of *La virgen de los sicarios*) rendered a virtual 'non-place' of anonymous streets and interior spaces, the cuckoo-clock and chintzy artificial Christmas tree giving more of an alpine flavour to the cramped apartment Pablo shares with his aunt than anything discernibly Latin American.

The director's preference for a rough, grainy image during the developing of the negative also recalls the 'dirty realism' of earlier examples of what some have termed 'New Argentine Cinema', though the documentary feel of Pablo Trapero's *Mundo grúa* (1999) and Caetano and Stagnaro's *Pizza, birra, faso* (1997) is most definitely mitigated by the deliberate colour saturation and mobilization of highly controlled camera work.[5] Whilst Sergio Wolf argues that these films 'resist globalization' by choosing different parameters and affinities or affiliations that are less standardized and that appeal to a different kind of spectator (in Falicov 2007: 116), *Un año sin amor*'s resultantly controlled image, combined with a meticulously electronically produced soundtrack (again devoid of national referents) and other stylized elements such as the 'quirky' end credits do recall what we might term a 'global' aesthetic arguably present in productions such as *21 Grams* (Alejandro González Iñárritu, 2003), *Memento* (Christopher Nolan, 2000) and Tom Twyker's *Run Lola Run* (1998).[6]

This is reinforced by the frequent nods to an internationally-orientated metropolitan gay culture contained within the film. In the opening sequence, for example, we see Pablo browsing a pile of glossy gay lifestyle magazines of the *Boyz* or *Attitude*[7] variety, the camera glimpsing a succession of attractive but ultimately interchangeable naked cover boys, their smooth, sculpted bodies drained of any national referents in apparent homage to the generic mould of the 'Global Gay'. Eventually the camera pauses to reflect on the wording of Pablo's entry printed in the magazine's personal columns and from which we infer him to be an openly gay man, comfortable with his sexuality: 'Edad 30. Altura 173 centimetros, peso 70 kilogramas, rapado, buen cuerpo. Busca amante o amigo varonil, activo, protector, bien dotado, para relación estable con sexo seguro' [Age: 30. Height: 173 cm. Weight: 70 kg. Shaved head, good body. Looking for lover or male friend, active, protective, well endowed, for stable relationship and safe sex]. The number of other entries in the columns, in turn, establishes the existence of an associated community whose physical presence is subsequently revealed by the camera's periodic forays into the busy cafes, bars and restaurants located at the intersection of Avenidas Puérredon and Santa Fé, traditionally one of the most important meeting points for gays and lesbians in the city. As Viviana Gorbato and Susana Finkel note, the area would become even more of an iconic location during the 1990s as it became colonized by the infamous *tarjeteros*[8] with their flyers, free passes and queue jumps to the new gay superclubs which had opened such as *América* and *Bunker* (1995: 192). Certainly at two points in the film, Pablo and his close friend Nicolás visit an unnamed gay nightclub, its appropriately rainbow-coloured stairwell, crowded dance floor and upbeat electronic music all exuding a sense of confidence, openness and cosmopolitanism of which Nicolás himself functions as the absolute embodiment. Employed within the creative industries (specifically publishing), well travelled, financially solvent, healthy and attractive, the latter fulfils all the prerequisites of the modern gay man, his stylish, contemporary apartment a monument to his success. Like the gay club, this space is characterized by a similarly 'universal aesthetic', its minimalist styling and muted tones seemingly pulled straight from the interior design sections of Pablo's gay magazines. The image, in one scene, of its trendily attired owner propped against a well-stocked bookshelf nursing a large glass of red wine completes the picture, a rather overly obvious visual shortcut to the gay man's reputed 'predilection for certain forms of art, décor, clothing, food and drink' (Fields in Champagne 1999: 1).

Whilst this 'global' aesthetic seemingly compliments the film's supposedly 'universal' thematic — described in various press interviews by the director simply as the 'búsqueda del amor' [search for love] (see, for example, Lerer 2005) — her decision to explore this through the dual prisms of HIV and sadomasochism can hardly be regarded as entirely arbitrary. Aside from the (sub)narratives of films such as Víctor Saca's *En el paraíso no existe el dolor* (Mexico, 1995) and Hector Babenco's *Carandiru* (Brazil, 2003), the region's HIV epidemic and most definitely the practice of S/M both constitute relatively uncharted territory in Latin American fictional feature film. The combination of these in a single film was no doubt intended, at least in part, to capture a degree of domestic media attention as well as to appeal thematically, as well as aesthetically, to the tastes of international audiences in North America and Europe, where cinematic mediations of such themes have asserted a greater presence both in the realm of fiction and documentary. The film was indeed undeniably critically successful: in 2005 it won the prestigious Teddy prize at the Berlin Film Festival, the FIPRESCI prize at Argentina's Mar del Plata Film Festival, the Grand Jury prize at the Los Angeles Outfest and the Best Foreign Narrative Film prize at the New York Gay and Lesbian Film Festival, as well as subsequently securing extensive international distribution rights.

The 'Mirror Effect'

Why Argentina should have become more prolific with regards to the production of an identifiably 'lesbigay' or 'queer' cinema than say Mexico or Brazil, both of whom have comparably-sized industries of a similar international reach, has no simple answer. Perhaps it serves as a reflection of what Jon Beasley-Murray notes is the Argentinian reputation for being 'unusually attentive to fashions and trends originating elsewhere' (in Sarlo 2001: xii). Buenos Aires, in particular, has been considered by some to 'exist only to the extent that Europe looks at it' (Dujovne Ortiz, in Pick 1989: 64), with Dujovne Ortiz claiming 'the city was born into this play of mirrors, in this complicity of reflection' (in Pick 1989: 64). They are perhaps crude and well-trodden stereotypes, indeed it could be said that North America these days wields far more economic and cultural influence in Latin America than Europe does. However, as Sarlo argues in her eagerness to reclaim the productivities of 'cultural mimicry on the periphery', what is significant is the accentuated and exaggerated manner this attentiveness takes. Such 'normative reproduction', as she puts it, can be regarded as 'an exercise of subjective autonomy' that actually marks

Argentinian *national* identity itself. In turn, as Beasley-Murray observes (referring in particular to Sarlo's account of the prevalence of (Miami-inspired) plastic surgery in Buenos Aires), this reproduction allows the consequences of what is initiated *elsewhere* to be 'more clearly and starkly visible' (in Sarlo 2001: xii). Perhaps it is this tendency towards the extreme which explains Berneri's decision to produce a film dealing *both* with S/M and HIV/AIDS, topics which even amongst gay and lesbian communities remain sensitive.

Certainly since the end of the country's military dictatorship (1976–83) and the resultant *destape* [opening] both on the level of sexuality politics and lesbian and gay culture, Argentina (especially Buenos Aires) has been particularly receptive to North American trends. The 1990s were particularly effervescent in this respect, not only in the greater convergence between Argentina and the USA on an economic level through the pegging of the peso to the dollar, but also in the way in which individual liberties were conceived. As Ernesto Meccia notes, the work of LGBT organizations, such as the Comunidad Homosexual de Argentina created in 1984, ensured that the issue of homosexuality began to be gradually politicized and its discussion brought into the public domain, with gays and lesbians increasingly demanding, in place of 'negative' rights to tolerance and privacy, concrete legal guarantees of equality and discriminatory protection (2006: 54–55), a phenomenon similar to that documented by Sinfield in North America in his book *The Gay and After* (1998). In 1992 Argentina would introduce a national programme to reduce the HIV/AIDS epidemic and burden, and by 1997 Law 24455 would guarantee universal and free access to treatment. In 1992 Buenos Aires also held its first gay pride march, now an annual event second in size within Latin America only to São Paulo's yearly celebration, which itself has become one of the largest in the world along with those of San Francisco and Sydney.

The greater climate of openness was reflected not least in the realm of television programming, traditionally subject to more scrutiny than the big screen. The year 1992, for example, heralded the first gay (male) kiss to be shown on the Argentinian small screen in the drama *Zona de riesgo 2: atendida por sus propios dueños* and a year later lesbians would have their turn in *Cartas de amor en cassette* (Bazán 2006: 380). By now the stipulations of the Ley de Radiodifusión [The Audiovisual Law] to 'abstenerse de exaltar el desvío sexual o el erotismo' [abstain from promoting sexual deviance or eroticism] had well and truly been consigned to the political dustbin with other programmes such as *Verdad / Consecuencia* (1996) and *Como pan caliente* (1996) soon following suit with their own (positive) gay story lines (Bazán 2006: 380). Seven years later, drama would, in turn, become reality with the small screen televising Buenos Aires's first civil union ceremony following the promulgation of La Ley de Unión Civil [The Civil Union Law] on 17 January 2003. It was the first city in Latin America to take such a step. It would serve as a true mark of how far things had come since the years of the so-called *Guerra sucia*[9] [Dirty War] and its conflation of homosexuality with political subversion resulting in the disappearance of hundreds if not thousands of people suspected of engaging in same-sex erotic activity.[10]

Carlos Menem, himself elected to presidential office in 1989 amidst the economic crisis presided over by his predecessor Raúl Alfonsín, can hardly be regarded as having given much importance to lesbian and gay rights. At a talk given at Columbia University, New York, in 1991, for example, a student's demand that he explain the contradiction between his plea for 'freedom for all countries' and the continued persecution and discrimination suffered by gays and lesbians in his own, was merely greeted with the rather evasive response: 'ese es un problema ya superado en la Argentina' [that is a problem we have overcome in Argentina] (Bazan 2006: 374). Nevertheless, his economic policies, namely a vigorous package of neoliberal reforms which would quickly make him the 'toast' of the neoliberal international establishment (North & Huber 2004: 147) could be argued to have allowed on some levels for the enrichment of gay life. The replacement of the 'máquina de impedir' [machine of obstruction], to use the words of the then Buenos Aires governor Eduardo Duhalde in reference to the bloated national state apparatus, with the 'Estado mínimo' [minimal state] in particular, opened up a new space for the accumulation of (trans)national capital.

The genesis of Argentina's 'culture of the shopping mall' that resulted from Menem's embracing of a form of mass commercial culture sponsored primarily by the global corporate elite (Falicov 2006: 77, but see Sarlo 2001 for more extensive discussion) would provide fertile ground for the emergence of a more visible commercial queer life of a distinctly international flavour to accompany these other gay cultural and political shifts (see Sívori 2005). As Argentine sociologists Menant and Siddig note, discussing the dynamics of neoliberalism, along with non-intervention in the economic realm, the privileging of competition and the free market, and the consolidation of representative democracy, 'the cultural realm [also] takes on characteristics of globalized "Western" values' (in Falicov 2006: 91).

Certainly a particular variety of popular literature (endowed with a quasi-sociological slant) that was being published at the time provides ample evidence of such 'global queering', at least as it was experienced in the capital and, to a lesser extent, the cities of Córdoba and Rosário.[11] Gorbato and Finkel's previously cited *Amor y sexo en la Argentina: la vida erótica en los 90* [*Love and Sex in Argentina: Erotic Life in the 1990s*] in particular the chapter entitled 'La nueva cultura gay' [The New Gay Culture] is one such example, the opening testimony given by a 31-year-old gay man reading:

> A los diciséis años hablé con mi familia de mi homosexualidad. Mi mama fue la primera en aceptarlo. Mi padre se abstuvo de opinar y mi hermano me rechazó abiertamente. Me enamoré con un chico de veintidós años [...] Con él conocí el gueto gay de Rosário y empecé también a viajar a Buenos Aires, a vivir la vida nocturna [...] Hoy, los cambios son brutales, abismales. Con el correr del tiempo se nos empezó a aceptar. Yo no me siento para nada discriminado. (Gorbato & Finkel 1995: 191)

> [When I was sixteen I talked to my family about my homosexuality. My mother was the first to accept it. My father didn't express his opinion and my brother openly rejected me. I fell in love with another boy when I was 22 [...] It was with him that I got to know Rosário's gay ghetto and I started travelling to Buenos Aires to experience the nightlife [...] Today, the changes have been immense. With time they've started to accept us. I don't feel discriminated against at all]

The changes were so 'immense' apparently that he then goes on to say that he began to positively avoid the city's gay clubs due to the fact that the 'majority' of the clientele in these establishments were now apparently heterosexual, a perhaps unwanted, though ironic, by-product of this greater climate of acceptance in which gay locales had become fashionable amongst the more open-minded sectors of the heterosexual population (Gorbato & Finkel 1995: 191).

Raquel Orella and Osa Orella's *Guía erótica de Buenos Aires* [*Erotic Guide to Buenos Aires*] (1994) and Gorbata's second study *Fruta prohibida* [*Forbidden Fruit*] (1999) provide further accounts of the rise of gay culture in Argentina, though again with a similar focus on Buenos Aires. There is not space to provide any extensive review of these here but *Fruta prohibida*'s opening chapter entitled 'El gay cliché' ['The Gay Cliché'] gives a flavour of the camp, tongue-in-cheek and irreverent tone which seems to be characteristic of these books, the latter featuring an amusing selection of sex tips, fashion advice, guides to *porteño* gay slang, price lists for sexual services rendered by *taxi-boys* [rent boys], a double-page 'quiz' to enable one to determine one's 'true' sexual orientation, as well as a map of gay Buenos Aires detailing the location of gay bars, clubs, porn cinemas, saunas, cruising areas, gay-friendly hotels and other services (1999: 42–72). The presence of the sexual orientation 'quiz' and the mapping of Buenos Aires's gay scene is particularly significant here in that it underscores the growing importance being attached in Argentina at the time, as elsewhere in the 'gay world', to naming and declaring one's homosexuality as an identity and assuming one's position within an accompanying community whose existence, as the map shows, had now become a material as much as an imagined reality. Indeed, the existence of the books themselves, which were seemingly targeted at a popular gay readership, attests to what was the increasing commodification of same-sex erotic subcultures occurring in Argentina at the time amidst the production of what Lisa Duggan has termed 'a new homo-normativity', that is a 'neoliberal sexual politics [...] that does not contest domi-nant heteronormative assumptions and institutions but upholds and sustains them while promising the possibility of a demobilized gay constituency and a privatized, depoliticized gay culture anchored in domesticity and consumption' (2002: 79).[12]

Disidentification

We will return to Duggan in due course, but for now it would be less than contro-versial to suggest that *Un año sin amor* (set incidentally in the mid-1990s, a period which marked the apogee of Menem's process of reform) clearly reflects the 'spirit' of the era with this ever more open, visible and 'homonormative' manifestation of gay life. The film's allusions to a transnational 'gay sensibility' produced through a shared set of '"devices", rituals, or practices' (Champagne, 1999: 145) and the presence of commercialized spaces in which these are represented or enacted, in particular, would seem to confirm the logic by which capital accumulation has been seen to encourage the dismantling of the 'closet' in space during the redevelopment and rebranding of cityscapes by urban planners (see Knopp 1992, or Bell & Binnie 1995).

Certainly a clear tension is established in the film between the fashionable space of the gay club in which Nicólas prefers socializing and that of the rather decrepit porn cinema that Pablo favours. In the case of the former, as we have seen, a high-angled shot reveals the two friends entering the establishment through a crowded, rainbow-coloured stairwell thronged with enthusiastic clubbers, the thump of a bass drum luring them down towards the dance floor. In the case of the porn cinema, however, Pablo's lonely descent to the establishment concerned is made via a completely deserted and low-lit set of stairs leading to a cinema box office, where he purchases his ticket before passing over his belongings so they can be stowed in a locker. Significantly, there is no human face to be seen, the transaction mediated via a muffled voice that emerges from behind the obscured glass which has been installed to ensure the anonymity of both customers and staff, in marked contrast with the openness of the gay club whose staff are clearly visible behind the bar. Beyond the threshold of the box office, in turn, the upbeat nature of the night club's dance floor with its energetic dance music is exchanged for the more sombre atmosphere of the sparsely populated cinema theatre, a rather sullen form of electronic music audible on the soundtrack simultaneously interspersed with the distant grunts and moans emanating from the rather dated porn film that is being screened. Not that the 'viewers' are paying much attention, of course, for whilst in the case of the gay club the most risqué behaviour we encounter goes little beyond the intertwining of tongues on the dance floor, here they are far too busy servicing each other's needs to pay any attention to what is happening on-screen. Pablo himself does not hesitate to make advances on the man seated next to him, a medium-shot revealing his head being lowered towards the man's lap where he presumably performs fellatio on the person concerned. Of course, when compared with his subsequent dalliance in a later scene, in which he penetrates another man against the cinema wall, this act of foreplay would appear remarkably discreet. Thus, whilst in the case of the gay club the use of generic dance music, 'clean' minimalist *mise-en-scène* and framing/editing techniques which underscore the fluidity of movement between its various sections (entrance, dancefloor, bar and so on), firmly established it as a safe, accessible, desexualized and 'non-threatening' space reserved primarily for socializing, the case of the porn cinema could not be more contrasting. This, quite clearly, is represented as a space of anonymous sexual pleasure, an 'unhealthy' or 'dirty' site of deviant and perhaps unsafe sex reminiscent of a bygone era in which gay life in Argentina was very much kept underground.

Yet although the film attributes a set of distinctly negative values to the space of the porn cinema, this is not to say that the more sanitized (and implicitly more 'respectable') spaces of bar and club culture we associate with Nicólas, appear as some sort of fantasy of globalized, neoliberal gay liberation. For, as we shall see, Pablo shares a rather ambivalent and distinctly uncelebratory relationship with the brave new commercialized gay world to which they pertain. Although in 1992 the *Economist* heralded a 'golden era' of new-found prosperity in Argentina (in North & Huber 2004: 147), by the mid-1990s the accompanying hangover of mass unemployment and social exclusion familiar to many countries that have followed the trajectory of neoliberal globalized modernity was less of a cause for celebration. Nearly all sectors of society were affected but North and Huber suggest that Menem's virtually instantaneous privatization of large swathes of the public sector was particularly detrimental to the middle classes, whose jobs were often unprotected by clientist networks, in contrast to the rich 'who looked after themselves' and the working classes who 'had their union-run social programmes' (North & Huber 2004: 148, see also Saborido 2006: 474). Although the protagonist of *Un año sin amor* can hardly be regarded as destitute (no specific reference is made in the film to the protagonist having been made redundant from a previous job), it is difficult to imagine that the sporadic French lessons he gives to his sole client — a rather tongue-tied female cabin crew member — pay him anything approximating a working wage. His 'career' as a writer is, for the majority of the film, similarly fruitless. Beyond the Manuel Puigs of this world it seems Argentina's intellectual resources are of little interest to 'big business' and Pablo is told unceremoniously by his agent that whilst it is possible that his poems could be included in an anthology, it probably would not be this year, or even the next. 'Local' writers, he laments, have a hard time getting published here, a comment suggestive of the more general trend of underinvestment (both public and private) in the arts under the Menem administration (see Falicov 2006, or Page 2009).[13]

Thus we can assume that without the support of his father, who pays the mortgage on the apartment he shares with his aunt, his existence would be a good deal more precarious, as the film's conclusion eventually does indeed suggest. This contrasts markedly with Nicolás, who has forged a successful career in publishing (a more lucrative sector of this business, we presume, than that within which Pablo is attempting to establish himself) and can afford all the trappings of the 'Global Gay' lifestyle — trendy clothes, a nice apartment, trips to the city's fashionable nightspots, international travel and so on. Indeed, arguably it is only through Nicolás that the protagonist is able to access the gay club they visit, in one scene the former luring a reluctant Pablo to go dancing with him with the promise that he will pay for his entrance ticket. As Judith Filc writes, the transformation of the urban landscape wrought by the erection of glittering skyscrapers, shopping malls and other spaces of commercial enterprise may have produced an attractive veneer of 'development' but frequently these have been the domains only of a privileged minority, what she terms 'espacios pseudo-públicos de circulación restringida' [pseudo-public spaces of restricted access], spaces which straddle the public and the private to which access is granted only to the 'ganadores' [the winners] of society (2003: 184).

Ultimately, though, to suggest that Pablo's experience of exclusion primarily owes itself to economic reasons is problematic and would be to overlook one of the film's overarching themes. For beyond the consolidation of metropolitan gay culture within Buenos Aires, the film also documents another manifestation of globalization, the HIV virus described by William Haver as the 'first true cosmopolitan' in that it 'respects neither geographic, cultural, sexual, class nor racial boundaries' (1996: 7).[14] Whilst 'uniting' millions of people who have become infected through same-sex erotic activity, HIV simultaneously destabilizes modern 'gay identity' as a coherent banner under which homosexuals may (or may not) identify. As O'Neill argues, 'nothing represents the postmodern moment in our history more than the transformation of our sexuality in its encounter with the HIV virus' (in Binnie 2004: 181).

This 'transformation' is made apparent in the film, not least through the conflict that the presence of Pablo's body now produces within the film's spaces of sanitized metropolitan gay culture. For whilst the HIV virus does not always produce necessarily visible markings on the body, Pablo's dwindling T-cell count, and consequently, the growing inability of his immune system to fight off even the most common of viruses, means for him the illness has now attained an increasing visibility. The opening minute of the film is replete with clues to this corporal deterioration. Here cross-cuts to his inhaler and an array of tinctures and herbal medicines are intersected by a series of alternating close-ups between the computer screen and the keyboard on which he is typing, suggesting that all is not well with the body to which these rather delicate looking hands belong. This is confirmed by Pablo's self-description in the accompanying voiceover as a 'profesor en sus años otoñales' [a teacher in his autumn years], a reference to his own sense of impending mortality which necessarily negates any aspiration to 'youthfulness and the "body beautiful"' embodied by the 'gay as now model' (Simpson 1999: 213). Such negation is implicit in the subsequent transition to the following scene in which we move from close-ups of meticulously sculpted young bodies as seen on the covers of the gay magazines to a high-angled shot of the bed-ridden Pablo coughing uncontrollably before a medium-shot then reveals him receiving oxygen in a dour hospital corridor.

A lingering spectre for much of the film, the cough, in turn, places an increasing burden on Pablo in his circulation around the material gay world to which these magazines pertain. For in contrast to the space of the porn cinema in which the lack of behavioural boundaries would seem to encourage 'risky' behaviour, here the metaphor of HIV as a 'polluting menace' to be contained and avoided is all pervasive. In one scene, for example, the protagonist is depicted sitting in a café-bar in the vicinity of Santa Fé and Puéyrredon shooting furtive glances at two men sitting at an adjacent table. Any flirtation, however, is quickly cut short as Pablo is suddenly overcome by a coughing fit, prompting nervous glances across the room from the men concerned. With the former unable to stifle his irritating affliction the two men eventually beat a hasty retreat, the integrity of this 'healthy', homonormative space now fractured by the perceived threat of contagion.[15]

Even when Pablo's health has considerably improved, leaving virtually no out-wardly visual markers of his illness, the protagonist, it seems, can never be totally immune either from the prejudices of those closest to him or from what emerge to be his own internalized ones. In a scene marking his second visit to the gay club, Pablo is framed from Nicolás's point of view as he dances with another man, before the two eventually become locked in a passionate embrace. At this point, a reverse shot cuts back to the image of Nicolás looking on from the bar, an obvious expression of disapproval besetting his face. Whilst this might be interpreted as a sign of jealousy pointing to his 'undeclared love' for the handsome Pablo, there is little evidence elsewhere in the film that he sees him as more than a friend. Rather, although not explicitly expressed, it would perhaps seem to serve as a reflection of his own preconceptions as to the moral legitimacy of the latter's pursuit of a liaison with the man in light of his HIV status.

My reading of the film in these respects both converges with and diverges from Subero's analysis in *Representations of HIV/AIDS in Contemporary Hispano-American and Carribean Culture: Cuerpos suiSIDAs* (2014b). For Subero the film's preoccupation with the protagonist's sickened body as it submits itself both to medical interventions and the punishing crack of the sadist's whip, buys into (perhaps inadvertently he acknowledges) the same 'visual rhetoric of plague imagery' that has dominated public discourse about HIV/AIDS, and therefore reinforces rather than challenges the sorts of stereotypes which frame the illness as a threatening, highly contagious, incurable, deviant syndrome that leads to other deviant practices (in this case S/M). The AIDS body here, Subero argues, is 'constructed from a position of difference and is portrayed as an abject body that has no place within heteronormativity' (2014b: 16).

That Pablo's body is rendered 'other' both through the film's narrative and visual devices is clear, and indeed the spatial dimensions of this will be discussed in due course. However, I would suggest that this process of 'othering' is more nuanced than Subero suggests, in that the distancing of Pablo's body takes place as much in relation to mainstream gay culture as to wider heterosexual society. As Mark Casey writes, developing Duggan's concept of a 'new homonormativity', amidst commercialized, mainstreamed and non-threatening gay spaces, one's ability to claim legitimate rights of citizenship previously denied to queer folk but increasingly being extended to them 'are nevertheless limited to "non-threatening" lesbians and gay men' (2007: 127), a category to which Pablo no longer belongs. Certainly, as a diary entry written several days later subsequently demonstrates, the protagonist himself seems to have internalized the view that he poses a latent risk to the gay men around him, recounting:

> Me llevó a su casa. Insistió que me quedara a dormir. Pero no quise. Si me ponía a toser y lo despertaba? Lo dejé dos mensajes pero no me respondió. Debería haberlo contagiado con mi micosis y por eso no me llama.

> [He took me back to his. He insisted I stay over. But I didn't want to. What would happen if I started having a coughing fit and woke him up? I left him two messages but he didn't get back to me. I must have infected him with my mycosis and that's why he hasn't called]

This heightened sense of self-awareness that Pablo experiences in the presence of other gay men (present within other scenes such as that relating to the coughing fit described above) arguably reflects the heightened meaning that these outward symptoms carried within gay communities on 'high alert' after their devastation in the 1980s and more alert to (perceived) traces of the illness invisible or unremarkable to people in other social milieu. Of course such collective neurosis, as we see in the film, only serves to reinforce these categories of 'threatening' and 'non-threatening' gay people on which 'homonormativity' (itself a production of patriarchy) is premised. The film in this respect does indeed play out the anxieties of a heterosexual audience as Subero suggests (2014b: 10), but it plays out those of gay audiences too who are confronted with the rife discrimination still experienced by those living with HIV within their own communities today.

The emotional impact of the episodes referred to above is certainly made clear in the film not least through specific techniques of cinematography and editing. In particular, the director privileges the use of close-ups at points where Pablo is depicted undergoing treatment or medical tests: blood being drawn into a syringe, stethoscopes pressing against his skin, oxygen masks being fitted around his mouth, his back being positioned so a chest x-ray can be taken, and so on. These can be juxtaposed with subsequent medium-/long-shots framing his passage through grim hospital corridors or his lone wanderings through empty city spaces in which the frame is devoid of other human activity. Pablo, it seems, is becoming increasingly alienated and disconnected from both his own body and the world around him, prompting a crisis of identity, something alluded to by the first line of his journal entry in the opening sequence, '¿Quién soy? ¿Qué busco?' [Who am I? What am I looking for?]. The words speak loudly of the subjective ambivalence produced by the HIV-positive body in which the 'self' as a supposedly secure, coherent entity suddenly becomes defined by the inevitability of death. Here, as Matthew Sothern suggests (quoting Haraway 1991 and Martin 1994), the extent to which there can be a 'stable identifiable 'I' within the identity claim of a 'Person living with AIDS (PLWA)' and whether the HIV-positive body itself can be regarded as a 'stable container in which that "I" is supposed to be self-identical', is highly questionable (2007: 189). Thomas Yingling, in this respect, argues AIDS not to be merely a physical undoing of the self, but rather as producing a 'no-longer self':

> That is the *thing* of AIDS, it is the signifier through which we understand the cancer of being, the oncology of oncology — not only in its threat to our being, its announcement that we are moving towards non-being, indeed are already inscribed with it, in it [...] It is the disease that announces the end of identity. (in Sothern 2007: 189)

I would therefore read the rather insistent gaze asserted by the film over the protagonist's frail, vulnerable body in less negative terms than Subero and suggest that it is at least partly bound up with the film's otherwise thoughtful inquiry into the interplay between corporal decay and subjective dissolution. Certainly the film refuses a 'positive account' of HIV/AIDS here, but living with the virus in the mid-1990s, when burgeoning combination therapies (though far more effective than previous treatments) nevertheless implied an extremely arduous drug regime and a range of unpleasant side effects, was still overwhelmingly defined by its corporality. Indeed, is it in Pablo's search for something *beyond* this experience that the film's principal narrative begins to emerge: namely a search for human connection, as well as a means of transcending his suffering in order to reclaim some tangible sense of self. 'Pablo [...] busca su lugar de pertenencia' [Pablo is searching for his place of belonging] explains the director, 'un espacio que no sea transitorio' [a space that is not transitory] (in Monteagudo 2005: 22).

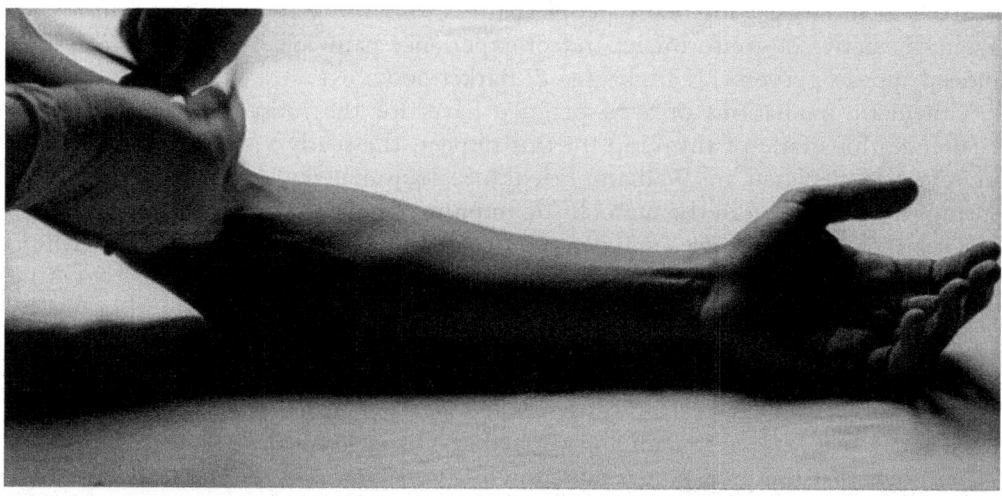

FIG. 2.2. Crisis of identity: Pablo's medicalized body juxtaposed with lone city wanderings in *Un año sin amor* (Anahí Berneri, 2005: Pecadillo Pictures)

S/M as (Dis)Pleasure

In light of the above discussion, that Pablo's search should lead him to the shadowy basements of Buenos Aires's S/M scene might seem somewhat surprising. Since the writings of Krafft-Ebing, Havelock Ellis and Freud, sadomasochism has been endowed with distinctly negative connotations and aligned with other sexually deviant behaviour such as child abuse and rape. Indeed, S/M is listed within the *Diagnostic and Statistical Manual of the American Psychiatric Association* (DSM-IV, 1994) and the *International Classification of Diseases* (ICD-10, 1992) as a psychiatric disorder. *The Shorter English Dictionary*, in turn, describes the practice as a 'form of sexual perversion' marked by a 'love of cruelty'. Certainly, as Darren Langbridge notes, bearing in mind that for many people pain is something they do their utmost to avoid, the active desire to inflict and/or experience pain, superficially at least, does indeed appear 'perverse' (Langbridge & Barker 2007: 95).

Cinematic mediations of S/M practice have, for the most part, done little to challenge this mode of thinking. In this respect, the seedy vision of the gay S/M underworld depicted in William Friedkin's documentary *Cruising* (USA, 1980) springs to mind, though the masochistic impulses depicted in the opening sequence of Gaspar Noé's *Irreversible* (France, 2002) are surely amongst the most unsettling. Here we witness the protagonist entering a male S/M club and subsequently taking revenge on his girlfriend's murderer, whom he bludgeons to death with a nearby fire extinguisher. Disturbingly, however, the 'punishment' appears to be a source of pleasure for the victim, each of his appreciative moans eliciting an even more forceful blow to the head from his frustrated assailant. It is only when the former's skull and jaw have been so badly pulverized that he is physically unable to make any more noise that the protagonist puts down his weapon and the unflinching long-take through which the whole episode has been represented then cuts away.

The notion of deriving pleasure from perpetrating or suffering acts of physical abuse and violence, in turn, might be regarded as doubly contentious in the context of countries whose recent political histories have been overshadowed by a tendency towards authoritarianism and the threat and/or use of torture as a means of suppressing and controlling populations, as in the case of Argentina. And yet as influential feminist thinkers such as Susan Sontag have made clear, the fetishization of symbolism and iconography associated with repressive authoritarian regimes, most obviously Fascism, is not uncommon to (or apparently particularly taboo within) the sadomasochistic ritual. Even in Germany, she claims:

> Much of the imagery of far-out sex has been placed under the sign of Nazism [...] Boots, leather, chains, iron crosses on gleaming torsos, swastikas, along with meat hooks and heavy motorcycles, have become the secret and most lucrative paraphernalia of eroticism. (Sontag 1991: 102)

Although no Nazi imagery appears in *Un año sin amor*, the fact that Baéz (Omar Nuñéz), the man who initiates Pablo into the S/M scene, performs his sadistic rituals dressed in military garb and is known by the pseudonym 'El comisario' [The Officer] amongst the other men within the S/M community, cannot have failed to remind older Argentinian film viewers of their own nation's history of political repression.

Yet not in a single interview reviewed for this book is the director asked to comment on or make any correlation between the film's theme of S/M and some lingering, unresolved sense of malaise within the national psyche regarding the *Guerra sucia* and the legacy of the 'disappeared', despite the fact that, as Sergio Wolf argues, 'the notion of being trapped or confined to a space' was a common theme that plagued the collective unconscious during the dictatorship period (1993: 276). In fact, I would contend quite the opposite: that the film constitutes a firm break with Argentina's past whereby the eroticization of pain need no longer be psychoanalyzed as an excising of the country's history of state repression. As Langbridge argues, there is a clear difference between torture and pain play in S/M, pointing out that in the case of the former the notion of consent is notably absent: 'the infliction of pain is a deliberate act of cruelty without regard for the agency of the victim in their wishes to be involved or not' (Langbridge & Barker 2007: 90). Quoting Elaine Scarry's *The Body in Pain* (1985), he goes on to describe torture as an 'almost obscene conflation' of inside and outside, public and private spaces that brings (again quoting Scarry) 'all the solitude of absolute privacy with none of its safety, all the self-exposure of the utterly public with none of its possibility for camaraderie or shared experience' (2007: 90). Contrastingly, he continues, the practice of S/M is constructed precisely around the idea of consent — people enter voluntarily into its practices 'fully aware of the consequences of their contracted relationship' (2007: 90). Similarly, he writes, the meanings of S/M acts are quite different to the practice of non-consensual torture since people who practise S/M enter into such contracts for the pleasure that they experience, that is 'the participants themselves mutually define the meanings of the acts that are perpetrated' (2007: 90). In this sense, he concludes: 'The double experience of agency, the dissolution of inside/outside and the disintegration of consciousness — crucially mediated through consent — provide a number of answers to the apparent paradox of pain play' (2007: 90).

Un año sin amor makes clear the centrality of these notions of consent and agency to S/M practice, most notably in Pablo's 'initiation' scene, which takes place in Baéz's apartment, the former having replied to an advertisement for a third play partner placed in the personal columns of a gay magazine by Baéz and Juan. Initially the power dynamic here between the three characters is unambiguous. The camerawork effectively 'belittles' Pablo through a series of high-angled shots from Baéz and Juan's point of view, which are then followed by cross-cuts onto a mirror which reveal the three characters grouped together, Pablo below in the lower section of the frame with Baéz and Juan standing above him. Pablo's 'inferiority' in relation to the other men is alluded to further in the dialogue between them. Here Pablo has difficulty in naming any of the Parisian leather bars he supposedly used to frequent whilst living in France, and then fails to address Baéz as 'señor' [sir] revealing his lack of S/M experience, much to the amusement of Juan, who jokes 'no sabe' [he doesn't know]. Pablo is thus effectively positioned as the submissive 'bottom' with the older and more experienced Baéz and Juan both fulfilling the role of dominant 'tops' who will mentor the young novice. This is confirmed moments later in a medium-shot from Baéz and/or Juan's point of view looking down onto the semi-naked Pablo, now dressed only in leather pants and a gimp-mask as he anticipates the crack of the sadist's whip. And yet despite the apparent appropriation and reification of normative gender/power roles so evident in this brief glimpse of Pablo's initiation, the scene is also careful to show how it is Pablo who sets the parameters for the type and scope of the activities in which they will participate. '¿Quieres contar que cosas te gustan, que límites tienes?' [Would you like to tell us what you like, what your limits are] suggests Baéz to Pablo before adding finally, 'si no te aguantas algo, grita "rojo"' [if you can't stand something, shout 'red'], demonstrating that ultimately the 'bottom' will be in control of the proceedings.

The representation of the acts themselves, in turn, seems keen to avoid scandalizing or shocking the viewer, the movement of the camera in the scenes relating to the S/M club being remarkably fluid, allowing us to glimpse only an impression of what is occurring between the various groups of men without directly implicating us in the action or forcing us to 'endure' a static image as occurs at several points in *Irréversible*. What instead becomes apparent is the latent *eroticism* of S/M practice, in marked contrast to the sexual encounters which we witness within the space of the porn cinema. Characterized by anonymity and emotional detachment, the latter are reduced to little more than an impersonal exchange of bodily fluids in which oral or anal penetration is privileged as the preferred means of erotic interaction between the men concerned. Indeed, the lack of intimacy established between the characters in the cinema is embodied in the very camerawork itself employed in these scenes, the camera tending to maintain a degree of cautious distance via the use of medium long-shots of the occurring action.

With regards to the spaces pertaining to S/M in the film, however, the dynamic could not be more different. The camera's gaze, often articulated from Pablo's point of view, is always at close quarters to the men concerned, privileging the sensual contact of skin on skin as it is conducted by a multitude of participants in what appears as a highly social and communalized activity. The use of extreme close-ups, in particular, reveals S/M to be a multi-sensory activity in which corporal stimulation is limited not merely to 'legitimate' erotic zones that are the genitals, nipples, mouth and so on, but to areas of the body that within the realm of hetero-normativity are deemed either to be un-erotic — the feet, back, torso, legs, ears, nose, for example — or whose arousal is considered dirty or aberrant, such as the anus. Also significant is the plethora of accompanying paraphernalia, straps, ropes, toys and other instruments, used to achieve this stimulation, and the simultaneous absence of conventional, phallo-centric forms of intercourse. Here, penetration, if it occurs at all, is articulated again through parts of the body which have been de-eroticized, hands and feet for example, or objects completely extraneous to the body such as sex aids or everyday items which are erotically appropriated for use in the S/M ritual. The director notes:

> Pudimos corrernos del estereotipo de lo que se piensa del sadomasoquismo, para poder ver eso como un juego sexual de mucho refinamiento. Asistir a un lugar vestido de una manera especial para llevar a cabo ese ritual tiene todo un encanto, una mística. (in Fontana 2005: 25)

> [We were able to get away from the stereotypes people have about sadomasochism, to show this as a highly refined sexual game. Going to a place, dressed up in a special way in order to enact this ritual has a certain enchantment about it, a mysticism]

Our discussion of notions of 'consent', 'agency' and 'eroticism' with regards to sado-masochistic acts necessarily raises the question as to what *meaning* these acts indeed have for those involved. Is S/M merely about 'pleasure', 'fun' and 'play' (however broadly these concepts need to be conceived) or, less superficially, does it hold a more profound significance? Certainly some critics such as Gary Taylor and Jane Usher go further by discussing how the (perceived) 'high' some S/M practitioners claim they receive, leads them to a 'heightened state of consciousness', making them 'more astute, more enlightened or more alive' (Taylor & Usher 2001: 305). This line of thinking is advanced by Andrea Beckmann, who goes as far as suggesting that S/M body practice may serve as a means of experiencing 'spirituality' or 'transcendence' in a similar manner to many religious and mystical belief systems which 'also involved the "lived body" as a whole' (2007: 111). She continues: 'Consensual "SM" can therefore satisfy the longing for religious and spiritual experiences for some practitioners and further provide them with the possibility of self-actualization (e.g. through boundary situations) [...] in many ways, re-enchanting the "life-world" of its practitioners' (2007: 111). Certainly the representation of semi-public spaces of S/M and the bodies which occupy them in the film seems to embody this sense of liminality. The use of extreme close-ups, for example, serves to fragment the bodies of the men concerned, their cinematic disembodiment appearing as an act of liberation in which the limits of the skin, famously argued by Judith Butler to be 'the limits of the socially hegemonic' (1990: 106), are essentially dissolved. In turn, the limits of space during these scenes tend to be the limits of screen space, giving the impression that these now dissected corporal forms are occupying an unhindered state of freefall.

This desire to feel more 'alive' or 're-enchanted', as Taylor & Usher and Beckmann respectively put it, does indeed seem to present itself as the prime motivation for Pablo's entrance into the S/M scene in *Un año sin amor*, the director stating that Pablo's role as slave serves as a metaphor for the possibility of finding love through suffering and the transformation of this suffering into pleasure, 'un placer que puede controlar, en cambio con la enfermedad en que eso no es posible' [a pleasure that he can control, in contrast to the impossibility of controlling his illness] (in Fontana 2005: 25). And certainly Pablo's adventures in this strange new world do seem to endow him with a new lease of life, the protagonist appearing after each session both invigorated and upbeat. The now diminishing sense of alienation that Pablo begins to feel in relation to his own body, in turn, opens up possibilities for exploring new relationships, both platonic and romantic, with other men on the S/M circuit, as those he shares with his family and more established friends (with the notable exception of Nicolás) grow ever more precarious and defective.

S/M Subculture: An Alternative Space?

To bring this discussion back to the realm of space then, the S/M subculture presented to us in the film would appear to emerge as an 'alternative' space, produced in opposition not only to dominant geographies of heterosexuality but also to those associated with 'homonormative' gay culture. And certainly on the level of cinematography the space of S/M is indeed established as one that is both hermetic and antagonistic, particularly in the manner in which the film's visual mapping is articulated. Consider, for example, the disparity which exists in this respect between those scenes depicting Pablo in the gay club, porn cinema or cafés at Avenidas Santa Fé and Puéyreddon and those relating to his amblings on the S/M circuit. Whilst the former tend to adhere to conventional framing and editing techniques whereby Pablo is positioned in an exterior location via an establishing shot or panning long-shot before we cut to the principal (interior) space of action, this is eschewed in the case of the latter in favour of direct cuts to close-ups and extreme close-ups of a plethora of leather-clad human bodies, precluding any ability on the part of the viewer to locate these said spaces within the wider cinematic geography of the city. The subsequent transition between these scenes and those which follow them is similarly abrupt. At one moment the image candidly reveals the various activities taking place between the men, the limits of space generally corresponding to the limits of screen space, thus imbuing their location with ambiguity. The next, we tend to cut to a (daytime) scene of utter banality: a close-up of a plate of food in front of Pablo as he has lunch with his father in a downtown restaurant, for example. The idea of S/M pertaining to a space that is 'other' or 'beyond' is reflected too in the conversations between Pablo and his friend Nicolás, which similarly serve to

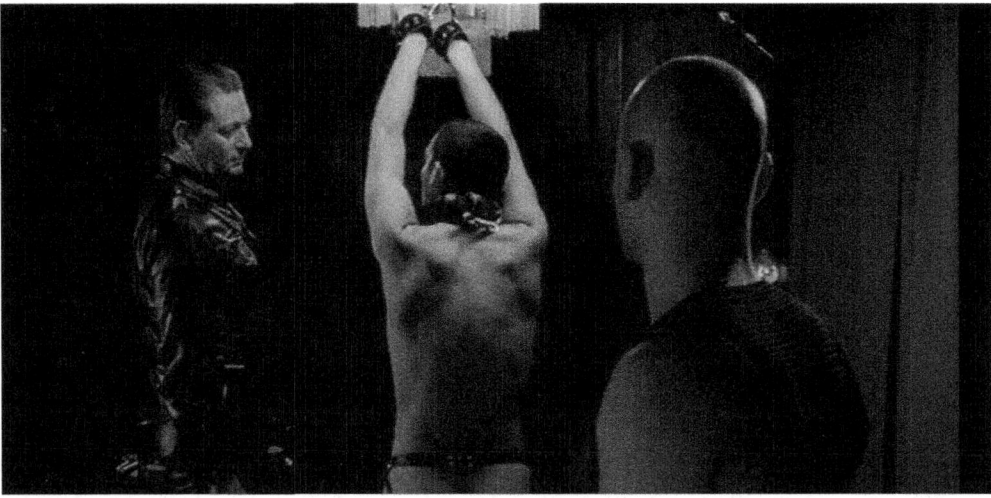

FIG. 2.3. Contrasting the 'other' space of S/M with the homonormative world of Nicolás in *Un año sin amor* (Anahí Berneri, 2005: Pecadillo Pictures)

underscore the distance between the respective ambits in which they socialize. In a thinly-veiled disparaging remark relating to Pablo's newfound penchant for leather, for example, Nicolás jokes that he is hardly surprised his friend is still single bearing in mind the *sorts of places* he goes to, as if for him they were a rather uncomfortable reminder of a more closeted era of days gone by and which are now 'out of place' amidst the more respectable, sanitized and internationalized contemporary gay culture of the 1990s.

However, a closer analysis of the film begins to unsettle such a reading of things. The rather decrepit, decaying basements in which the S/M parties are played out may lack the glamour, polish and sheen of the trendy gay club which Pablo and Nicolás attend, but they still nevertheless show themselves to be spaces of commercial enterprise. As with the former, entry to these spaces and participation in their associated activities does not come free, but is granted only to those who have the means to pay. Significantly, on one occasion Pablo does not, and Juan and 'El comisario' offer to subsidize his entry as their 'treat' in exactly the same way in which Nicolás enabled Pablo's access to the gay club in an earlier scene. In this sense, access to the space of S/M in the film, like that pertaining to mainstream gay culture, appears similarly restricted to the 'ganadores' [winners] of society, as Filc terms them (2003: 184). This is confirmed by the visual and aural cues to wealth and prosperity that we receive with regard to certain characters associated with the scene, in particular Baéz and Martín: a shot of a plush apartment lobby or a nocturnally-lit swimming pool, for example, or a close-up of crystal spirit decanters or a mobile phone, the mention of holidays and periods abroad in Europe or the USA and so on.

What the S/M venues depicted in the film lack in terms of interior design and aesthetic appeal is more than made up for by the apparent investment that has been made by the practitioners with regards to the accompanying paraphernalia which, as we see, is so crucial to the enactment of the S/M ritual. In the initiation scene, for example, before cutting to the image of Pablo on all fours waiting obediently for his punishment to begin, a close-up reveals a selection of apparatus and toys arranged on a glass table — handcuffs, ropes, chains, blades, and cigars, by way of example. As we then move from this to the scene which subsequently takes place in the S/M club, similar attention is paid to the costumes of the practitioners, the camera honing in on the men concerned, whom we see dressed in a variety of rubber and leather garb, boots, restraints, overcoats, masks and so on. Many of these objects and items of attire, of course, have their own, often more mundane uses in the world 'outside', as demonstrated by the rather bemused reaction of Pablo's cabin crew student to the thick metal chain she finds lying on the his desk, asking innocently '¿Tienes perro?' [Do you own a dog?]. Amidst S/M's specific spacio-temporal parameters these, however, take on wider significance, becoming theatrical props in the parodic enactment, reappropriation and/or subversion of dominant societal power roles and identities.

The production of S/M space, in turn, appears in the film as necessarily dependent on its successful integration into the very 'network society' that, as Castells argues, has now come to define late capitalist development and modernity, something we might initially presume it would strive to resist.[16] In this respect, references to communications technology abound. The initial encounter between Pablo, Juan and Baéz, for example, is contingent on the telephone messaging service which accompanies the gay magazine's personal section and which we presume has been previously used by the latter as a means of finding new S/M partners. Later on in the film, it is the internet which comes into play with Pablo, having set eyes on Martín in the S/M club, using email to subsequently pursue his love interest, who is registered with an ISP aptly known by the name of 'Top.com'. Their mutual attraction then established, Pablo is subsequently invited by Martín to speak with him, their first conversation, significantly, realized not in person but again, via a telephone line. Here cross-cuts of Pablo anxiously dialling Martín's number and the latter emerging from a swimming pool to answer his mobile phone subsequently merge into a split-screen format. The two share the frame as they converse, a fitting visual metaphor, we might argue, for the phenomenon of time-space compression which David Harvey claims, in *The Condition of Postmodernity: An Enquiry into the Origins of Cultural Change* (1990), is so characteristic of the information age.[17] The notion of S/M culture as being most definitely connected to and interactive with the 'outside' world is further alluded to by Baéz's tales of his travels abroad, in which he fondly recalls his trips to the leather bars of Paris, San Francisco and Berlin. 'Me gusta ir y venir' [I like to come and go] he explains to Pablo before stating that Juan 'también conoce el territorio' [is also familiar with the territory], a remark which alludes to S/M culture as being a transnational space firmly assimilated into the 'global village'.

S/M as (Un)Becoming and 'Non-self'

These subtle but crucial details have significant implications for the way in which the space of S/M must be conceived, for it appears as highly dependent on patriarchal capitalism for its production and survival and very much located within a strategic field of power relations. But does this mean that the practices as they are represented in the film serve merely as a handle or support for power, or might, as Foucault suggests, they act as adversary too? As Beckmann's account suggests, beneath this desire for the pursuit of (dis)pleasure on the part of S/M practitioners often exists underlying dissatisfaction with 'normal life' itself, and an 'awareness of the limits of "progress" and "reason" and of the dis-enchantment of modernity and consumer culture' (Beckmann 2007: 112). This raises a more complex debate (touched upon in Chapter 1) surrounding S/M's status as a (potentially) subversive practice whose enactment may serve to challenge hegemonic power structures and identities produced within modern, industrialized and patriarchal capitalist societies. In this respect, writing in the *The History of Sexuality, Volume 1* (1978), Foucault argues that since the seventeenth century, the state's power over the life of its population has evolved in two basic forms. The first, itself a direct product of industrialization, was centred on the notion of body as a machine; 'its disciplining, the optimization of its capabilities, the extortion of its forces, the parallel increase of its usefulness and its docility, its integration into systems of efficient and economic controls' (1978: 139). The second, which occurred later, revolved around the idea of the human body as 'species', the domain of biological processes: 'propagation, births and mortality, the level of health, life expectancy and longevity and all the conditions that can cause these to vary' (1978: 139). The coalescence of these two forms of asserting sovereignty marked, he continues, the beginning of an era he terms 'bio-power'. This was characterized by an explosion of numerous and diverse techniques for achieving the subjugation of bodies and the control of populations of which perhaps the most important was, as he puts it, the 'deployment of sexuality' in the nineteenth century (1978: 140).

As John Noyes and others have suggested, the subversive force of (sado)masochism lies precisely in the *eroticization* of this body-machine complex that Foucault identifies, a 'reduction ab absurdum of disciplinary technique' (Noyes 1997: 11). Here 'transgression' pertains not merely to the transformation of submissiveness, pain and discomfort into sexual pleasure. Rather, it is the way in which this is achieved through the mobilization of the disciplinary technologies and ready-made identities (and this might include 'gay' identity) used in dominant culture to perpetuate submissiveness, their erotic appropriation simultaneously serving to negate and disqualify them. Pat Califia, speaking on lesbian S/M, writes:

> The socially sanctioned repertoire of identity is an oppressive and superficial regime of sexual control, a world of arch-conformists with their cardboard cunts and angora wienies. S/M recognizes the erotic underpinnings of our systems and it seeks to reclaim them. (in Noyes 1997: 213)

From this perspective, then, if we are to apply a psychoanalytic reading to Pablo's participation in S/M practice, beyond the pleasurable eroticization of pain, the masochistic impulse in Pablo's case might be regarded as a strategy to confront the subjugating mechanisms which, through medical intervention, seek to regulate, control and ultimately contain the protagonist. For whilst initially Pablo forthrightly rejects conventional treatment for his condition, on account of his plummeting T-cell count he does eventually succumb to the wishes of his doctor and begins taking combination therapies. His reluctance is understandable: the treatment is both arduous and unpleasant as one scene indeed makes clear. Here the detailed hand-written timetable we see alludes to what is now a highly regimented existence on his part, structured almost entirely around the timing of his next dose of medicine. As a close-up traces the movement of the protagonist's highlighter as it methodically crosses off the completed instalments of his daily schedule, he reflects ironically:

> ¿Lo llaman coctél para volverlo atractivo y que se imagine un delicioso nectar en una copa de cristál con dos cerezitas? Sólo la vista de un comprometido de DDI me provoca nauseas. Ayer conté quince minutos hasta que se disolvió por completo.

> [Do they call it a cocktail to make it seem more attractive so you imagine a delicious beverage served in a crystal glass with cherries on top? Just the sight of an AZT pill makes me feel sick. Yesterday it took fifteen minutes to dissolve entirely]

Physically and psychologically at the mercy of an often fatal disease and enslaved to a gruelling regime of drug-therapy providing only short-term relief, the practice of S/M for Pablo serves as a (pleasurable) means of neutralizing these disciplinary mechanisms which render the HIV-positive body, as Sothern argues, 'a cyborg space in which flesh and biomedical technology become indistinguishable and is thus a space that is precisely not-normal, not fully human' (2007: 188). Furthermore, it allows for his experience of 'un-becoming' to be lived not as a 'crisis of identity' (as it is in the 'world outside') but as a celebration of the fragmentary. Here self-reconciliation and achieving a 'tangible sense of self', as I earlier phrased it, corresponds to the parodying of hegemonic power roles, whose theatrical appropriation exposes the notion of a unified and abiding self as illusion.

The film, however, true to its queer credentials, refuses such an affirmative, clear-cut view of things and ultimately seems to question whether Pablo's descent into the S/M world can ever hope to bear its initial promise. For whilst the director states that the protagonist is looking for 'su lugar de pertenencia, un espacio que no sea transitorio' [his space of belonging, a space which is not transitory], S/M practice would, by its very nature, appear less than conducive to fostering any sense of 'belonging' in the sense that it necessarily negates any aspirations to an essential identity around which a concept of community may be constructed — it is, to quote Noyes, 'a celebration without synthesis' (1997: 200). For Foucault, of course, this is precisely the point: within the space of the sauna, the sex club or the S/M dungeon he argues that connection, community and belonging occur precisely through this process of desubjectivization whereby identity is subordinated to the production and the experience of pleasure (in Halperin 1995: 86). These are spaces where 'one can meet people who are to you what one is to them: nothing else but bodies with which combinations, fabrications of pleasure will be possible', Foucault argues (in Halperin 1995: 94). Anonymity is crucial here 'because of the intensity of the pleasure that derives from it' (in Halperin 1995: 94).

The highly commodified nature of S/M subculture as it appears in the film, however, mitigates against such a sanguine reading of things.[18] For as previously discussed, this is hardly some sort of utopian space of 'free love' (or pleasure) open to all: rather an elite club to which access is granted only to those who have the means to pay. The plethora of paraphernalia required to participate in its activities is another manifestation of its commodification and also potentially exclusory. Indeed, from this perspective the space of S/M subculture arguably functions precisely *as* a material production of heteronormativity firmly calling into question its status as 'alternative'. As Michael Brown reminds us in his enlightened study *Closet Space: Geographies of Metaphor from the Body to the Globe* (2000), such 'closet' spaces may, due to their invisibility, certainly *appear* antithetical to the more explicit and visual production of sexualized heterosexual urban spaces (strip clubs, massage parlours or simple 'pick-up' bars, for example) or indeed those relating to mainstream 'homonormative' gay culture. Yet, he writes, in a world where the increasing dissection, categorization and commodification of sexual experience offers endless possibilities for new sexual activities to be profitably exploited (even if these are socially disruptive) their objectives are ultimately the same — the achievement of material gain from the stimulation and satisfaction of desire. As the author notes, 'spaces of sex are commodified regardless of their orientation' (2000: 83). Their invisibility and concealment therefore is a product of capitalism's strategy to achieve what Harvey in his essay 'The Geography of Capital Accumulation' (1996) has termed 'a spatial fix', a production of space that functionally enables the commodification of (homo)sexual relations to occur whilst efficiently maintaining the traditional heterosexual coding of the urban landscape (in Brown 2000: 56).

Thus whilst Foucault argues that S/M is disruptive because it imbues strategic power relations (which in the world 'outside' are highly institutionalized and 'very, very difficult to supress', in Halperin 2005: 86) with fluidity and mobility, it arguably loses this transgressive edge in this context of commodification. This is because by rendering power relations harmless and profitable, S/M colludes (at least partially) with the very founding dynamics underpinning the modern industrial city it seeks to subvert. Here S/M shows itself to function around the same exclusionary practices that we see in Buenos Aires's 'homonormative' gay world, with material wealth serving as a necessary prerequisite to access and participate in its associated activities. And as Noyes aptly reminds us, 'once the technologies of control become the object of erotic attachment, who is to say whether control is subverted by eroticism or whether eroticism is reintegrated into control?' (1997: 14).

Even S/M's supposed embracing of the HIV-positive body in the face of its rejection from hegemonic spaces of (homo)sexuality ultimately proves to be far from unconditional. In this respect, one hitherto undiscussed detail in the film relates to the fact that Pablo's immersion into the S/M world occurs at roughly the same point in the film in which he begins taking his combination therapies. Although, as we saw, the treatment is initially regarded with considerable ambivalence on the part of the protagonist, ultimately he appears to embrace it, admitting in one scene that he 'loves' the design of the branded capsules, describing them as 'una obra del arte de los años 90, un unicornio que me llama' [a work of art from the 1990s, a unicorn which beckons me]. As we cut from an extreme close-up of the capsule in question, to a close-up of Pablo's chess board and the image of him manoeuvring a knight (aptly laden with an empty drug-capsule), knocking over his opponent, we then see Pablo in the following scene power-walking in sports attire in the outskirts of Buenos Aires, now apparently in rude health. In this sense, regardless of whether Pablo owes his rejuvenation of mind, body and spirit primarily to a multi-national drug company or to the punishing crack of the sadist's whip (something that remains ambiguous), ultimately it is only *through* his submission to the three-drug cocktail that the protagonist is actually able to garner the physical strength to pursue his regime of 'pleasure through suffering' in the first place. Here, therefore, as in the ambit of the 'homonormative' gay world, a healthy, functioning body holds equal importance, it seems, albeit for different ends. As Casey argues in his account of sexuality and space:

> As specific gay urban sites are assimilated into the wider urban framework, one door is opening and another is being closed as to who may enter and be visible within such sites and as to what spaces and sexual identities can emerge. (Casey 2007: 127)

With these exclusory/collusive material considerations in mind, the film's denoue-ment is perhaps unsurprising. For S/M proves itself to pertain precisely to the sort of space that the director states Pablo seeks to avoid, one that is indeed 'transitory' and in which the search for (lasting) human connection ultimately appears as a futile quest. Accordingly, after two encounters, Martín quickly forgets Pablo and melts away into obscurity. Then, when Pablo is thrown out of the apartment by his father his telephone calls to Juan prove similarly fruitless, the latter apparently also having disappeared, an absent friend, it would seem, in the protagonist's time of need. As Pablo, in the final scene, trudges down the steps to the porn cinema we saw him frequenting in earlier scenes, the significance of the film's title thus becomes apparent. This literally has been 'un año sin amor' [a year without love] with Pablo ending his story as he began it, 'solo con lo solo' [alone, with the alone].

Decentring the 'Global Gay'

To conclude, then, the above discussion in its discursive 'untying' of the 'Global Gay' somewhat paradoxically frustrates any attempt to dismiss 'global queering' merely as a form of western homogenizing imperialism. Certainly the emergence of a commercialized and visible gay scene in the Argentinian capital during the 1990s, as it is evidenced in Berneri's film, would appear to confirm the logics surrounding capitalism and gay identity proposed by the likes of D'Emilio and Knopp and outlined in Chapter 1. However, the tensions displayed in the film between mainstream 'homonormative' gay culture and the sexually dissident spaces pertaining to a similarly internationalized S/M culture show the globalization of sexuality to be multilayered in nature, resulting in the simultaneous dismantling *and* production of the closet in space and the proliferation of a range of sexual prac-tices and accompanying (non-)identities which vary across space and time. These are indeed products of capitalism, yet they share a highly ambivalent relationship with it. S/M strives to subvert society's machinery of domination and shatter the hegemonic constructs of sexuality and identity it produces, so we might imagine alternative modes of articulating desire and subjectivity. And yet as a highly commodified sexual practice one cannot help but wonder, to borrow Quiroga's phraseology, whether 'the translocalised body of the homosexual does not stand at this point so much for personal liberation as for the liberation of global capital to pursue its aims' (2000: 11).

However, as Buenos Aires's status in the film as a host to the HIV virus, the world's 'first true cosmopolitan' (Haver 1996: 7), implies, 'globalization' and the questions of 'inclusion' and 'exclusion' it raises, are not, to put it crudely, always about money. Despite the fact that Pablo appears as what some sociological accounts of Latin American homosexualities have constructed as the paradigmatic Latin American privileged 'gay' man — white, educated, middle-class, an inhabitant of a major metropolitan centre — none of these factors in the end mitigate his sensation of exclusion. For what is significant about the HIV virus is that it has collapsed spatial scales precisely *without* discriminating. As Binnie writes, 'the cosmopolitan does not respect boundaries and difference — but annihilates them'

(2004: 121). And it is here, amidst the film's allusions to this alternative metaphor of globalization where we might conceive of a more nuanced understanding of Latin American cities such as Buenos Aires. These arguably correspond less to what Sinfield terms 'localised versions' of the queer metropolis (2000: 21) and the notions of co-optation and slavish replication this implies, but rather represent constituent elements of a highly decentred supra-territorial space produced and sustained through a plethora of multi-directional and sometimes antagonistic flows. These most often are understood in terms of capital, but they may also be cultural and, in this case, biological, wielding equally transformative effects.

Notes to Chapter 2

1. Parts of this chapter have been previously published in an article entitled '(Re)Traçando o armário de celulóide: espaço, homoerotismo e identidade no cinema latino-americano contemporâneo' (Hoff 2008).

2. Christophe Honoré's *Homme au bain* (2010) and Gaël Morel's *Le Clan* (2004) serve as two further examples, films which are marketed in such a way that they satisfy both the consumer demands of independent distributors such as Pecadillo Pictures and gay high-street sex shops such as Prowler or Clone Zone. The participation of the famous French gay porn actor François Sagat in a lead role in *Homme au bain* aptly embodies this cross-over of genres.

3. In an essay and book of the same title, *Non-Places: Introduction to an Anthropology of Supermodernity* (1995), Augé coined the phrase 'non-place' in reference to spaces — motorways, airports, hotels and so on — whose transient and generic nature impinge on one's ability to construct a sense of place within them. Sarlo's account of the 'shopping mall' as a globalized space in *Scenes from Postmodern Life* (2001) echoes on many levels Augé's idea.

4. *Porteño* refers to somebody from the city of Buenos Aires.

5. See Hugo Colace and Ezequiel García's interview with director of photography Lucio Bonelli for more detailed discussion (Colace & García 2005).

6. In this respect, David Martin-Jones argues that such films, on a formal level, are characterized by a 'blending' of 'various cinematic styles once associated with, or at least marketed as belonging to, different parts of the globe [...] in an attempt to cross over into different markets [...] thereby increasing the profitability of a film' (2006: 8).

7. Both are popular British gay (male) magazines, *Boyz* being available free from gay bars, clubs and organizations, whilst *Attitude*, a glossy 'lifestyle' magazine, is widely available from most major newsagents.

8. *Tarjetero* can loosely be translated as 'flyerer' in English slang.

9. The *Guerra sucia* refers to the state-sponsored violence in Argentina waged against thousands of (suspected) left-wing militants and sympathizers primarily by Jorge Rafael Videla's military dictatorship, which was installed on 24 March 1976 and which continued until the return of civilian rule in 1983.

10. Carlos Jáuregui notes in *La homosexualidad en la Argentina* [*Homosexuality in Argentina*] that 'uno de los integrantes responsables de la CONADEP [Comisión Nacional por la Desaparición de Personas] afirma la existencia de, por lo menos, 400 homosexuales integrado en la lista de horror' [an official from the National Commision for Disappeared People affirmed the existence of at least 400 homosexuals on the list of horror] (1987: 171). For extensive analysis of cinematic mediations of the *Guerra sucia* in the context of gender and sexuality see Constanza Burucúa's *Confronting the 'Dirty War' in Argentine Cinema, 1983–1993* (2009).

11. For an account of gay life in Rosário during the 1990s see Sívori 2005.

12. In this respect Óscar Guasche in *La crisis de la heterosexualidad* [*The Crisis of Heterosexuality*] argues that homosexuality has become so heterosexualized that its status as a 'subculture' is now highly questionable. He writes, 'la progresiva normalización de la realidad gay implica su institucionalización: el Estado pasa a regular la afectividad gay através de medidas legislativas' [The progressive normalization of gay reality implies its institutionalization: the state now

regulates gay life through legislative measures] (2000: 91).

13. Falicov notes that paradoxically, however, at a time when the state itself was being 'downsized', the system of state-subsidized film was not only left intact but was actually strengthened during Menem's second term in office, with legislation introduced in 1994 stipulating that new avenues of funding (taxes on home video rentals and television advertisements), in addition to the original tax on box-office receipts, be directed towards the production of national cinema (2006: 88). State funding (in tandem with private support, often from the television networks), however, tended to favour more commercially-viable, 'blockbuster-style' domestic productions of which some notable examples would include *Commodines*, *La furia*, *Dibu, la película* and *Cenizas del paraíso* (all 1997).

14. In 1996, according to data from the Programa Nacional de Lucha contra los Retrovirus del Humano y Sida [National Programme for the Fight against HIV/AIDS] there were 9,189 confirmed cases of AIDS in Argentina (putting the country in third place behind Brazil and Mexico in terms of prevalence rates in Latin America), though other estimates such as that made by EPIMODEL put the figure as high as 17,725 (in Kornblit 1997: 20). HIV infections were estimated to be around 150,000, 70 per cent of which were concentrated in the Buenos Aires metropolitan area (Kornblit 1997: 21).

15. These episodes can perhaps be regarded as symptomatic of Casey's argument that, 'as specific gay urban sites are assimilated into the wider urban framework, one door is opening and another is being closed as to who may enter and be visible within such sites and as to what spaces and sexual identities can emerge' (in Browne & others 2007: 127)

16. When interviewed by Harry Kreisler from the University of California, Berkeley, Castells defined 'network society' as 'a society where the key social structures and activities are organized around electronically processed information networks. So it's not just about networks or social networks because social networks have been very old forms of social organization. It's about social networks which process and manage information and are using microelectronic-based technologies' (2001).

17. Harvey's notion of 'time-space compression' refers to the technologies that have collapsed spatial and temporal scales into a culture of instaneity in which he argues 'space is annihilated by time'. These technologies might include those pertaining to communications (internet, telephone, fax), travel (cars, trains, aeroplanes) and economics (the need to penetrate trade barriers, speed up commodity production and make the turnover of capital more time-efficient).

18. Bienvenu in this respect noted that initial American S/M practitioner networks originally formed precisely around the producers of S/M-related products (in Langbridge & Barker 2007: 15). By the 1930s, he continues, practitioners' range of behaviours had expanded to such an extent that it now began to incorporate 'elaborate restraints, specialized equipment, highly stylized fashion and electrical and medical technology' (2007: 15). The 1960s, in turn, would herald the genesis of mass-produced fetish clothes and equipment with the opening of 'House of Milan' in the USA (2007: 18). Such availability has undoubtedly expanded beyond all recognition with the advent of online retailers in the age of the internet and the scope for anonymous transactions that this affords. And beyond the domain of S/M products, big business, of course, has found other ways of profiting from S/M culture — the holding of mass S/M events, for example, at leisure resorts and hotels, which, despite frequent protests from local residents go ahead regardless, with profit, of course, taking precedence over the concerns of the 'moral majority' (2007: 15).

CHAPTER 3

Medellín: *La virgen de los sicarios*

Sicarios, Shotguns and Sugar-Daddies: Reclaiming Metropolitan Sexualities in the Valley of Death

'Unofficial' Global Cities

The preceding chapter considered to what extent the ambits of S/M practice were proposed as an 'alternative' space in Berneri's film, produced in tension with those of 'homonormative' gay culture in Buenos Aires. I argued that although S/M practice is antithetical to the heterosexual gender relations underlying the industrialized city, the way in which it emerges as a highly commodified dissident sexual practice dependent precisely on the sort of transnational communication networks that have been produced and facilitated by the expansion of global capitalism necessarily problematizes such a reading of things. In this respect I concluded that despite initial appearances, this sexually dissident subculture appears in *Un año sin amor* as firmly integrated into the 'global village'.

Taking forward this discussion, we might, in turn, argue that the terms on which cities are qualified as being 'global' perhaps need to be re-evaluated, expanded and diversified. According to Sassen, 'global cities' can be defined as 'centres for servicing and financing international trade, investment and headquarter operations' (2001: 171). Beyond familiar first-tier cities such as Tokyo, London and New York, she proposes that an increasing number of second-tier cities beyond 'the core' (many in the majority world) are now assuming such functions, resulting in a 'new geography of centrality [...] that cuts across national borders and the old North-South divide' (2001: 169).[1] She also argues that concurrent to the 'explosion' of wealth and power now concentrated in these cities, other localized economic spaces are simultaneously being produced through increasing informalization of labour markets (2001: 172). Castells goes somewhat further, moving beyond the idea of 'other' spaces of capital accumulation merely as localized, micro-level phenomena.[2] For him there exist many 'unofficial' global cities the world over, cities whose strategic positions as centres of drug smuggling, arms dealing, money laundering or people trafficking position them as highly important drivers of *macro-level*, global, capitalist economic processes, even if this role is played out illicitly and not officially acknowledged.

Medellín might be invoked as one such example of an 'unofficial' global city. Colombia's second-largest conurbation, it is perhaps the city which has experienced the most profound penetration of the drugs trade into its economic, civic, political and cultural life, symptomatic of the consolidation of the Medellín drug cartel (headed by the infamous Pablo Escobar) towards the end of the 1970s as one of the world's richest, most powerful and far-reaching trafficking networks. As Castells writes, these cartels were internationalized from the outset, exporting initially to the USA, then to Europe and then to the rest of the world:

> Their strategies were, in fact, a peculiar adaptation of IMF-inspired export-orientated, growth policies towards the actual ability of some Latin American regions to compete in the high-technology environment of the new global economy. They linked up the national/local crime organisations in America and Europe to distribute their merchandise. And they set up a vast financial and commercial empire of money-laundering operations that, more than any other criminal organisation, deeply penetrated the global financial system. (Castells 2000: 177)

This chapter builds on my discussion in Chapter 2, shifting from the globalized neoliberal urban cinematic landscape of Buenos Aires to that of the 'unofficial' global city that emerges in Barbet Schroeder's *La virgen de los sicarios*, considering what kind of impact Medellín's globally integrated criminal economy is imagined to have on the production of dissident sexualities in the film. Here I provide a rereading of the relationship between protagonist Fernando and two teenage *sicarios* [hitmen or hired assassins], arguing that it goes beyond *pornomiseria*, the rather evocative label sometimes applied to the films of Víctor Gaviria with which *La virgen de los sicarios* arguably shares a certain dialogue. In this respect, I consider how the dynamic between the two protagonists, rather than pointing to a 'traditional' (and assumedly exploitative) model of sexuality as their class and generational differences might suggest, might be indicative of a metropolitan, and more egalitarian, understanding of things. Of particular importance to my discussion here are the processes of urban socio-spatial realignment imaged in the film, whereby organized crime and illegal transnational flows of capital appear to collapse the once peripheral *comunas*[3] into the centre, dehermeticizing previously distinct social groupings and accompanying cultural models. Whilst from one perspective this realignment endows the *sicarios* with the 'space' in which to reclaim their (dissident) sexuality as a lived identity, as in Chapter 1, I question to what extent the imbrication of the body with the urban economy can be regarded as emancipatory or affirmative.

Medellín, Violence and Cinema

Before discussing these aspects, however, let us return to the initial contextual discussion above in order to further situate *La virgen de los sicarios* within its local and national, social and cinematic contexts. As previously mentioned, the power, influence and wealth of the Medellín drugs cartel at its peak in the 1970s was virtually unrivalled both within Colombia and beyond, with Escobar and his colleague Jorge Luis Ochoa controlling a significant portion of the world's global market.[4] That the rise of the Medellín cartel should coincide with the decline of the city's manufacturing industries in this period, the major basis of its prosperity for the previous seven decades, is perhaps no coincidence. Large-scale unemployment and economic insecurity created a pool of excluded and disenchanted young men who would swell the ranks of Escobar's criminal network, working, in particular, as *sicarios*, whose culture was most famously documented by sociologist Alonso Salazar in his book *Born to Die in Medellín* (1992). Although the Medellín cartel fell in 1992, life in the city's poor *comunas* continued to be defined by youth gang culture, which simply diversified into small-scale drug-trafficking and organized crime. City space, in turn, became more and more divided as an increasing variety of armed actors fought over territory (Riaño Alcalá 2006: 3). By 2001 levels of violence had begun to rise towards the levels of the early 1990s, when they had peaked at 444 homicides per 100,000 inhabitants per year, the highest of any urban centre in Latin America (Riaño Alcalá 2006: 3).

These were merely new constellations within a pre-existing 'galaxy of conflicts' (Safford & Palacios 2002: 346). Its major foundations were laid during *La violencia*, a period of intense partisan rivalry between the unionist *Conservadores* (Conservatives) and the federalist *Liberales* (Liberals) from the mid-1940s to the mid-1960s. Of its major flashpoints, the assassination of Liberal leader Jorge Eliécer Gaitán in 1948 and the resultant *Bogatazo*, one of the bloodiest riots in Latin American history, are perhaps the most notorious. By the 1960s a new type of political violence began to emerge in the form of insurrectional struggle between leftist guerrilla organizations such as FARC (Fuerzas Armadas Revolucionarias de Colombia [Revolutionary Armed Forces of Colombia] created in 1964) and ELN (Ejército de Liberación Nacional [National Liberation Army] created in 1962), the government and emerging paramilitary groups. In the mid-1970s these conflicts would intersect with violence associated with the narcotics trade, translating in the 1980s into a bewildering convergence of 'violences' pertaining to drug mafias, guerrillas, paramilitaries and hitmen, in alliance or in conflict with politicians, the military and the police (Safford & Palacios 2002: 356).

Historically, Medellín has always held a strategic importance in terms of these armed struggles and, amidst the frequent mediations of violence so characteristic of Colombian national cinema, the city itself has come to occupy a privileged position. The films of Víctor Gaviria, notably his Medellín triptych consisting of *Rodrigo D, no futuro* (1990), *Don Isa* (1992) and *La vendedora de rosas* (1998), are in this sense iconic, making frequent allusions to the intersection of the city's marginalized communities with the dynamics of the narcotics trade. Certainly *La virgen de los sicarios* can be said to share certain similarities with Gaviria's *oeuvre*, most notably by way of its hyper-realist aesthetic and use of non-professional actors. Widely regarded as a fairly faithful adaptation of the original novel written by Fernando Vallejo (1994), the film also betrays a heavy reliance on non-professional actors, most significantly Anderson Ballesteros (who plays co-lead Alexis), himself a former gang member. A similar concern with presenting the 'brutality of the facts' is also embodied in the somewhat jarring image created by what at the time was the unorthodox use of HD-digital video and which, as Desson Howe aptly puts it, 'rubs our noses in the grimness of Colombia's second city' (2001). Most significantly perhaps, like Gaviria's films, as Geoffrey Kantaris notes, the film can also be juxtaposed with mass, globally marketed cultural forms (Hollywood-style cinema, for example) in the way it works against the 'well-nigh Pavlovian association between violence and spectacle' (Kantaris 2002). Here, instead of veiling or disavowing the symptoms of violence as occur in films which peddle violence as spectacle, it is precisely the symptoms which are of concern, acts of urban violence depicted as 'the aftershocks of cataclysmic geopolitical displacements' (Kantaris 2002). And whilst the constant repetition of violence in itself might be argued as being somewhat gratuitous, the director's aim here, it would seem, is to *desensitize* the viewer to violence, inspiring within them a 'moral panic' at their growing indifference to the murders taking place (Kantaris 2002). The director notes: 'I wanted the viewers to feel, like the characters, a kind of progressive anaesthesia towards violence, like anyone who wants to continue living in Medellín' (in Kantaris 2002).

In these respects the film is perhaps suggestive of Gaviria's brand of *pornomiseria*, so called, claim Carlos A. Jáuregui and Juana Suárez because it exports a 'deteriorada' [degraded] image of Colombia through 'un deleite morboso de la cámara en la abyección [...] la indigencia y la basura' [the camera's morbid delight in capturing destitution [...] debasement and trash] (Jáuregui & Suárez 2002: 373). In terms of its perspective, however, the film could not be more different. If Gaviria's work is characterized by an emic, interior point of view from the city's social periphery (2002: 370) then the dystopic world of *La virgen de los sicarios* is viewed from a more privileged standpoint: that of Fernando, Vallejo's alter-ego, whose return to Colombia after a thirty-year hiatus abroad marks the film's narrative point of departure.[5] As we learn somewhat bleakly, Fernando, who we presume to be in his late fifties or early sixties, has come back to his native Medellín 'para morir' [to die], only to discover that the city he remembers no longer exists. The idyllic farm of his childhood memories has instead been replaced by a sprawling metropolis of four million souls fractured by gaping social inequalities and riddled with seemingly endless cycles of violence that appear to be spiralling out of all control. Simultaneously appalled and fascinated in equal measure by the new city before him — now affectionately known as *Metrallo* by its armed gangs[6] — Fernando, however, is not quite ready (as he literally does in the film's closing sequence) to draw the curtains on this distinctly Dantesque incarnation of twenty-first century Latin American urban society, and instead embarks on two relationships with young *sicarios* Alexis and Wílmar, around which the intervening narrative is structured.[7]

In the 'Butterfly Room': Differing Sexual Dynamics

In light of the brief contextualization of the film provided above, the urban backdrop of *La virgen de los sicarios* clearly constitutes a very different proposition from that which we encounter in *Un año sin amor*. Indeed it is perhaps difficult to see exactly where Schroeder's film could possibly begin to image 'a more enriched consideration of gay life in Colombia and Latin America', as Foster puts it in his analysis of the film (2003: 76). *Paisa* culture, has always remained somewhat 'provincial' in its outlook, with political conservatism, religious devotion, family values, thrift and frugality often proudly evoked as the key tenets of this culture upon which the success of Colombia's economic powerhouse was built.[8] Amidst this highly patriarchal Antioquian society has prevailed what Diana Lucía Sarabia describes as: 'el mito paisa' del hombre luchador y emprendedor [...] el héroe incansable, patriarca fecundador de las montañas que más tarde impulsa la modernización y industrialización del departamento y de la nación' [the *paisa* myth of the brave pioneer [...] the tireless hero and fertile patriarch of the mountains who would later spur on the modernization and industrialization of the province and the nation] (2007: 34). Medellín's recent history of industrial decline, high levels of unemployment, increasing socio-spatial exclusion and spiralling incidence of homicide would, in turn, seem similarly incompatible with the genesis of a more open gay culture if we are to subscribe to the logics supposedly underpinning the 'production of gay' discussed in Chapters 1 and 2.

From this perspective, the film's opening sequence is perhaps unremarkable, giving the impression that gay life in Medellín continues to be played out behind closed doors. Certainly the construction of cinematic space that we see in the film's opening sequence alludes to Brown's notion of a 'closet' space, which, as previously mentioned in Chapter 2, is a secret, hidden and concealed space which enables same-sex desire to be successfully (and spatially) commodified for profit whilst simultaneously maintaining the traditional heterosexual coding of the urban landscape (2000: 56). After the passing of the initial credits, for example, a tracking shot frames Fernando walking down a busy city street before pausing outside a residential building and buzzing the intercom. The lock is released and the front door slams firmly shut behind Fernando, who ascends the stairs towards an upstairs apartment, the muffled sounds of gramophone music and excited chitchat becoming gradually audible as he approaches the white door. Eventually the door is opened and Fernando is welcomed in by his friend, the former's intervening journey between the street and the apartment itself thus having firmly delineated the separation of public and private spheres.

In turn, the opulent *mise-en-scène* pertaining to the low-lit room we see beyond the threshold of the doorway — antique furniture, red drapes, classical nude male statues and other items of 'flamboyant' paraphernalia — contrasts with the austerity of the preceding whitewashed lobby and stairwell, further establishing this as a 'safe', almost cocoon-like space protected from the surveillance of the world outside. Here, an informal gathering of generally older gay men appears to be in full swing as they chatter excitedly amongst themselves whilst proffering furtive glances and witty one-liners to the selection of adolescent males strewn amongst them. 'Esto es el mejor regalo que te pudiera haber traido' [This is the best gift I could have brought you] beams his host, as he leads Fernando over to Alexis, apparently the evening's 'prize'. The three exchange complimentary niceties, before Fernando and Alexis quickly take their leave for the more intimate surroundings of the 'Butterfly Room' where the latter is then paid for his sexual services.

FIG. 3.1. 'Closet space': the apartment where Fernando and Alexis first meet in
La virgen de los sicarios (Barbet Schroeder, 2000: Paramount Pictures)

Within this protective space of the apartment the dynamics between the guests
do not substantially depart, it would seem, from the 'traditional', 'non-metropolitan'
model typically associated with Latin America, inflected, as discussed in Chapter
1, by differences in age, gender (identification), class and race. This infers the idea
of a younger, feminized, socially inferior and resultantly stigmatized (read 'homo-
sexualized') insertee. However, as Sinfield points out in a more general global
context, if the crucial point here is power difference, the social categories through
which this difference is articulated may therefore be interchangeable or reinforce
or significantly complicate each other (2000: 30). For example, if youth co-occurs
with femininity, he explains, it may do the *opposite* when it is inflected by class,
referring in this respect to admiration of middle-class 'effete' gentlemen for the
alleged masculinity of working-class boys between the eras of Oscar Wilde and the
Stonewall riots (2000: 30).

This inversion has been a striking presence in the realm of male sex work where
the 'macho', heterosexually-identified sex-worker has functioned in many parts of
the world as an erotic doppelgänger to his 'transvestite' female- (or sometimes gay-)
identified other (see, for example, Aggleton 1999). Certainly, in this particular scene,
the *sicarios'* 'butch' demeanour, caustic use of slang and baggy street-wear function
as markers of 'authentic' masculinity (and thus presumably their heterosexuality)
which clash visually and aurally with the 'delicate' nature of the older guests.
With regards to the latter, a rather obvious set of visual cues — limp wrists, tightly
crossed legs, exaggerated mannerisms and so on — clearly evoke the image of the
effeminate *maricón*.[9] The correlation here between effeminacy and homosexuality
is, in turn, alluded to by the host in his jovial revelation to Alexis that he and
Fernando have known each other 'practicamente desde que nos volvimos maricas'

[practically since we first became fags].[10] According to this paradigm, the sexual role of the *sicarios* would remain strictly prescribed, their masculinity (and therefore heterosexuality) contingent on their rejection of receptive anal or oral sex and fulfilment of the active penetrating role during the sexual act. Indeed, amidst what Patrick Larvie terms the 'erotics of the closet' the boundaries of age, class, race and sexuality between client and sex-worker and the (supposed) rigidity of accompanying behavioural codes function as a source of erotic investment, thus heightening the sexual appeal of the encounter (1999: 162–63). 'El angelito tiene en su consciencia tres o cuatro muertos' [This little angel has three or four deaths on his conscience], recounts the host at one point in reference to Alexis, eliciting a theatrical gasp from his friend, underlining the social distance between the older men and the killers in their midst, as well as the (sexual) titillation such a 'dangerous' encounter with the 'other' might provide.

And yet whilst, as Sinfield suggests, power and hierarchy may be 'sexy' (and through implication, their subversion[11] too), the notion of transaction in sex work always implies a degree of control on the part of the client due to his or her financial solvency. In this sense, whatever role 'transgressions' take place during the sexual act itself, these are still generally enacted within a framework of existing social hierarchies. 'Era de la banda de no sé que, de la comuna nororiental que ya están muertos. Fue el único que quedó' [He's from such and such gang from a *comuna* in the North East, I don't remember which, [but] they're all dead now anyway. He was the only one who survived], imparts the host in continued reference to Alexis. Turning to the latter's friend La Plaga [The Pest] he then enquires 'o fueron más?' [or were there more?], the question's vapid delivery implying the question was purely rhetorical. His position of privilege will always ensure that the grim realities of gang culture and life in the *comunas* remain detached and ultimately inconsequential, the 'danger' of the *sicarios* invoked merely as an evening 'show' that indulges sexual fantasy but which, within the protective space of the host's apartment, will always remain on the latter's terms.

Significant amidst this, however, is the rather more contrasting dynamic existing between Fernando and Alexis. Fernando, as he indeed reminds his host on entering the apartment, has been abroad for nearly thirty years. Their subsequent conversation hints at a shift in Fernando's view of his own sexuality during this time away, the latter resisting his host's suggestion that he should define himself under the traditional epithet of 'marica'. Instead he replies sarcastically: '¡Qué va! ¿Marica yo? Marica vos y el presidente' [No way! Fag? Me? It's you and the president who are the fags]. And although his subsequent question, '¿Como se hace marica un tipo que ha acostado con mil muchachos?' [How can someone who's slept with a thousand boys be a fag?], might suggest that Fernando's rejection of the term is a reflection of a denial of his own homosexuality justified through self-identification as an older 'active' male, in reality I would suggest the underlying implication is that this latter 'observation' is merely a tongue-in-cheek jibe at his host's more 'outdated' conception of homosexuality. Alexis, in turn, corresponds tenuously to the mould of the 'macho', heterosexually-identified male sex worker. With the sexual act transacted, Fernando hands over to Alexis the money he is due, and says, apparently in accordance to what he believes etiquette dictates, 'para que te vayas de paranda con tu novia' [so you can take your girlfriend out]. Yet Alexis's candid response conflicts with this presumption. '¿Cuál novia?' [What girlfriend?], he demands, 'no me gustan las mujeres' [I'm not into women]. Fernando is visibly pleased with this admission and quips, 'eso si está pero muy bien' [I'm glad to hear it].

The dynamics of the sexual act itself would also appear similarly conflictive. On entering the 'Butterfly Room' it is Fernando who takes control of proceedings and he immediately instructs Alexis to strip, the boy objectified by the camera's gaze which is articulated from the point of view of Fernando, who watches whilst seated on a chair. After conversing briefly on the subject of Alexis's gunshot wound, the latter then walks naked towards the bed, with only his *tote* [gun] (lit. 'heater') covering his modesty. He then switches off the bedside light and reclines obediently on his back to await Fernando, who takes his turn to undress, the implication being that it will be Alexis who assumes the passive role in the proceedings which follow.

This, however, always remains an implication since the sexual act itself is left largely unrepresented. The only glimpse we receive of their shared intimacy is via a momentary reflection in a mirror in which, as if to mark the passing of time, we see two bodies morphing fluidly in and out of various positions. Lighting here is absent, however, and the image is so ghostly it is all but impossible to determine which is Alexis and which is Fernando. This affords plenty of room for speculation as to who, in fact, penetrates whom in the 'Butterfly Room', something in which Foster's analysis of the film does indeed indulge. He suggests that Fernando's gesture of transaction in fact *confirms* 'the formula of the passive male paying the active male for sex', arguing that if Alexis were, in reality, the passive male, the film's narrative conventions would be very different:

> Alexis would either be the transvestite prostitute paid for her services as any female prostitute, no matter what penetrative role might take place between prostitute and client, or he would be the passive male grateful for the attentions of the macho. (Foster 2003: 77)

And yet the reflection we see in the mirror is so brief — the camera cuts within a few seconds to the postcoital image of the two characters dressing again — that to clearly discern what we are seeing requires rewinding the film and viewing it several times. In this sense, one cannot help wondering whether the question of sexual role was something the audience was intended to attach much importance to. Rather, from another perspective, I would contend, the muteness of the scene in this respect is symptomatic of the way in which the relationship between Fernando and Alexis operates *outside* the ideological parameters to which Foster refers.

The initial exchange between the two characters on entering the 'Butterfly Room', in this sense, is telling. '¿Dónde están las mariposas?' [Where are the butterflies?], Fernando asks Alexis, prompting a response of similar candour to that which he receives in relation to his suggestion that Alexis might have a girlfriend. 'Aqui no hay mariposas' [There are no butterflies here], he replies with a measure of indignation, 'nosotros somos las mariposas' [it's us who are the butterflies]. A euphemism for 'gay' in the Spanish language, the irony in Alexis's use of the word 'mariposa' is hardly subtle; nevertheless it is indicative of his experience of homoerotic desire not merely as practice but as an identity and, more importantly, one which he believes he *shares* with Fernando.[12] This is something effectively confirmed by the latter's reply that 'Lo importante no es el nombre sino la substancia de las cosas' [Labels aren't important, it's the essence of things which matters]. Here he seems to insinuate that *regardless* of what name, if any, is given to those who participate in same-sex erotic practice, and whatever acts they may or may not perform according to their gender identification, age, class, race or otherwise, their 'essence' is still the same and ultimately inescapable. It is this sense of reciprocity produced through Fernando and Alexis's shared idea of same-sex erotic practice as an expression of something 'innate' that, I wish to argue, sets their relationship apart from that shared by the other older guests and *sicarios* such as La Plaga. In turn, it opens up the narrative possibility of its extension beyond the realm of mere transaction to incorporate an emotional (loving?) element which transcends the standard hierarchies around which the erotics of this 'closet space' are structured.[13]

Out of the Closet: Respatializing Same-Sex Desire

One of the most immediately noticeable features of Schroeder's film, particularly when contrasted with *Un año sin amor*, in which the general cityscape of Buenos Aires is largely invisible, is the strong presence that Medellín itself asserts over the viewer in many scenes. As the director himself states, 'I wanted the city to be one of the characters' (in Foster 2001), something that is effectively achieved through his use of HD video, whose extreme depth of field affords penetrating views across the city to the opposite side of the Aburrá valley itself. Indeed, the opening sequence

FIG. 3.2. Fernando and Alexis kiss against the backdrop of Medellín in *La virgen de los sicarios* (Barbet Schroeder, 2000: Paramount Pictures)

discussed in the previous section is something of an anomaly with regards to the overall construction of cinematic space in the film, its nocturnal interiority then 'opened out' in subsequent scenes via the frequent use of panoramic long-shots of the city and the surrounding mountains articulated either from exterior locations or interior ones which afford similar views. A notable example would be Fernando's high-rise apartment, a space to which the camera returns time and again to gaze through its wrap-around windows. The crisp HD image reveals in these moments a brash, modern, high-rise city bursting unapologetically from the verdant hills of the surrounding valley, which gives little superficial evidence of the staid conservatism for which Medellín has traditionally been known.

And it is against the backdrop of these windows, and thus the city itself, which sweeps across the front aspect of the living room like a gigantic film reel, that Fernando and Alexis share their two most intimate moments in the film. In one scene, having thrown a hi-fi out of the apartment window in apparent emulation of Fernando's actions in a previous scene, where the din of Alexis's music prompted him to do the same, Alexis proudly celebrates his recklessness with a swig of *aguardiente*. The chuckling Fernando meanwhile, checking that no one has been 'killed' by the falling object, lingers by the windows before sitting down on a chair, the cityscape clearly visible behind. 'Abre la boca' [Open your mouth], demands Alexis, approaching him. '¿Para qué?' [Why?], enquires Fernando suspiciously. Alexis answers his question with a mouthful of *aguardiente*, which he dribbles slowly from his mouth into Fernando's, the camera swooning in such a manner that the only thing separating the couple from the city outside at this moment are the two vertical bars of the window frame traversing the screen.

Later on in the film, after Alexis has committed one of his many shootings, the couple are framed again in front of the windows mimicking, amidst fits of laughter, what they believe to be the rather overdramatic response to the murder from a bystander. Quickly, however, a more reflective tone besets the scene and, as some rather saccharine extra-diegetic piano music becomes audible on the soundtrack, we cut to a close-up taken perpendicular to Fernando which frames the couple looking into each other's eyes, their hands laid on each other's shoulders. As we revert to a reverse shot from Alexis's point of view, Fernando declares, 'Alexis, niño, tu eres lo más hermoso que me ha dado la vida' [Alexis, kid, you're the most beautiful thing life has given me], before the two then kiss, the camera panning slowly round to reveal Medellín's high-rise skyline through the gaps in their embracing bodies, beautifully bathed in orange light from the setting sun. As the array of ticking clocks present within the 'Butterfly Room' in the opening scene might, on a metaphorical level, imply, Fernando and Alexis's relationship seems to be one that embodies disjuncture, change and something new, the shift in outlook palpable in the 'exteriority' of cinematic space pertaining to these scenes, which clearly contrasts with the oppressive, closet-like milieu in which the party at which they first met was conducted.

Of course, if we are to subscribe to Michel de Certeau's opinion that the 'panorama-city' seen from above is little more than a fictional visual 'simulacrum' which totalizes and immobilizes the 'most immoderate of human texts' — that is, street life as it is lived below (1984: 92) — then the unlikely relationship that we see budding between Fernando and Alexis might similarly be regarded as highly idealized, one that whilst *appearing* to be conducted in full view of the city, is, in fact, highly removed from it, lifted, to use Certeau's phraseology, 'out of the city's grasp' (1984: 92). Yet the couple do indeed bring their romance to the streets below, any sense of 'detachment' embodied in the apartment relieved through their frequent flaneurial wanderings through the city. These weave their way through the chaotic downtown area, taking in Medellín's decaying relics of colonial architecture and monuments to liberation. The latter are now dwarfed by the glittering towers of the central business district in a fitting visual metaphor for the apparent demise of the city's traditional institutions and their accompanying values, which are so vehemently rejected in the scathing commentaries that characterize Fernando's rather unusual form of 'guided tour'. 'Sin sexo la humanidad se enloquece' [Without sex, humanity goes crazy], declares the latter on one such occasion as they approach one of the city's churches, before continuing: 'Si no, mira este papa lo loquito que anda. Habla de huévonadas... besando pisos. Que los homosexuales que eso es pecado. ¿Qué pecado es huévon? El pecado es seguir pariendo. Si no acabemos el planeta va a explotar' [And if you don't believe me: look at how mad the pope is. Spouting crap... [saying] that homosexuality is a sin. What's sinful about it? The sin is [humanity] carrying on reproducing. If we don't stop the planet's going to explode]. Barely has he finished this rather provocative dismissal of heterosexuality as a valid or productive sexual orientation or institution before his ire becomes redirected to one of the city's most iconic role models of 'triumphant masculinity', Simón Bolívar, whose statue presents itself in their path: 'El libertador! Cobardón! Maricón! La única vez que pudiste lutar con alguien saliste huyendo [...] Pero quítate, le van a cagar las palomas! Anda, métete bajo la falda de tu mujer, ¡pirobo!' [The great liberator! You coward! You fag! The only time you got into a fight with someone you ran away [...] Go on, go hide under your wife's skirt you dickhead!].[14] In a timely fashion a pigeon then defecates on Bolívar's head, prompting Fernando to conclude caustically, 'la gloria es una estátua que cagan las palomas!' [glory is a statue shat on by pigeons!]. It is difficult to decide which of the two tirades would be considered more blasphemous by the Colombian establishment. For not only does Fernando publically refuse to define his sexuality and gender identity according to the dominant system of values, he does this by invoking the glorious masculinity of the continent's 'Great Liberator' as little more than a performance in the charade of heteronormativity.

Once inside the cathedral the 'profanities' continue as Fernando points out to the mesmerized Alexis three of the saintly statues which look down upon them — Santo Inácio de Loyola, El Emperado de la Colombière and Santo António. Santo António, remarks Fernando, is the 'patrón de los novios' [the patron saint of lovers], an observation which Alexis qualifies with the words 'de nosotros' [our saint], recalling his earlier comment to La Plaga at the beginning of the scene that the purpose of their visit to the cathedral was to 'casarse' [get married]. Not, of course, that there is much in the way of religious ceremony occurring, the pious congregations of yesteryear now most definitely dispersed in place of a throng of drug-dealers, pimps, prostitutes and beggars who have now also apparently claimed this once sacred space as their own.

The examples cited above are certainly not exhaustive, but they are nevertheless indicative of how Fernando and Alexis's dissident same-sex union crosses the threshold of the private sphere into public space in a way in which the 'sexual contracts' maintained between the other *sicarios* and Fernando's middle-class friends certainly do not. As previously argued, these contracts, hidden and concealed within a 'closet space', ultimately do not disturb the heterosexual coding of the wider urban landscape. The same, however, cannot be said for Fernando and Alexis's city wanderings in the 'city below'. For if we are to subscribe to Certeau's argument that the act of walking itself, as a spatial practice, 'produces meaning', then the circulation of the homosexual body through heterosexually-coded spaces arguably constitutes a process of 'rewriting'. Here, heterocentrism, as the dominant narrative of Medellín's 'urban text', is deconstructed and destabilized in what ultimately is a queering of public space reflecting the manner in which walking, as Certeau argues, 'suspects, tries out, transgresses [...] the trajectories it "speaks"' (1984: 99). And it is a queering that only serves to be embellished by the verbal commentary which accompanies Fernando and Alexis's ambulant traversing of the city, an apt allusion to the idea of walking as a space of enunciation, a 'statement' that the above critic terms a 'pedestrian speech act' (1984: 96).[15]

Class, Socio-spatial Realignment and Sexual Identity

The question necessarily poses itself, however, as to how we (re)read this representation of same-sex desire in the film as manifested in Fernando and Alexis's relationship. In Fernando's case, his enlightened attitude towards his sexuality would appear to confirm socio-anthropological accounts of sexual identity in Latin America as referred to in Chapter 1, and by extension the underlying logic which informs the arguments of John D'Emilio and Larry Knopp. Educated and well-travelled, Fernando arguably constitutes the paradigmatic 'modern' white, male, middle-class Latin American 'gay', easily able to 'import' his experience of homoerotic life abroad back into his native Colombia due to his relative financial solvency and accompanying ability to exist independently, both materially and spatially, of potentially unaccommodating family structures. Arguably this is further facilitated by his place within a cultural elite that is perhaps more tolerant of alternative lifestyles than other sectors of society and an accompanying socio-economic status, which, to a degree, mediates the stigma attached to his same-sex erotic preferences.

As for Alexis, however, his distinctly candid attitude towards his sexuality and experience of this as a personal identity appears perhaps more surprising given his (working-class) social background. Or is it? As Colin Hardy reminds us in the introduction to the English translation of Salazar's book, Medellín's violence in the 1980s and 1990s was not the violence of decline, rather, that of a city which was 'booming economically, even as the murder rate spirals' (in Salazar 1992: 10). For where Medellín's industry had gone into decline, the burgeoning narcotics trade had soon taken over, representing, as Castells notes more generally in relation to

Latin America, 'a sizeable and most dynamic sector' of the city's economy, 'with proven global competiveness' (2000: 201). Consequently, concurrent with the exclusion of Medellín's poorer inhabitants from the official employment market, new openings simultaneously began to emerge within this burgeoning criminal economy of which drug 'couriering' to the USA and contract-killing within the city's sub-market of violence both constitute notable examples. These soon became a standard mode of employment, not merely as a means for 'getting by' but, more importantly, as a lucrative source of income with the potential to facilitate access to a status and lifestyle which had previously been beyond the reach of Medellín's traditionally lower-income sectors (Safford & Palacios 1992: 362; Salazar 1992: 114). The respective accounts of Salazar, Riaño Alcalá and Castells, in this respect, all make reference to this rise of the 'narco-bourgoisie' and a phenomenon of 'conspicuous consumerism' attesting to the manner in which, as Mary Roldán puts it, 'the aura of privilege, the sense that political and economic entitlement was limited to a select few, was breached' (1999: 174).

La virgen de los sicarios certainly features ample reference to this process of economic destratification and social realignment. Ironically, however, in an overtly queer take on the hyper-masculine culture of the *sicario*, it is through hustling and transactional romances with (financially) well-endowed sugar-daddies such as Fernando that they seemingly earn their 'keep' rather than through (monetarily) contracted killings, as the opening sequence of the film indeed suggests. Nevertheless, in terms of their appearance there are certainly traces of social and economic mobility. Alexis, La Plaga, El Difunto and the other unnamed *sicarios* we meet are clean, apparently well-nourished and clothed in fashionable sports attire, visually contrasted with the hotch-potch of unwashed beggars sometimes seen in their midst, whose 'ragged' appearance is so meticulously attended to by the film's costume artist that it verges on the parodic. Indeed, the apparent social distance between these two groups of marginalized characters is made explicit in one scene when La Plaga decides to share out a box of cakes with the local beggars. '¡En fila desechables!' [Get in line you trash!], he shouts to a rag-tag selection of vagabonds. They then obediently arrange themselves in a line and proceed to kneel, mouths open, in hungry anticipation of their 'communion', to the obvious delight of the onlooking Alexis and Fernando. An act of charity this clearly is not, rather an opportunity for La Plaga to assert his own authority over these other errant characters who he clearly believes are inferior to him, something implied by his reference to them as 'desechables' [trash] (lit. 'disposable') — an insult commonly used to refer to *sicarios* themselves.

This increased sense of social status is claimed by the *sicarios* themselves *and* bestowed upon them by certain members of the moneyed elite as represented by Fernando. On one occasion, in a disturbingly fascist-style oratory, the latter reflects to Alexis: 'Juntan una pareja de pobres y verás que en los quince minutos se cruzan y producen diez pobres. Odio la pobreza. La única manera de acabar con esta plaga maldita es terminar con los que la transmiten' [Put two poor people together and you'll see that in fifteen minutes they'll breed and produce ten more. I hate poverty. The only way to finish with this plague is to exterminate those who transmit it]. Significant here is the question of positionality, since the use of the verb 'verás' [you'll see] essentially aligns Alexis with Fernando, thus not only excluding him from the category of 'pobre' [poor] but also valorizing his profession as a potential 'solution' to the spread of poverty, which he imagines as a form of contagion which must be contained. The frequent use of the word 'ellos' [them] in reference to the city's poor in Fernando's other musings performs a similar function, repudiating Alexis as a subject of his tirades whilst also implicating himself verbally as a passive accomplice in their deliverance.

A shifting positionality is reflected too — and perhaps more noticeably — in the film's (re)mapping of the cinematic landscape, which, as we have seen, marks one of the film's major points of divergence from Gaviria's *oeuvre*. Whilst in the latter, the *comunas* strike an overbearing presence within the film's topography as the primary space of narrative action, in *La virgen de los sicarios* they constitute an overwhelmingly absent space or one that is viewed from afar. At one point in the film, Alexis and Fernando admire the view across the valley from a local body dumping ground, the former reciprocating the latter's tours of the city's historic centre with his own unique lesson in geography. 'Las comunas de La Salle, El Popular, La Francia, Villa Socorro, Santo Domingo Savio', he recounts, pointing into the distance, the camera shifting with each neighbourhood's name to another location on the horizon before eventually arriving at the farthest and highest point constituted by Santo Domingo Savio, Alexis's *comuna*. Clearly, this is not a moment of nostalgia, however, with Fernando's subsequent suggestion that one day they visit his home patch eliciting a negative response from Alexis, pointing to his increasingly weak connection with the neighbourhood. '¿No a qué? Por allá está muy caliente' [What for? Things are pretty heated over there], he replies, moments later fixating on a metro train as it snakes through the densely populated valley *away* from the *comunas* to which they have just been referring.

This process of 'distancing' and reversal of perspective is continued at other points in the film, particularly in those scenes occurring in Fernando's living room. Here Alexis is afforded the same spectacular vista across the city to the mountains opposite and the *comunas* that he might have enjoyed when living in Santo Domingo Savio. However, this is mediated by a series of panoramic windows, suggesting a certain detachment on his part, as if the scene beyond the glass were no more real than those which he views on the nearby television screen. The nature of the space from which this view is articulated is also significant. A plush, high-rise, centrally located apartment, it is the absolute antithesis of the ramshackle building in which he was raised and which Fernando visits at one point in the film to inform Alexis's mother of his death, one of the film's rare forays into the warren-like space pertaining to these terraced hillside neighbourhoods.

Accompanying this general absence of the *comunas* as a principal space of action in the film comes, in turn, a privileging of the city's central district, a part of the city where, as the protagonist of *Rodrigo D, no futuro* demonstrates, the experience of many *comuneros* has traditionally been one of exclusion and alienation. In one of the most iconic scenes of Gaviria's film, we see the protagonist taking an elevator to the top of an empty office tower in the business district from which he contemplates the opposing towers and city below. Beset by increasing despair he begins to bang his head repeatedly against the glass of the window before a jump-cut glimpses his body in a suicidal freefall towards the ground. As in the testimonies found within Salazar's book, the centre of Medellín is envisioned here as a 'cannibal, a living organism ready to consume slum dwellers on the hillside above' (Roldán 1999: 173).

In *La virgen de los sicarios* the relationship of young *sicarios* with the downtown area, however, could not be more contrasting. The camera, for example, returns on several occasions to the setting of the cake scene to reveal Alexis's friends such as La Plaga and El Difunto, relaxing and socializing in a busy pedestrian shopping street, giving little hint of feeling 'out of place'. At other points in the film, the assertion of their presence is a good deal less congenial. In this respect, the sound of the *sicarios'* motorcycles freely traversing the city's otherwise traffic-clogged arteries bears an increasing audial presence through the course of the film and one which Fernando finds progressively unnerving, particularly after Alexis is gunned down in front of him from a black Kawa motorcycle. For Fernando, the motorcycle's piercing high-pitched whine serves as a constant reminder of the latent threat of violence which now pervades this once secure area of the city — an aural recoding of urban space symptomatic of what Roldán describes as the dissolving of 'the last of the cultural barriers between sectors of the city amidst the deployment of armed youths into the heart of what had once been off-limits to the poor' (1999: 174).

Thus the film quite clearly alludes to the fact that despite the apparent social distance which exists between them, the circumstances in which their sexualities are produced are perhaps not so different after all. For concurrent with the existence of the *comunas* in the film as an absent space, that relating to the family home is similarly invisible, the existence of the *sicarios* presented as overwhelmingly rootless

FIG. 3.3. Reclaiming urban space: gun-toting *sicarios* riding through Medellín in *La virgen de los sicarios* (Barbet Schroeder, 2000: Paramount Pictures)

and nomadic. Of course on one occasion, as previously mentioned, we do indeed visit the house in Santo Domingo Savio where Alexis's mother lives, but it hardly gives the impression of having provided a stable adolescence for the boy. This, as her testimony to Fernando confirms, has developed against a backdrop of domestic violence courtesy of her second partner, an alcoholic with whom Alexis appears to have shared a particularly dysfunctional relationship and which prompted his exit from the rather precariously constructed dwelling they call 'home'. Now apparently having been abandoned by the man in question, Alexis's mother has been far too busy single-handedly bringing up her two younger children to ponder the whereabouts of her errant older teenage son, who at this point is already dead. The point is here, though, that it appears that Alexis does not apparently *need* the support — material, emotional or otherwise — of his family (or what is left of it), the implication being that it is his implication in Medellín's criminal underworld that sustains him, allowing him to exist outside family structures. In this sense, he too, just like Fernando, as the cinematic mapping described above implies, quite literally possesses the 'space' in which to organize a personal life around his erotic/emotional attraction to members of his own sex.[16]

Reclaiming Metropolitan (Dissident) Sexualities

The above account is significant in the sense that it allows for a rather less restrictive (and reactionary) interpretation of Alexis and Fernando's relationship than that provided by the likes of critics such as César Alzate Vargas and Diana Lucía Sarabia. These two both focus their analysis on the power differential existent between Fernando and Alexis, arguing it to be wholly exploitative in nature. However, this critique is undertaken at the expense of any serious consideration of the convergence that is established by the film between the two characters at the level of their respective (homo)sexual identities and of the film's narrative and cinematographic bridging of the socio-spatial gap existent between the two characters. For as my discussion clearly demonstrates, Fernando and Alexis's relationship goes beyond a simple 'reconstrucción del antiguo paradigma: artista maduro se enamora de hermoso efebo' [reconstruction of an ancient paradigm whereby the mature artist falls in love with the ephebically handsome boy] as Alzate Vargas puts it (2001: 159). Neither can it be explained away simplistically as being one that is 'escandalosa, típicamente carnavalesca [que] expone la pederastia y la explotación sexual del pobre' [scandalous [and] typically carnivalesque, exposing the pederasty and sexual exploitation of the poor], as Sarabia, in turn, proposes (2007: 37). Rather I would suggest that the film does indeed begin to image a *metropolitan* reading of things. This might seem at first sight an unlikely proposition. As Sinfield writes, it is a defiantly *egalitarian* rhetoric that has underpinned 'modern' understandings of metropolitan sexualities in which ' "(gay) identity" is so compelling that it makes *difference* irrelevant and inappropriate — at best invisible, at worst undesirable' (2000: 25). And no matter how much one attempts to align the two characters, Alexis ultimately needs Fernando much more than Fernando needs him.[17] As Sarabia herself writes of Fernando: 'Su edad, posición económica y educación lo sitúan en una posición privilegiada que de ninguna manera es compartida por sus amantes' [His age, economic status and education put him in a privileged position which is in no way shared by his lovers] (2007: 37).

However, as Sinfield goes on to argue, the dominant ideology that posits differentials as something that can and must be 'avoided or overcome', is at best misguided and worst, purely hypocritical:

> If metropolitan lesbians and gay men in fact succeeded in wiping out power relationships, all we would have to do is enjoy our egalitarian practice and let everyone else in on the secret. But that is far from the case. The prevailing sex-gender system, we have every reason to know, is geared to the production of hierarchy and, as part of that, to the production of anxious, unhappy and violent people. It produces us and our psychic lives — straights and gays — and it is not going to leave us alone […] it cannot be realistic to suppose that we can simply, through good intentions sidestep hierarchies of capitalism and patriarchy. It is a liberal-bourgeois delusion to suppose that 'private' space can be somehow innocent of and protected from the real world. (Sinfield 2000: 33–34)

Instead he urges a recognition of the realities, and more importantly, the *productivities* of power in sexual relations and an exploration of the 'ways to assess and recombine power, sexiness, responsibility and love' (2000: 35). It is here perhaps where Alexis and Fernando's relationship acquires a queer, dissident dimension. For although their mutual understanding of same-sex desire as the expression of something 'innate' hardly goes against the grain, the social and generational divide between them certainly does, not only because it lays bare the hierarchies (supposedly) concealed within 'homonormative' relationships but also the *productivity* of these hierarchies. From this perspective, refracted through Sinfield's prism of reasoning, Alexis and Fernando's relationship might therefore hint at how power differentials in metropolitan same-sex relationships, far from being inherently repressive, might be reconfigured instead 'as potentially rewarding' (2000: 35).

Most obviously, Fernando has the financial means to support Alexis and possesses at least the *potential* to assist his young lover in changing his status quo by providing a place to live and access to education, thus offering him a way out of the gang culture in which he has become involved. Indeed, in one scene he even mentions perhaps helping Alexis to establish his own business, though it is an idea he then quickly rejects on the grounds of the excessive bureaucratic impediments which he believes would stand in his way. Nevertheless, the domestic setup that Fernando establishes in his apartment with his young lover does provide the latter with a degree of stability, a point of reference, and even a tentative feeling of 'home'. This contrasts markedly with the more transient presence that the other *sicarios* have in the lives of Fernando's friends who we encounter in the opening sequence. Whilst for a few brief hours the likes of La Plaga and his friends might enjoy the comforts and protection of their host's showy apartment, it is anybody's guess what the night will bring for them once the party is over and they are roaming the streets again. Fernando's dwelling, in contrast, is constructed in the film as a 'safe' space for Alexis, in which the latter is able to circulate freely, its position on an upper floor of the apartment block, intercom system and security gate at the front door establishing it as a secure refuge from the violence of the city below.

Alexis himself, of course, possesses nothing on the material front that Fernando does not already have, but nevertheless brings light and albeit short-term purpose to an existence which until such time as Fernando takes leave of the living world (whether that be via suicide, natural causes or murder) we assume would otherwise be one characterized by sombre monotony. For Fernando's life is now as empty as the fortified abode he has inherited from his sister and which serves as a poor substitute for a writing career (which for one reason or another has now reached its conclusion) and family members who are either dead or estranged. Set in relief against the neutral backdrop of the apartment, with its meticulously attended to scarcity of *mise-en-scène*, the figure of Alexis glows with a youth and vitality that functions as a source of fascination for the ageing Fernando, the latter proclaiming in one scene, as previously mentioned, that 'usted es el mejor regalo que me ha dado la vida' [you're the best present life has given me].

Fernando's words speak of an attraction that goes beyond the purely libidinal, whilst Alexis seems to profit from the relationship in a manner that cannot simply be read in terms of material gain. As the director himself states, 'the movie became a *dialogue* rather than a monologue' (in Foster 2001, my emphasis), a reference to what is in fact a clear process of mutual intellectual reciprocity between the two characters, which far from being stunted by a generational gap and two highly diverging respective social backgrounds is, in fact, nourished by them. For whilst Fernando's attention to grammatical correctness, his love of literature and classical music and fondness for the city's historic centre and colonial architecture may position him as a relic of 'old' Medellín, their nostalgic wanderings through the city arguably provide Alexis with a bridge to the past and a way of *contextualizing* the present.

As Salazar suggests, it is all too easy to regard the demographic which Alexis represents simply as an expression of a purely 'new' culture, when in fact the evidence suggests that a form of 'cultural intermixing' has taken place whereby both modernization *and* longstanding, specifically Antioquian, social traditions have coalesced into the phenomenon of contract killing (1992: 115). Medellín's value system, he writes, has always been constructed around the idea of entrepreneurism and making money, with the pursuit of profit traditionally prioritized over social integration. It is perhaps no surprise then that the narcotics trade and associated sub-markets such as contract killing should collectively constitute one of the most dynamic sectors of the country's economy — it is, writes Salazar, indicative of a culture in which the popular saying goes 'son, make money honestly, but if you can't, make it anyway' (1992: 115). Here, God's pardon for killing someone is something that has, throughout Colombia's long tradition of violence, been taken for granted. Alexis in *La virgen de los sicarios* is no exception, his devotion to the Virgin Mary, regular pilgrimages to Sabaneta and the bizarre ritual of having his bullets blessed with holy water all respectively ensuring the successful execution of his crimes and their eventual absolution in the Kingdom of Heaven. We can, then, perhaps regard it in Salazar's terms as 'the culture of the rosary and the machete which nowadays has become the religious medallion and the mini-Uzi' (1992: 115).

And whilst Fernando can be deemed representative of the 'old guard', as the director himself states, from another perspective he also assumes the status of a 'rebel who speaks against the world as an adolescent would' and is thus someone Alexis can 'connect and laugh with easily' (Schroeder in Foster 2001). Fernando, continues Schroeder, connects with the boy 'because he's learning from him — about the new realities of Medellín and the vernacular now spoken in the town of his childhood' (in Foster 2001). This sense of reciprocity and dissolving of difference is aptly embodied at the beginning of the film in a verbal exchange that takes place between the two characters as they walk back from Sabaneta having witnessed a shooting outside the church there. Here Fernando reflects on the event, musing philosophically that before disagreements were settled with a machete and that now gunpowder is used. Alexis interjects, arguing that 'a la final, viene a ser lo mismo plomo o machete' [*at* the end, bullets or machete, it's all the same], with Fernando quick to pick up on his grammatical mistake, informing him that the correct expression is, in fact, 'al final' [in the end] or 'al fin de cuentas' [at the end of the day]. Fernando, however, quickly reminds himself that such corrections are futile and perhaps even unnecessary 'porque a la final da lo mismo' [because *at* the end it's the same thing], his replication of Alexis's incorrect use of the Spanish language insinuating that whichever way they express themselves, they are still nevertheless speaking from the same page.

Alexis and Fernando's relationship emerges in these respects as an embodiment of Medellín's curious blending of old and new, symptomatic of the fact that as Riaño Alcalá argues, the cultural proposal whereby the drug trafficking lifestyle and its conspicuous consumerism became simultaneously anchored in a 'return to tradition' regarding values, musical styles and religious practices, was one that ultimately 'blurred generational differences' (2006: 160). The grandiose fireworks display that erupts one night over Medellín as Fernando and Alexis survey the city from the apartment terrace can be invoked as a fitting metaphorical endorsement of this uneasy union, the classical tones of an opera from Fernando's beloved Callas which plays on the living-room stereo serving as an audial backdrop to what Alexis enthusiastically reveals to be in fact a celebration marking another successful shipment of cocaine to the USA.

(Trigger) Happy: Til Death Do Us Part

In theory, then, Fernando and Alexis's relationship does at least possess the potential to flourish as a productive, metropolitan (though not 'egalitarian') form of same-sex union. The operative word here, of course, is 'potential' since Fernando's ability to steer Alexis onto a different life trajectory, and a destiny other than an early grave, is ultimately dependent on his ability to remain sufficiently affected by Medellín's culture of violence and the 'career' which Alexis has forged within it to feel any motivation to do this in the first place. In a city where murder is so commonplace that it has come to constitute an 'everyday' expression of Medellín's street life, this ability is necessarily limited. As the director implies, indifference itself is perhaps the only survival strategy left for 'anyone who wants to carry on living in Medellín' (Schroeder in Kantaris 2002). The world of *La virgen de los sicarios* is, in short, characterized by a sheer *banalization* of violence.

Superficially Fernando does indeed express the sort of emotions — shock, distress, disapproval — towards Alexis's profession and the murders being committed in his midst that the film's presumably educated, middle-class audience would expect. 'Estoy contra toda violencia' [I'm against all kind of violence], he declares on one occasion before continuing, 'simplemente no hay que andar armado' [there's simply no need to go around armed with guns], the sentiment confirmed in his subsequent reaction to Alexis's murdering of the *punkero* [punk] who lives in the adjacent apartment. However, beneath the many instances of self-righteous indignation lies a latent hypocrisy that makes any claim he may have to holding the moral high ground extremely tenuous. Despite his 'surprise' at the boy's shooting of the *punkero*, for example, he certainly cannot claim to be a stranger to Alexis's impulsive tendencies or his supposed inability to distinguish between 'el pensamiento y la acción' [thought and action]. For only several scenes earlier, after Alexis has threatened to 'kill' the president as he watches him giving a national televised address, Fernando looks on in amusement as the boy then fetches his gun from the bedroom and aims it at the image of their national leader before obliterating their newly acquired television set. Indeed, as Fernando himself admits at one point in the film, 'si no se aparece en la televisión, no se existe' [if you don't appear on television then you don't exist], a comment which attests precisely to his awareness of the fact that amidst the increasingly scopic regime around which 'civilization', as he calls it, is constructed, distinguishing between the tangible and the intangible can no longer serve as a legitimate means of discerning what is 'real' and what is not, that is, if we are to believe in the objectivity of such a concept in the first place.

Even more significantly, Fernando's self-positioning as an innocent onlooker to the crimes which Alexis commits is, on closer examination, also highly questionable. His complaints about the *punkero*, for instance, and subsequent threat that 'una de estas noches le pego un tiro así hijo de puta' [one of these days I'll put a bullet in that son of a bitch] may initially only be a 'mal pensamiento' [bad thought] as he claims, but it is one that he subsequently puts into action when he raises Alexis's gun and pretends to shoot the boy as an accompaniment to this verbal threat, and which precipitates the actual murder itself several scenes later. Similarly, when Alexis rushes over to the window of the apartment to photograph mentally the *punkero* so he may be easily identifiable when the time comes to shoot him, Fernando too rushes over to join him in what from the boy's perspective can only be regarded as an act of encouragement.

The scene which takes place in the metro train similarly problematizes Fernando's status as somehow being exterior to the murders committed by his young lover. Apparently attempting to lead by example by avoiding recourse to verbal or physical abuse, the erudite Fernando instead asserts his authority over his two critics by shaming them through the exposure of their own stupidity and lack of education. 'Si supieron con quien están hablando' [If only you knew who you were talking to], he says before clarifying, 'Soy el último gramático de Colombia, el que descubrió el pronombre... ¿Qué saben que es? Es la palabra que está en lugar del nombre' [I'm the last grammarian of Colombia, the one who discovered the pronoun... Do you even know what that is? It's the word that goes in place of the noun].

As intended, his brief grammar lesson is clearly lost on the two men, who gormlessly stare back at him in utter confusion, much to the satisfaction of Fernando, who, from their point of view, may as well be speaking a foreign language. Fernando then attempts to clarify the knowledge he has just imparted by using a spoken illustration. 'Os doy un ejemplo' [I'll give you an example], he proposes, 'le dijo que lo iba a matar, y lo hizo' [I said I was going to kill him and I did it], and it is at precisely at this point that Alexis's gun emerges from behind Fernando and delivers its lethal payload into the two men.

The scene illustrates how Fernando is not only passively implicated in the murders through his physical presence at the scene of the crime. Rather, he assumes an active role through his example of the grammatical rule, which is in and of itself a generative act of violence to which Alexis's pulling of the trigger serves as the natural conclusion. Similarly, the former may erroneously believe that responding to Alexis's request for more bullets following the shooting on the metro may somehow prevent or at least delay his lover's death, but in reality it only serves to suck Alexis further into a vortex of violence in which his chances of also becoming a victim increase the deeper he travels.

From this perspective then, despite the initial promise of the power differentials between Alexis and Fernando, it would ultimately appear difficult to reclaim their union as the sort of 'productive' metropolitan gay relationship proposed by Sinfield. For it is precisely the supposedly 'rewarding' imbrication of Alexis's and Fernando's respective lives which serves as the Achilles heel that ultimately tears them apart. Here Fernando finds himself receptive not only to the culture of Alexis and his contemporaries in terms of their cultural references and vernacular but, most crucially, to their understanding of killing not only as a valid method of social interaction and conflict resolution but one which remains their only method of social advancement. His resultant implication in the acts of murder from which he tries to distance himself, far from altering the course of his lover's passage to the grave, only serves to consolidate it and propel it forward. And yet the insidious manner in which this occurs arguably mitigates a reading of their relationship in terms of pure 'exploitation' as per Sarabia's account. This is because the role he effectively assumes in Alexis's death has less to do with a conscious abuse of power than with these dehumanizing effects of violence. Here, just like the viewer, Fernando too becomes 'anaesthetized' to violence and experiences a similar 'emptying out' of his 'stock moral responses' (Kantaris 2002). Staring numbly into the lifeless eyes of his now dead lover as his body bleeds onto the seats of their hospital-bound taxi, the shell-shocked Fernando like us, it seems, has also been 'caught in a very devilish situation' without having 'the normal time to protest' (Schroeder in Foster 2001).

Bent Logics

And it is here amidst the film's dehumanization of violence where the logics proposed by D'Emilio and Knopp discussed in Chapter 1 begin to 'short circuit' and implode. Certainly, as I previously argued, the coalescence of Alexis's homosexual desires into an assumed, lived identity would, as per D'Emilio's account, seem contingent on his ability to construct a personal life outside the family unit and to live independently of its structures as a waged/subsidized individual. Similarly, the dismantling of the 'closet' that characterizes the construction of cinematic space, in turn, could be possibly read as symptomatic of processes relating to capital accumulation and their accompanying (queer) reappropriation of urban space mentioned by Knopp. Here the landscape's dominant narrative of heterocentrism, embodied by Medellín's civic and religious colonial architecture and monuments to the country's wars of independence, is rewritten by new constructions such as the towering buildings of glass and steel. These, whilst they can be psychoanalyzed as monumental phallic symbols of patriarchal capitalism (see, for example, Pile 1996), simultaneously attest to the alternative (albeit commoditized) lifestyles that have proliferated under this economic system and of which Alexis and Fernando's union, played out sexually in the latter's high-rise apartment, serves as the most poignant example.[18]

Yet in spite of the film's visual references to Medellín's narco-induced make-over,[19] significantly, and in marked contrast to *Un año sin amor*, there are no tangible references whatsoever to an emergent commercialized gay culture, nor to an associated community beyond the social group we encounter in the opening sequence. They frequent bars on several occasions but none of them are perceivably 'gay' spaces. Similarly, the establishment to which Fernando takes his second lover, Wílmar, towards the end of the film appears, judging by the pornography playing on the television above their bed, to cater to a primarily heterosexual clientele. Indeed, as the couple leave the building a medium long-shot confirms it to be a run-of-the-mill sex motel, as opposed to any sort of gay 'sauna' which often feature private rooms for more intimate male same-sex encounters. Also absent are any material signs of gay culture in Fernando's apartment — books, magazines, films, posters, pornography, for example — or evidence of a connection to a 'virtual' gay community such as we see in *Un año sin amor*, something which might perhaps not be entirely antithetical to Alexis's character given his voracious appetite for popular culture and technology. Nor does the film hint at any engagement on the part of Fernando and Alexis with the rhetoric of minority group politics. Both, as we have seen, are remarkably forthright about their sexuality and reject the values and institutions associated with heterosexuality, marriage and the nuclear family. However, this fails overwhelmingly to translate into any form of social consciousness — lesbigay, queer or otherwise. Indeed, Fernando's scorning of the presidential television address and Alexis's subsequent metaphorical assassination of the man in question, are representative of their mutual contempt for, and, in Alexis's case, exclusion from, the political process with its rather shallow promises of inclusivity and rights for all.

Of course, from one perspective this perhaps has more to say about Alexis and Fernando's individual tastes than anything else — being 'gay' after all certainly does not necessarily imply an interest either in the commercial gay world itself or in politicizing one's sexuality. Yet from another and perhaps more important perspective, I would suggest that it speaks loudly of how the supposed inevitability of minority world narratives surrounding the 'production of gay' and 'gay emanci-pation' become radically *destabilized* in contexts such as that pertaining to Medellín.

A booming, 'free-market' economy it may indeed be, but ultimately it is one that owes its growth largely to the successful cultivation, processing and exportation of Colombia's primary cash crop — coca. In this sense, as Foster rightly points out, the city we see in *La virgen de los sicarios* functions as a 'grotesque parody of economic success', one that 'can only be sustained through high-tech violence' (2003: 80), violence which has developed into an entire industry in itself and has become self-sustaining. Here, 'efficiency' is determined by the complete trivialization of death whereby it becomes normal to kill and to be killed, so much so that the shooting of a lame dog is likely to elicit more of an emotional response than that of a fellow human being. In turn, life itself assumes the status of a material product that can be bought and sold at whatever price the market dictates. It is reduced, as Salazar remarks, 'to an instant' (1992: 120), something embodied by *sicario* slang for the verb 'to shoot': 'tomar un foto' [to take a photo]. Thus whilst Medellín would, like the Buenos Aires featured in Berneri's film, appear to offer fertile ground for 'men and women to organize a personal life around their erotic/emotional attraction to their own sex' and for the 'formation of urban communities of lesbians and gay men, and more recently, of a politics based on a sexual identity' (D'Emilio 1983: 104), in fact it does quite the opposite. For existence has become so ephemeral, and death so inevitable, that the very ideas of preserving human rights, raising political consciousness, building communities, celebrating shared identity and even investing in one's own personal relationships become increasingly redundant. As Koonings and Krujit note more generally of the city's *comunas*, 'people tend not to make plans for the immediate future, let alone for a lifetime' (2007: 64).

The status of the homosexual body as a potential space of transgression, in turn, emerges as necessarily ambivalent. In many ways, as director Karim Aïnouz says of João Francisco, the protagonist of *Madame Satã* (discussed in Chapter 5), Alexis's body is similarly 'a única coisa, objetivamente, que ele tem' [the only thing he has] (Ainouz 2003: 181) — the sole possession through which he might define himself against and transcend the dominant order and its system of values, which have relegated him sexually and socially to a status of marginality. For it is precisely *through* its insertion into the city's economy of violence, which as we have seen permits Alexis to reclaim his sexuality as something positive that may be lived, enjoyed and ultimately used to his advantage its erotic enmeshing of youth and danger constituting an alluring aphrodisiac for older middle-class men such as Fernando. And yet it is difficult to see how this insertion might be regarded as in any way emancipatory or affirmative since the price he must pay for this willing submission to Medellín's submarkets of contract killing and male prostitution is ultimately his own life. Alexis and his contemporaries become, to use Riaño Alcalá's phraseology, 'factors of production in and of themselves whose value is determined by markets of supply and demand' (2006: 46). It is in this rather perverse form of corporal commodification that arguably the film becomes most disturbing, with the body of the *sicario* gradually reduced to the status of a disposable object which, like the detritus we see littering Fernando's apartment following Alexis's death, is wholly *desechable* [disposable].

Free to Die: Bodies, Commodification and 'Life in an Instant'

It is Fernando's subsequent relationship with another *sicario* named Wílmar which serves as the ultimate testament to this cheapness of life in Medellín. Certainly Alexis's death has affected Fernando, of that there is no doubt. Following his trip to the hospital, which proved fruitless in reviving the boy, Fernando is plunged into a profound existential crisis, returning in a rather surreal scene to the church, where he is plagued by the demons which now inhabit this once sacred building and encounters the sight of his very own tomb ensconced somewhere amidst the shadows. The scene, we presume, corresponds to a nightmare, with the sight of Fernando sobbing on the tiled floor between the pews quickly transitioning to a high-angled shot of him slumped over his dinner table back in the apartment. The next time we see the protagonist he is sporting several weeks' beard growth, dark rings around his eyes, and he struggles to remember the date or recognize the image of the new national president on the television in the bar in which he is sitting, asking on both counts for clarification from the owner. Fernando, it seems, has been in mourning, and for quite some time. The apparent sight, in one scene, of his deceased lover contemplating the window display of a city-centre shop one day is then naturally arresting for him. Staring in disbelief at the spectre before him, Fernando gingerly approaches the boy, identifiable by the much cherished blue and yellow sports jacket worn in other scenes, most notably that in which Alexis eventually loses his life.

Of course, when he eventually turns around to face Fernando, he in fact reveals himself to be Wílmar — these supposedly 'prized' blue and yellow jackets are ten to the dozen in Medellín it would appear. And so too, as Fernando discovers, are boys like Alexis, the film establishing here a clear interchangeability between the two lovers. Beyond the obvious use of identical jackets in Fernando's first liaison with Wílmar, the former's invitation to visit the church with him after lunch mirrors Alexis's suggestion that Fernando accompany him on his weekly pilgrimage to Sabaneta in their first encounter. And once they have returned to the apartment, the sexual proceedings are initiated with exactly the same request that he made to Alexis, 'quítate la ropa, niño' [take off your clothes, kid], the words eerily articulated in an identical tone of voice. Even Fernando himself seems to have trouble at times distinguishing between the two, waking in the night and futilely attempting to arouse the attention of the boy sleeping next to him by calling out Alexis's name, then remembering that it is, in fact, Wílmar.

Despite Fernando's claim that he is 'la cosa más bonita' [the most beautiful thing] life has given him, Alexis, like the television set the boy himself unceremoniously destroys, is apparently wholly replaceable, a fact alluded to by the film's association of the body of the *sicario* with purchasable material goods and the equivalency that is established between them. In the scene in which Alexis and Fernando visit the seminary-turned-shopping mall to purchase items for the latter's empty apartment, for example, the two are framed travelling down an escalator with the afternoon's 'prize' — the Aiwa sound system — in hand. Here, Alexis is depicted carrying the item in question, his torso substituted by a large cardboard box emblazoned with the Aiwa logo, with only his head and shoulders remaining visible. In what is also another indication of the interchangeability of Fernando's two lovers, this particular scene is later recalled following one of Wílmar's spending sprees (made courtesy of Fernando), where the former is depicted arriving back at the apartment laden with branded shopping bags that hang from him as if they were appendages of his own body. And later, when the couple have decided to escape Medellín together, it is a Whirlpool refrigerator, bought as a parting gift for Wílmar's mother, against which the young *sicario* is juxtaposed. Here, having decided for security reasons that he should accompany the delivery men on their journey to the *comuna* where his mother resides, we see Wílmar also being 'loaded' into the back of the van along with the white goods Fernando has just purchased for him.

It will, of course, be the last time Fernando ever sees Wílmar. For just like Alexis, the boy also meets his death, leaving the older man to wait in vain for his lover back at the apartment, thus necessarily precluding the 'happy ending' implied by their plan to leave the city. All Fernando finds as he checks in desperation for any sign of his lover outside the front door is an empty plastic bag, which blows in through the open doorway, and a subsequent telephone call from the city mortuary requesting him to come to identify the deceased boy. And it is here where the notion of the 'body as commodity' becomes most macabre, the following scene revealing the scale of the facility to be so huge that it is more akin to a processing plant than a mortuary, the final destination on the city's industrial conveyor belt of violence. On arrival Fernando quite literally has to fight his way through the crowd of people gathering at the perimeter fence apparently in search of missing loved ones. Once inside, a crane shot from above reveals him entering the reception area where a family can be seen trying to identify the image of their child. This will be no mean feat, for it is one amongst hundreds that can be found in the mortuary's 'catalogue of death', a file several hundreds of pages long containing photograph after photograph of murdered adolescents identifiable only by a serial number laid across their chests. They might as well be browsing a mail-order directory, it seems, so detached and impersonal has the claiming of a deceased loved one become, the face of their son eventually revealing itself amidst sobs and cries from the family concerned. The camera then moves across the next room, a large administrative office where several officials can be seen at their typewriters efficiently processing the latest batch of corpses to arrive, before entering the clinical area of the mortuary where we presume the autopsies are performed. As the camera pans slowly across the room, a dozen or so naked dead bodies are revealed, each lying illuminated by harsh overhead lighting against a backdrop of white tiles and stainless steel, their clothes and possessions tied in a bundle at their feet. So obviously artificial are the 'corpses' that whilst one might regard this scene as somewhat risible, their mannequin-like forms and waxy, artificial complexions arguably only serve to embellish their status as (now damaged) 'goods'. Eventually we arrive at Wílmar's body, which has been given only the most rudimentary of 'window dressing', his traumatized chest having been stitched crudely back together by the duty doctor, whom we see explaining matter of factly to Fernando the cause of death, namely cardio-respiratory failure from excessive blood loss.

FIG. 3.4. The industry of death depicted in *La virgen de los sicarios*
(Barbet Schroeder, 2000: Paramount Pictures)

It is a disturbing scene and one which appears as a highly perverse rendering of
the Foucauldian idea of 'bio-power' or, to quote the latter once more, 'the notion
of the body as a machine; its disciplining, the optimization of its capabilities, the
extortion of its forces, the parallel increase of its usefulness and its docility, its
integration into systems of efficient and economic controls' (1978: 139). Superficially
Alexis and Wílmar may indeed appear to use 'capitalism's tools to undermine its
repressive paradigms' (Quiroga 2000: 12), yet in doing so, they submit body and
soul to the full control of the market into which they become subsumed, necessarily
negating any claims to transgression, liberation or transcendence. In this sense, we
might identify clear similarities between the fate of the *sicarios* and that of Pablo in
Un año sin amor, whose body, as I suggested in Chapter 2, seems to be 'reintegrated
back into control'. However, in contrast to Berneri's film, no psychoanalytic reading
of events here is required, for the entire existence of the *sicario* is quite literally, in
and of itself, an act of masochism. Unlike the 'games' played out between Pablo and
his companions in the safety of the S/M club or Baéz's apartment, it has nothing
to do with 'theatrical (re)appropriation', rather, it is what defines their everyday
reality, a reality whose only certainty is the inevitability of an early grave. *La virgen
de los sicarios* thus firmly puts to bed the vision of the 'market' as the harbinger of
social change — whether that be the promotion and acceptance of gay rights, racial
equality, distribution of wealth or otherwise.

Death, Growth and Capitalism

The 'unofficial' global city that is Medellín emerges then in *La virgen de los sicarios*
as a highly ambivalent site with regards to the production of homosexualities and
same-sex erotic subcultures. Superficially the socio-economic backdrop against

which the film's narrative is articulated would appear limited in its ability to foster the emergence of the 'modern' metropolitan gay model. High levels of social inequality, the resultant cycle of violence and a cityscape that is consequently ever-more fractured and confused with regards to the distribution and organization of urban space, would hardly appear conducive to the accumulation of national and transnational capital witnessed in 1990s Buenos Aires, and to which the development of the Buenos Aires gay scene discussed in Chapter 2 would, at least in part, appear to owe itself. Paradoxically, however, as I argued, contrary to conventional wisdom, the violence we see in *La virgen de los sicarios*, as Hardy puts it, 'is not the violence of decline' (in Salazar 1992: 10), rather that of a prosperity born from a city that is, in fact, just like Buenos Aires, highly integrated into the world economy, although in this case due to its position at the hub of Latin America's narcotics trade. In this sense, the resultant process of socio-spatial realignment alluded to in the film produces, as we see, a *decoupling* of the longstanding (perceived) correlation between class, financial solvency and family reliance in Latin America, and as a result, entertains a more nuanced, metropolitan reading of Fernando and Alexis's relationship. As Castells points out, 'globalization and identity interact in the criminal economy of Latin America [and] organize the perverse connection that redefines development and dependency in historically unforeseen ways' (2000: 206). Nevertheless, whilst the application of minority-world logics surrounding the 'production of gay' allows us to deconstruct and take forward socio-anthropological accounts of Latin American homosexualities, as the final two sections of this chapter demonstrated, these ultimately become 'bent', with the supposed inevitability of (market-driven) 'liberation' severely curtailed in the specific context of Medellín's economy of violence.

In no way, however, does capitalism win out in the film. Indeed, it is ultimately shown to sow the seeds of its own destruction. To return to Foucault, 'bio-power', as he terms it, has been undoubtedly an 'indispensable element' in the development of capitalism. The latter, he writes, 'would not have been possible without the controlled insertion of bodies into the machinery of production and the adjustment of the phenomena to economic processes' (1978: 141). However, as mentioned in relation to *Un año sin amor*, 'it also needed the growth of both these factors [...] their reinforcement as well as their availability and docility; it had to have methods of power capable of optimising forces, aptitudes and life in general' (1978: 141). This, he continues, has been achieved through a 'bio-politics of the population', a careful regime of supervision, interventions and regulatory controls in the domain of public health and social policy which have been mobilized in the 'calculated management of life' (1978: 139). This perhaps explains why, until relatively recently, suicide itself was considered a criminal offence in many countries since it usurped the sovereignty of the state, which had assigned itself the role of primary 'administrator' of life (1978: 139). And yet in the Dantesque world of *La virgen de los sicarios*, somewhat paradoxically, economic growth is, to a large extent, dependent on precisely the opposite process — an investment in death and the complete *devaluation* of life. Here Medellín's economy of violence can only be nourished through the extermination of the living human bodies on which it feeds, and in this sense is quite literally an economy that is 'growing itself to death'. The city therefore may indeed be the proud purveyor of skyscrapers, shopping malls and light-rail systems but, having been built on a foundation far less stable than sand, that is, the blood of its citizens, one has to question for how long they may stand.

Notes to Chapter 3

1. Josef Gugler makes a distinction between 'first tier' cities 'at the core of the world's cities', namely the 'triumvirate' of New York, London and Tokyo, and 'second tier' cities 'beyond the core' which 'play major regional and global roles' such as Mumbai, Shanghai, São Paulo, Johannesburg, Bangkok and Seoul (2004: 1).

2. For more discussion on 'other' spaces of capital accumulation see also Gibson-Graham 1996.

3. The term *comuna* in Colombia literally corresponds to an administrative unit of a given city composed, in turn, of *sectores* or *barrios*. In popular parlance, however, particularly in Medellín, the plural, *comunas*, is used to refer (sometimes pejoratively) to peripheral working-class neighbourhoods such as La América, San Javier, El Popular and Villa Hermoso, often situated on the surrounding hillsides of the Antioquia Valley. Many of these are now established neighbourhoods with access to electricity and running water; some, such as Santo Domingo Savio and El Popular, have also been integrated into the wider urban infrastructure through a cable-car extension to the city's metro system. Others, however, may lack basic services in their newer, more peripheral *sectores*.

4. By 1980 it was estimated that 75 per cent of all US cocaine was transported from Colombia, largely through the Medellín cartel (Simons 2004: 67).

5. The real-life author himself moved to Mexico in 1971, where he continues to live, but in contrast to his fictionalized self in the film, he has returned regularly to his native Colombia.

6. *Metrallo* is an adaptation of *Medallo* — the informal name by which Medellín is often known — and incorporates the word 'metralleta' [machine gun] in reference to its reputation for armed violence.

7. For an excellent in-depth overview of Colombian film that moves beyond a focus on the cinematic depiction of violence, see Suárez 2012.

8. *Paisa* is the name given to inhabitants of a region in northwest Colombia comprising the departments of Antioquia, Caldas, Risaralda and Quindío. The administrative capital of Antioquia, Medellín, is also sometimes referred to as the 'capital' of the *paisas*.

9. Ramírez and Casper argue in *What it Means to be a Man: Reflections on Puerto Rican Masculinity* that the *maricón* is 'the total negation of masculinity, an individual who is devalued and despised, and calling a man *maricón* is the worst insult that could ever be given to him (in Subero 2014: 21).

10. *Maricón* and its adjective, *marica*, are often translated into English as 'faggot', 'fag' or 'queer' but these translations do not really capture the distinctly feminine connotations of the word, which derives from the name 'María' (Mary). I have opted to use the translation of the noun 'fag' here lest 'queer', which has been reclaimed and reappropriated in English-speaking cultures, give the (erroneous) impression of any kind of politicized identity on the part of the protagonists in this film.

11. Of course, as many of the essays in Aggleton's book go on to note, behind closed doors the 'rules' are often (quite literally) bent, something which rings particularly true in the Latin American-themed papers relating to Brazil, Costa Rica, the Dominican Republic, Peru and Mexico respectively. This, I would suggest, is almost inevitable: if we follow Larvie's logic that cross-class and cross-race sexual contact marked as unacceptable in the public domain 'charges up' (my phraseology) sexual relations in highly stratified societies, then it would seem almost inevitable that so too would the transgression of the rules of acceptable sexual conduct that these accompanying social categories imply.

12. The indication of 'identity' is particularly explicit in the use of the verb 'ser' [to be] which in the Spanish language implies a degree of permanence, in contrast to 'estar' (also 'to be') which indicates a temporary state.

13. In some respects Fernando's assertion that 'lo importante no es el nombre' is suggestive of a 'queer' understanding of his sexual identity which views it as something fluid, unfixed and undefinable. However, his subsequent qualification 'sino la substancia de las cosas' suggests an

alignment more towards a metropolitan gay model which has tended to view sexual identity as the expression of something 'innate' and in the context of modern identity politics to view gay people akin to an 'ethnic group' (Binnie 2004: 60).

14. Simón Bolívar (1783–1830) was a Venezuelan political leader who together with José de San Martín played a key role in Spanish-speaking Latin America's successful struggle for independence from Spain.

15. In this respect Certeau claims that the act of walking fulfils three enuciative functions. Firstly, he writes, it is a process of 'appropriation of the topographical system on the part of the pedestrian', in the same way that a speaker appropriates language. Secondly, he continues, walking can be regarded as a 'spatial acting-out of the place' just as the speech act is an (acoustic) acting out of language. And thirdly, he proposes that walking implies '*relations* among differentiated positions', that is, 'pragmatic "contracts" in the form of movements', in the same way that verbal enunciation is an ' "allocution", "posits another opposite" the speaker and puts contracts between interlocutors in action' (1984: 98).

16. Alexis's 'broken' home would appear symptomatic of what Jurado argues to be the demise of the traditional extended *paisa* family as an organizing unit amongst the city's working classes, the once pivotal father figure being only a transitory presence or else a complete absence in family life, with the mother instead often fulfilling the dual roles of chief care provider *and* breadwinner. In contrast, amongst the supposedly 'liberal' middle classes, the nuclear family model has increasingly reasserted itself as 'una esfera intocable que todos resguardan y defienden en medio de las inclemencias del ambiente social' [an untouchable sphere protected and defended by all amidst a harsh social environment] (2003: 134). This would appear to further destabilize the notion that social background constitutes a reliable indicator of one's freedom to declare and live one's sexuality without interference or repercussions from one's family.

17. The same here can be said for his second lover, Wílmar, who tells Fernando that he has not eaten for 'two weeks' during the restaurant meal they enjoy at their first encounter.

18. Steve Pile in *The Body and the City: Psychoanalysis, Space and Subjectivity* writes that monuments are phallic because they are 'erect, tall and associated with power' whilst high buildings such as skyscrapers exhibit corporate power by being 'erect, tall and associated with wealth' (1996: 221). In this sense, he argues, from a Lefebvrian or psychoanalytic perspective, the Manhattan skyline, by way of example, is concerned with a phallic 'formant of space' produced through three intersecting, aligned lines of power: masculinity, the bourgeois family and capitalism' (1996: 221).

19. Castells in this respect remarks how the Colombian economy appropriated a much larger share of the profits from *narcotráfico* than, for example, its Bolivian counterpart. He argues that although it is difficult to link rigorously this appropriation with the significant boom of construction and real estate development in the 1980s, the 'prudent distance' of regular foreign capital from Colombia at the time would suggest that some of this investment can be related to a recycling of drug trafficking profits into legitimate business (2000: 201–02). In the specific context of Medellín, Roldán makes a similar correlation between drug trafficking and the transformation of the city's urban landscape in the 1980s, in particular, manifestations of conspicuous consumerism such as shopping malls and imported car dealerships (1999: 169).

CHAPTER 4

Recife: *Amarelo manga*

Living on the Edge: Marginality, Liminality and the 'In-Between'

'In-between' Spaces

Chapters 2 and 3 focused on films depicting spaces located both physically and socially at the 'centre' of their respective settings of Buenos Aires and Medellín. But what of the spaces within these spaces — the fissures or cracks which have opened up within this highly fragmented and dislocated Latin American urban fabric? Within the abstract and obfuscatory space of maps and plans these often go unacknowledged, simply appearing as voids or gaps. And yet as argued in the Introduction, Latin American cinema has played an important role in making visible such spaces and giving voice to those who speak from within them. These spaces are often ones of ambivalence, what we might term 'interstitial' or 'in-between' spaces. Often physically located at or near the 'centre' of things, their status as what Rob Shields terms 'social peripheries' nevertheless inscribes them with a degree of marginality which means that within the geographical imagination at least, they are still often imagined as being 'out-of-the-way' and 'on the edge', having been placed on the periphery of 'cultural systems of space' (1991: 3). Within the general economy of sexuality, as Phillips and Watt argue, this metaphorical distance from the 'centre' — the locus of the medical, legal and political institutions responsible for the production and regulation of sexualities and sexual discourses — suggests that such spaces may be sites where sexual subjects may be least stable and hegemonic sexualities most open to challenge (2000: 1–2). They are, in this sense, what we might term 'liminal' spaces where, to quote Shields, one might experience, due to their interstitial nature, 'a liberation from the regimes of normative practices and performance codes of mundane life' and 'moments of discontinuity in the social fabric [and] in social space' (1991: 83–84). Indeed, in *Dramas, Fields, and Metaphors: Symbolic Action in Human Society*, Victor Turner goes as far as to argue 'in this gap between ordered worlds, almost anything may happen' (1974: 13).

The perceived liminality of such 'in-between' spaces might be regarded as being especially pronounced in the case of Brazil, where according to renowned anthropologist Roberto Da Matta, the national spatial imaginary has been structured around highly dichotomized divisions between centre and periphery, the space of the *rua* [street] and that of the *casa* [home], and between interior and exterior spaces. According to Da Matta, the *casa* might be regarded as a microcosm of Brazilian society, a 'universo controlado' [controlled universe] constructed around strict hierarchies of sex, age and lineage, with men and elders at the pinnacle, a static space where 'as coisas estão nos seus devidos lugares' [things are kept in their due places] and protection is provided from the disputes and hostilities of the world outside (1997b: 90). Indeed, the sanctity of the *casa* and its status as a 'safe-haven', as Richard Parker argues, has its roots firmly in Brazil's colonial past and legacy of slavery. Here the *casa-grande* [big-house] of the *engenho* [sugar mill] served as a type of 'prison and fortress' for a mill-owner's wife and, more importantly, his daughters, who were kept under the constant surveillance of a *mucama* [female house servant] in order to protect their virginity (and by extension, the honour of their father) from outside 'threats', in particular those posed by male slaves (Parker 2009: 38).[1]

Contrastingly the public space of the *rua*, in addition to the *engenho*, *cidade* [city] and *praça* [square], was most definitely a male domain, a world of economic, political and social interactions which was 'sharply opposed to the relatively inactive [and] guarded and bounded society of his [the mill-owner's] women' (Parker 2009: 37). The *rua* has, in this sense, emerged according to Da Matta as a 'Hobbesian' universe of unforeseen events, accidents and passions, the domain of linear time and individualism where, in contrast to the *casa,* hierarchal distinctions, at least between men, are less perceivable (1997b: 90). And whilst such strict delineations might appear incongruous in an age of postmodern spatial fragmentation, the continued importance attached to the country's annual celebration of carnival would suggest otherwise. Here, in a celebration lasting five days and nights, according to Da Matta, the *casa* and the *rua* dissolve into a space of anarchic liminality where sexual transgression, homoeroticism and gender-bending are unashamedly encouraged, attesting to the symbolic currency these spaces (and their dissolution) continue to hold within the collective psyche with regards to hegemonic discourses of gender and sexuality and the behavioural codes these imply. According to Da Matta, the confluence of these two spaces always creates confusion or even conflict (1997a: 22).

This chapter builds on the discussion of the previous two by now considering how the 'metropolitan', both at the level of the spatial and the sexual, has been reimagined in Latin American cinema through marginal perspectives articulated from inside the 'gaps' within the region's urban fabric. Focusing on the specific case of the north-eastern Brazilian city of Recife as it appears in Cláudio Assis's *Amarelo manga* (2002), it explores the relationship between the 'in-betweenness' of the film's setting — the city's historic centre — and the film's treatment and representation of gender and sexuality. More specifically, it assesses to what extent the apparent 'sexual anarchy' which characterizes this particular space in the film can be said to evidence a liminal space of sexual transgression which exists in counterpoint to the 'regulation' of the (new) economic 'centres' of the city. If this is a space in which the characters are supposedly 'liberated in their desires', how are we to interpret the cycles of misogyny, homophobia and domestic violence which propel the film's narrative? Are they symptomatic of the exclusion of this social sphere from 'progressive' Brazil and its emancipatory discourses of feminism and gay liberation? And if they are, can they merely be read as traits of a 'sexual hinterland' which continues to articulate gender and sexuality according to supposedly 'traditional' models, or do we require a more nuanced reading of things?

Voices From the Edge

Amarelo manga constitutes Cláudio Assis's feature-length directorial debut, with his short film *Texas Hotel* (1999) representing the precursor or calling card for the film in question. *Amarelo manga* was critically acclaimed both at home and abroad, winning over twenty-eight awards and thirteen nominations on the festival circuit, including the audience and critics' awards at the Brasília Film Festival in 2002, the Best Cinematography and Best Newcomer awards in Havana in 2002, and the Grand Prix at the Toulouse Latin American Film Festival also in 2003. The film even received endorsement from the then Brazilian president, Luiz Inácio Lula da Silva, who deemed it 'necessário' (Mendonça Filho, 2003b).

Opening a rare window on Brazil's north-eastern raw urban underbelly, the film recounts twenty-four hours in the lives of a hotchpotch of colourful yet marginalized personalities who orbit the worlds of the dilapidated Texas Hotel and Bar Avenida and include: a hotel cook, Dunga (Matheus Nachtergaele); his love interest and local butcher, Wellington (Chico Díaz); Kika (Dira Paes), Wellington's evangelical wife; Dayse (Magdale Alves), Wellington's lover; Isaac (Jonas Bloch), the hotel's resident necrophiliac; Lígia (Leona Cavalli), the jaded owner of Bar Avenida and love interest of Isaac; and Dona Aurora (Conceição Camaroti), a retired sex worker. The plot is driven principally by Dunga's obsession with Wellington, on the one hand, and Kika's plan to avenge her husband's infidelity on the other, though clashes between the other characters, particularly Lígia and Isaac, also constitute narrative strands.

To some degree, the film's marginal discourse and Assis's self-confessed concern to film 'o povo' [the people] might be argued to give nods to the films of Brazil's *cinema novo* [new cinema] movement. The inclusion of real footage of the city's street life to complement the dramatic performances of its professional actors, in particular, points to the neorealist-inspired ethos of 'an idea in your head, a camera in hand, the people in front, but not only in their festivities' so evident in films such as *Cinco vezes favela* (Miguel Borges & Joaquim Pedro de Andrade, 1962), *Vidas secas* (Nelson Pereira dos Santos, 1964) and *Os fuzis* (Ruy Guerra, 1964).[2] And yet this is given an ironic twist by director of photography, Walter Carvalho, who actually shot the film in Panavision, thus endowing the film with a panoramic grandiosity normally only seen in popular Hollywood cinema and which, of course, *cinema novo* reacted so virulently against.[3] However, far from compromising its status as a piece of social filmmaking, the use of Panavision arguably serves, albeit in an unconventional sense, to reinforce it, quite literally on a representational level giving these downtrodden characters a greater aesthetic presence and voice.

Similarly, if *cinema novo* was sometimes accused of paternalism in its representation of the *povo* [people], no such criticisms can be directed at Assis. Instead, in the sections of the film enacted by professional actors, the viewer is presented with a richly constructed cast, whose sordidness and despair mingle with a palpable sense of defiance, thus erasing any sense of victimization and inspiring both sympathy and repulsion in equal measure. Certainly the film, in terms of its aesthetic, is unmistakably a type of grotesque and distinctly off-kilter social realism which Kleber Mendonça Filho aptly describes as 'decorando multiplexes do país com um enorme vagina em close [...] seus pêlos pubianos pendurados junto de Arnold Schwarzenegger, Bruce Willis e Renée Zellwegger' [decorating the Brazilian multiplexes like an enormous vagina in close-up, its pubic hairs dangling next to the likes of Arnold Schwarzenegger, Bruce Willis and Renée Zellwegger'] (2003b). Although *Amarelo manga* carries here clear traces of *cinema marginal* with its depiction of a grotesque yet absurd sub-world of crime, sex and exploitation, within the more contemporary typology elaborated in Tatiana Heise's *Remaking Brazil: Contested National Identities in Contemporary Brazilian Cinema* (2012), *Amarelo manga* largely falls within the category of what she terms 'Opposition' cinema.[4] If 'Reformist' cinema (to which she correlates *cinema novo*) documented social problems, using the nation as a central reference point without fundamentally questioning whether a coherent nation and national identity was desirable or even feasible, then films of the 'opposition' category, rather more pessimistically, suggest them either to be so broken that they are beyond repair or conceptually impossible:

> They represent Brazil as a fractured society made up of groups whose ethics and ways of life are so much in conflict and so mutually unintelligible that no sense of solidarity between them is possible. Brazil is constructed in these films as the opposite of a racial democracy, as a place where ethnic and sociocultural differences are unbridgeable. National identity is thus seen as a shallow façade seeking to disguise the fissures that tear open the social fabric. (Heise 2012: 109–10)

Certainly the Brazil we encounter in Assis's film is a world away from the 'Brazil' that foreign audiences have customarily encountered on the silver screen — defined overwhelmingly by (often romanticized) images of Rio de Janeiro and to a lesser extent São Paulo. Although it is the country's fourth largest city, Recife's appearances in the cinema have, contrastingly, been conspicuous by their absence and films with north-eastern settings have often unfolded in the 'mythical' *sertão* [rural backlands] such as Paulo Caldas and Lírio Ferreira's *Baile perfumado* (1997), Walter Salles's *Central do Brasil* (1999) or, more recently, *Cinema, aspirinas e urubus* (Marcelo Gomes, 2005) and *Viajo porque preciso, volto porque te amo* (Karim Aïouz and Marcelo Gomes, 2009). The director laments ironically in this respect: 'O Recife está sempre na vanguarda... na vanguarda da fudição' [Recife is always at the vanguard... the vanguard of oblivion] (Mendonça Filho 2003a). His decision to set *Amarelo manga* in his native city is therefore significant in that the film joins a burgeoning body of productions offering a more decentred view of Brazilian urban life in the north-east with a view from 'the edge', such as *Cidade Baixa* (Sérgio Machado, 2005), *Mulheres do Brasil* (Malu de Martino, 2006) and *Capitães da Areia* (Cecilia Amado, 2011).

Informality, Social Exclusion and Decay in Recife's Historic Centre

Whilst the above statement by Assis serves as a fitting metaphor for the city's marginalized status within Brazilian cultural representation, it also attests to its economically chequered history. During the colonial era Recife's position as the world centre of sugar cane production saw it emerge as a wealthy city, characterized by the baroque architecture of its many monasteries and churches (Zancheti 2005: 16). By the nineteenth century, however, the south-eastern region had consolidated its dominance in the Brazilian economy due to the gold boom in Minas Gerais, which had begun in 1695, resulting in large numbers of north-eastern dwellers emigrating to the interior regions and, in turn, labour shortages and agricultural decline in the traditional 'motherland' of Bahia and Pernambuco (Burns 1970: 61–63).[5]

Efforts to modernize sugar production in the state of Pernambuco, coupled with the expansion of cotton production in the interior, did prompt, however, another period of accentuated growth which was followed by decades of explosive growth from the 1940s due to further modernization of the sugar industry and the emergence of modern forms of cattle ranching, as the cattle-cotton complexes of the interior disintegrated (Assies 1991: 43). The benefits, though, were tempered by massive migration from rural areas to Recife itself, which the city struggled to accommodate in terms of both production (employment) and reproduction (housing) (Sousa Santos 1992: 236). Indeed, even before 1940, 30 per cent of the population of 350,000 already inhabited *mocambos*, the notorious shantytowns which traditionally lay at the edges of the city's waterways and marshes, though which nowadays are more commonly found on the hills of the city's periphery (Cabral & Sobreira de Moura 1996: 58). Recife, therefore, has evolved as a divided city characterized by stark dichotomies between formal and informal, legal and illegal, planned and substandard, the result, according to John T. Cabral and Alexandrina Sobreira de Moura, of extreme financial, social, cultural and political inequalities that exist within the metropolis (1996: 54).

Interestingly, though, it is not the city's infamous *mocambos* which constitute the principal spaces of narrative action in *Amarelo manga*, rather its historic centre.[6] As S. M. Zancheti writes, until the 1980s its status as the most important economic area in the metropolitan region had gone unchallenged, and the area featured a concentration of the most important companies with a multitude of services aimed at high-income earners (2005: 17). However, between the early 1980s and early 1990s the city's economy suffered a major process of deindustrialization due to the repealing of federal industrial subsidies, particularly those channelled towards the sugar-cane industry (2005: 19). In its place emerged a service-based economy, a shift which, as businesses were closed or transferred, meant the loss of many ancillary activities and the emergence of new economic centralities within the city (2005: 19).

The migration of commercial and economic activities, and consequently the middle and upper classes themselves, occurred to the detriment of the city centre, which was afflicted with a shrinking population and saw the arrival of informal, predominantly stall-holder-type businesses targeted at low-income groups (Zancheti 2005: 19). Zancheti continues that the over-occupation of spaces by street vendors and (permanent) illegal stalls impeded circulation and the maintenance of sanitation in the area, accelerating the deterioration of public spaces, including its listed buildings (2005: 20). Thus, from being one of the city's most vibrant areas, the historic centre was transformed into one of its most, dirty, run-down and depressed, symptomatic of the way in which, concurrent to its appropriation of formerly rural land, the city, according to Tomás de Albuquerque Lapa, 'se mutilou por dentro' [mutilated itself from within] (Lapa 1987: 5).

As we will see in the discussion that follows, the notion of Recife's historic centre being somehow 'dirty', or to put it rather less crudely, a space of both physical and social 'impurity', is certainly all-pervasive in *Amarelo manga*'s imaginings of this particular part of the city. Since the 1990s parts of Recife's historic centre such as Recife Antigo have, in actual fact, undergone a vigorous process of regeneration. This has resulted in the emergence of leisure and recreation services, design, fashion and information technology outlets and a partial return of higher-income earners to some of its restored residential buildings (Zancheti 2005: 22). However, any reference to this gentrification is distinctly absent from the world of *Amarelo manga*, with the film's representation of the area articulated overwhelmingly through a predominance of medium shots and close-ups which reveal the area's squat, decaying colonial architecture and fetid, pot-holed sidewalks in all their faded glory. The Texas Hotel, in particular, appears as particularly 'run-down' not just in terms of its physical state of repair, but also through its status as an alternative and highly peripheral social space produced to accommodate those now unable to maintain their position in 'respectable' mainstream society.

As Tim Cresswell states, 'dirt', at its most basic level, is simply something 'in the wrong place or wrong time' and therefore is entirely relative (1996: 38). It is 'a mismatch of meanings', 'meanings that are erroneously positioned in relation to each other' (1996: 38). Thus 'dirt' can be indicative not just of the spoiling of a material surface but of 'a problem which lies much deeper': poor health/hygiene, social and sexual depravity, and other phenomena which are 'out of place' in the 'civilized' and ordered environment that modern societies seek to produce. And because 'dirt appears where it shouldn't be', he continues, it is almost always placed 'at the bottom of a hierarchical scale of values' and is 'valued by very few people'. In this sense, as something that is to be avoided, as Julia Kristeva observes, dirt is often 'pushed beyond a boundary to its other side, its margin' (in Cresswell 1996: 39), whether that be in a physical sense or within the social ordering of space that takes place within the geographical imagination.

Certainly the cinematic mapping of the principal space(s) of narrative action within the wider geography of the city evokes a sensation of detachedness and disconnection. In the scene immediately following the opening sequence, for example, we follow Isaac as he drives through Recife in his old yellow Mercedes, with a prolonged shot lasting well over a minute which tracks the high-rise skyline through the car windscreen from his point of view. The shot is interrupted, however, by a reverse long-shot framing his car travelling across Ponte de Boa Vista before it cuts abruptly to his arrival at the hotel (from his point of view), the resultant 'ellipsis' in his journey firmly disconnecting the principal space of narrative action from the cityscape previously framed in the tracking shot. The 'distancing' effect produced by the windscreen is replicated in further images of the city's glittering towers which are consistently shot from 'afar' through a series of long-shots and extreme long-shots. This again diminishes the viewer's association of the film's characters with the city's new upwardly mobile economic centres such as Boa Viagem and its environs. And yet, of course, whilst on one level this contributes to the viewer's perception that physically as much as socially the city's historic centre is now 'living on the edge', at the same time, the mere fact that Recife's historic centre is privileged as the centre of the film's action means that as an imagined space, this area of the city simultaneously redefines its position at the periphery of cultural systems of space, returning once more, albeit temporarily, to a position at the centre of things.

Recife's Historic Centre as a Space of Liminality

Particularly symbolic of the setting's 'impure' nature is the colour yellow, which aside from being central to the film's title reoccurs as a constant leitmotif throughout the film with which to index downtown Recife's affliction of physical and social decay. As body-trafficker Rabecão recounts wistfully in one scene while the camera cuts between the Bar Avenida and the image of Isaac's old, mango-yellow Mercedes:

> Amarelo é a cor das mesas, dos bancos, dos tamboretes, dos cabos de peixeira, da enxada e da estrovenga [...] Amarelo das doenças: das remelas nos olhos dos meninos, das feridas purulentas, dos escarros, das verminosas, das hepatites, das diarréias, dos dentes apodrecidos.

> [Yellow is the colour of tables, benches, stools, fish knife handles, the hoe and the sickle [...] The yellow of sickness, of children's runny eyes, of purulent wounds, of phlegm, of worms, of hepatitis, of diarrhea, of rotten teeth]

The words are taken from Renato Carneiro Campos's essay 'Tempo Amarelo' ['Yellow Time'] (1980) in which the Brazilian sociologist ponders the significance of this particular colour in the Brazilian context, writing that in contrast to the positive evocations of 'happiness and life' that it prompts in (colder) European countries, in Brazil it holds distinctly dystopic associations:

> É a cor do desespero, da miséria, do medo, como resultado, talvez, das doenças tropicais que se manifestam com intenso amarecelecimento da pele, da ausência da riqueza num país subdesenvolvido, [dàs] terríveis secas e, finalmente, das nossas raízes ibéricas, do fato de ser o amarelo a cor de luto para o povo árabe. (Campos 1980: 66)

> [It is the colour of despair, poverty, fear, of those tropical diseases which cause an intense yellowing of the skin, the absence of wealth in an underdeveloped country, terrible drought and, due to yellow being the colour of mourning for Arab peoples, our Iberian roots]

Yellow, he continues, is particularly indicative of the condition of the north-eastern worker, and he quotes in this respect (1980: 69) a verse from João Cabral de Melo Neto's poem 'Dois Parlamentos' ['Two Parliaments'] (1960):

O cassaco de engenho
É amarelo de corpo
É o amarelo tipo
E de estado de espírito.

[The millworker / Is yellow in body / The type of yellow / Of the state of the spirit]

The words, according to Campos, speak of a 'tempo amarelo interior' [interior yellow time] that is 'velho, desbotado, doente, de água estagnante, rasa' [old, washed-out, sick, shallow, stagnant] and which dominates enterprise, institutions, organizations, working efficiency and social relations (1980: 69). And although João Cabral's poem is written in the specific context of the rural north-eastern worker, it is the 'drone' of 'interior yellow time' which would appear to drive the degraded and specifically urban world of *Amarelo manga*, something made apparent in the film's opening sequence. Here, a dolly shot frames Lígia from above as she wakes up in bed, the murmur of street traffic audible in the background. The camera then follows her as she sleepily pulls on a dress over her naked body and trudges into a large, adjacent room, the Bar Avenida. Shot from behind, we then see her resignedly opening the bar to the street outside via a series of large ceiling-to-floor shutters to reveal a man, lying face down, sleeping off the previous night's festivities on the pavement. As she sets about removing the chairs from the table tops, a mango-yellow tea-towel slung over her shoulder, we hear her voice speaking in a weary monologue on the extra-diegetic soundtrack:

Às vezes eu fico imaginando em que forma as coisas acontecem. Primeiro vem o dia, tudo acontece naquele dia. Depois chega a noite, que é a melhor parte. Mas logo depois vem o dia outra vez. E vai, vai, vai, e é sem parar! A única coisa que não tem mudado ultimamente é o Santa Cruz, nunca mais tem ganhado nada, nem título de honra! E eu, não tenho encontrado ninguém que me mereça. Só se ama errado. Eu quero que tudo o mundo vá tomar no cú!

[There are times when I wonder about the way things happen. First the day comes, everything happens on that day. Then comes the night, the best part.

FIG. 4.1. The dilapidated Texas Hotel in *Amarelo manga*
(Cláudio Assis, 2002: Global Film Initiative)

But then soon after, day comes again. And on and on, never ending! The only thing which hasn't changed lately is that Santa Cruz has never won anything again, not even an honorary title! And I haven't found anyone who deserves me. Love always goes wrong. I wish the whole world would go fuck itself!]

The same sense of lethargic monotony that characterizes this idea of 'yellow time' is evident too in our first glimpse of the Texas Hotel. Beginning with an extreme close-up of a pair of feet and the image of a broom being passed around a dirty floor, the camera then cuts to a medium shot of the hotel's reception area (aptly painted yellow) to reveal Dunga jadedly singing the homonymous song 'Amarelo manga' by Otto to the rhythm of his brush strokes:

> Mangō de mim
> Amarelo
> Não vai ficar de graça
> Mango de mim
> Amarelo
> Não vai ficar de graça
> E dentro desta caixa
> Um corpo indigente.

[You took the piss | This will not go amiss | You took the piss | You are yellow | This will not go amiss | Inside this box | Is an indigent body]

His memory of the song though, extends little further than the set of lyrics cited above, which he repeats ad infinitum, pausing only to request that Dona Aurora, the retired sex worker, lift her feet so he can clean under the rather shabby sofa on which she is reclined. Behind the reception desk, a frail old man, Seu Bianor, can be seen rummaging for a key in a cupboard behind him, the drone of a crackly radio audible in the background. Although his demeanour suggests otherwise, he turns out to be the manager of the hotel, though it is increasingly apparent that he would be lost without Dunga. The latter directs him to the location of the said key, joking that he is 'ficando meio cego' [going half blind] and pointing out that the key is in the same place it has always been.

What is significant in these scenes is the lack of clear distinction between the space of the *rua* and that of the *casa*, which, as mentioned in the introduction to this chapter, have traditionally served as strong structuring elements in the Brazilian spatial imagination, according to Da Matta. The supposedly public space of the bar (an interior extension, we might argue, of the *rua*) simultaneously has connotations of *casa* due not only to its storage room doubling as Lígia's bedroom but also to its daily occupation by the same set of male characters. If the *rua* has literal or metaphorical connotations of a space to which those who lose their social footing are physically or metaphorically relegated in Brazil, then within the Texas Hotel, with its disparate population of down and outs, any sense of *casa* is, in turn, severely diminished.[7] The confusion of the *rua/casa* dichotomy is reflected not least in the film's set design, with both the Bar Avenida and the Texas Hotel opened to the world outside through open doorways, verandas and ample, glassless window spaces, blurring any clear division between public and private space. This confusion is further enhanced by the fluidity of the mobile camera used to track the passage of

FIG. 4.2. The confusion of *rua* and *casa* at the Texas Hotel in
Amarelo manga (Claúdio Assis, 2002: Global Film Initiative)

characters between interior and exterior spaces at various points in the film, in place
of more static framing devices which would otherwise consolidate the demarcation
of public and private space.

Gendered divisions of space and the resultant hierarchies of sex and age they
imply, would, subsequently, also appear to be confused. Seu Bianor's position as the
white heterosexual male patriarch of what might be described as his 'alternative
family' within the Texas Hotel is precarious and increasingly undercut by Dunga.
Confronted by the old man's increasing frailty (as demonstrated by the lost key
incident), Dunga effectively assumes day-to-day running of the hotel whilst also
presiding over the emotional well-being of the hotel's motley selection of residents,
such as Dona Aurora. This control essentially becomes *de jure* two-thirds of the way
through the film when Seu Bianor passes away. Here, Dunga's discovery that the
hotel's assets are, in fact, hidden in a package wrapped around the deceased's now
most definitely flaccid penis, serves as a fitting metaphor for the apparent demise
of patriarchy.

Bar Avenida, in turn, is characterized by the glaring absence of any patriarch, and
instead the establishment is managed by a young woman, Lígia, who, through her
assumption of authority over what is both a 'household' and an interior extension
of the *rua*, would definitely appear 'out of place'. Significantly, she is assisted only
by an elderly lady, the latter remaining nameless and frequently relegated to the
background of the set, underscoring an inversion of *both* hierarchies of sex and age
within this particular space. The situation is perhaps symptomatic of the changing
nature of gendered participation in the north-eastern labour market noted by Linda-
Anne Rebhun in her book, *The Heart is Unknown Country: Love in the Changing
Economy of Northeast Brazil* (1999). Here she writes that during her fieldwork the
majority of men either appeared to be without work or were employed in the
economia paralela [parallel economy] relating to the unregulated activities of the poor
— construction work, street selling and so on (1999: 119). Opportunities here for
men, though, she continues, were generally sporadic, with women taking the lion's

share of positions. The market was dominated by a demand for domestic maids and female factory workers who, she remarks, were more likely to arrive sober than men and who would be more likely to tolerate lower salaries (1999: 119). The result was a significantly reduced male participation in the labour market, and an increased financial independence amongst lower-class women, 'despite the cultural ideal of female economic dependency' (1999: 121). Judging by the clutch of empty beer bottles which seem to populate eternally the various tables of Lígia's establishment, her almost exclusively male clientele certainly seem to have time, though perhaps not money, to burn.

To return then to Cresswell's account of 'dirt', what we begin to see here is how the status of Recife's historic centre as a space of impurity is cinematically inscribed through what is essentially a 'mismatch' of spatial meanings, in which the 'controlled universe' of the *casa* and the 'Hobbesian' world of the *rua* come together. Here, not only do we see a dissolution and/or inversion of gendered hierarchies but simultaneously the production of a liminal and (apparently) sexually transgressive space in which the characters are seemingly free to express and pursue their own libidinal urges. Lígia, for example, appears not the least bit sexually inhibited, at one point in the film standing on a bar table and exposing her vagina to a group of highly appreciative male customers. In turn Wellington's lover, Dayse, who runs a stall/shop and thus like Lígia retains her economic independence, seems similarly in control of her emotional affairs. In our first encounter with her, Wellington enters the frame and tries to kiss her, to which she responds by shrugging him off, complaining that he stinks. Apparently sick of being the 'other woman', Dayse declares that she has had enough of their affair and that Wellington needs to choose: 'Eu não vou levando o nome de puta por aqui, tá?' [I'm not going to go around being known as the whore around here, get it?]. Attempting to pacify her, Wellington whispers sweet nothings before muttering the name of his wife under his breath as if to draw her attention to his painful dilemma. The ploy, however, inspires little sympathy from the furious Dayse, who spits back in a typically no-nonsense fashion, 'Kika caralho, porra!' [Fuck Kika, goddammit!]. For Dona Aurora, contrastingly, sexual satisfaction is an altogether more personal affair, and comes in the form of an oxygen mask, which as well as providing moments of welcome oblivion from her chronic lung condition, doubles at one point in the film as a rather bizarre form of sex aid.

Dunga's audacious pursuit of Wellington and the subsequent transformation that this inspires in Kika, Wellington's wife, is also significant. Positioned clearly as a very one-sided attraction, the first interaction we witness between Dunga and Wellington occurs in the kitchen of the Texas Hotel where the former waits impatiently for a delivery from the abattoir where Wellington works. 'Bota seu carne aqui perto de mim' [Come and put your meat over here near me], he requests suggestively, as the ever irascible Wellington arrives before setting about removing the skin from the said piece of meat. Wellington, obviously accustomed to Dunga's advances, shoots a glance towards him and growls: 'Eu te vejo... a qualquer hora tu pode dar o bote, né?' [I can see you... you're waiting to pounce aren't you?], before Dunga playfully throws flour over him. Failing to see the funny side,

Wellington then brandishes the carving knife in Dunga's face, rasping, 'um dia eu te fodo, te fodo!' [one day I'll fuck you, you hear?]. Wellington's 'threat', somewhat unsurprisingly, proves to be more of a source of delight than dissuasion and Dunga quips back without hesitation, 'com certeza' [with pleasure].

The apparent resistance to Dunga's attractions which Wellington displays in this scene forces the former to consider more drastic measures in order to win over the object of his affection. Inspiration strikes during a phone call from Dayse, who informs Dunga that she has decided to end her affair with Wellington and asks if he can pass on her apologies to Padre Adão, whose Umbanda[8] ceremony she will accordingly not be attending. Erroneously believing that if deserted by both his women Wellington will somehow direct his affections towards him, Dunga decides to write a letter to Kika informing her of her husband's infidelity and the time and place of his next furtive liaison, details of which he is now privy to thanks to Dayse's phone call. A young boy chosen as the messenger duly delivers the said letter under Kika's door before reporting back to the expectant Dunga. He hands the boy a coin in payment whispering suggestively that 'mais tarde te dou outra coisa' [I'll give you something *else* later on]. The boy's reply is fairly unambiguous: 'sai pra lá viado safado!' [piss off you dirty queer!]. Again, Dunga's response is typically nonchalant and comes this time in the form of a mere shrug, insinuating that he is more disappointed with the boy's lack of sexual interest in him than the blatantly homophobic insult which was directed towards him. The incident serves to highlight that it is not just Dunga's pursuit of Wellington which is remarkable, but the distinctly unapologetic attitude the former has to his own homosexuality, which he flaunts ostentatiously with little or no regard for the disapproving reactions of those around him.

But it is the dramatic shift in Kika's character which perhaps most obviously attests to the supposed liminality of the film's setting and underscores its presumed status as a space of transgression in which the characters really are 'liberad[os] em seus desejos' [liberated in their desires], as Luiz Fernando Carvalho, writing in the *Jornal do Brasil* puts it (2004).[9] Significantly, for most of the film's proceedings, Kika, at a spatial level, remains cut off from the ambit of the other characters and is established as being most definitely 'apart'. In one scene, having left the evangelical church, for example, Kika is framed amidst the hustle and bustle of Recife's downtown area before a bus pulls up beside her, suggesting clearly that she lives 'beyond' the film's principal space of action. This is confirmed several scenes later when she arrives home. As the camera cuts to a high-angled extreme long-shot of the city's skyline, Kika's head slowly enters the frame from below as she climbs the steps towards her house, her previous location established as both distant, and someway physically (and morally) 'beneath'. Her eventual arrival home, in turn, reveals a small, well-maintained, single-story, white-washed dwelling (somewhat at odds with the other properties which surround it), which contrasts with the ramshackle Texas Hotel and its crumbling façade and peeling, garishly coloured interior walls. Combined with window grills, tightly closed shutters, a locked front door and a strict demarcation between the immaculate interior spaces of the entrance hall, living room, and kitchen, Kika's world is thus firmly established as *casa* in a way that is rendered impossible in the case of the Texas Hotel, with its confusion of interior/exterior and private/public spaces.

Indeed, the sense of 'order' which pervades the marital home serves as a reflection of Kika herself. First encountered piously repeating the proclamations of the minister at the evangelical church which she attends, we then see her dutifully preparing dinner before her husband's imminent return from work, her scraped-back hair, crisply ironed white blouse and stiff, below-the-knee skirt alluding to an unyielding and ultimately repressed young woman. These suppositions are confirmed during the dinner scene, a dour affair in which Kika seizes on the opportunity self-righteously to lecture her husband about his bad language before reminding him of her attitude towards adultery, of which he is clearly under suspicion: 'Baixo este teto exigo respeito! No nome de Jesus! Uma coisa Wellington, uma coisa que não tolero é traição. Assasinato, violência, roubo, tudo isso perdo, [mas] traição não' [Under this roof I demand respect! In the name of Jesus Christ! Something I won't tolerate Wellington is betrayal. I won't tolerate that. Murder, violence, robbery, all that I can forgive. But betrayal, no].

Her meticulously scripted existence, however, is quickly thrown into freefall on receiving confirmation of her husband's infidelity through Dunga's letter, triggering, it would seem, a crisis of faith and consequently a rapid reassessment of the value of her own carefully maintained monogamy, as well as a blood-thirsty desire to avenge her husband's betrayal. Accordingly, Kika quite literally descends into the den of iniquity occupied by the other characters and, privy to the time and location of Wellington and Dayse's (final) amorous encounter in Campo de Euclides, she succeeds in ambushing the proceedings just as they move into full swing. Significant in these scenes are the changes in her appearance, outward signs of an internal transformation triggered by her presence in this unfamiliar space manifested in her now free-flowing hair and considered application of red lipstick, which is soon complemented by the blood pouring from Dayse's ear lobe, the result of Kika's savage (and successful) attempt to bite off the former's earring in her act of revenge.[10]

Several scenes later, apparently now having lost control of all her senses, the frenzied Kika is framed walking down a darkened street, presumably near the Texas Hotel, before Isaac's Mercedes draws up beside her, the driver demanding that she gets in. Kika does not hesitate in complying with the command, her subsequent presence in the passenger seat of the luridly coloured mango-yellow vehicle symbolic of the manner in which she too has now been marked as 'impure'. Turning to Isaac, amidst a hysterical fit of laughter, she proudly proclaims: 'Arranquei a orelha da amante do meu marido [...] Era uma mulher morta por dentro!' [I've just ripped off the ear of my husband's lover [...] I was a dead woman inside!]. The two then return to the Texas Hotel for sex, where amongst other things, we witness Kika roughly flipping Isaac onto his front before penetrating him with a hairbrush, something received with a surprising degree of ease, suggesting that Isaac is rather well-rehearsed in this particular activity. As Cresswell argues, 'transgression' itself is concerned with the 'questioning of boundaries', in this case that which, metaphorically as much as physically, demarcates the dual domains of the *casa* and

FIG. 4.3. Kika completing her transformation in the denouement of
Amarelo manga (Claúdio Assis, 2002: Global Film Initiative)

rua and the contrasting values and behavioural codes that these imply and which
Kika herself has now violated. And as Cresswell continues, things that transgress are
therefore in the wrong place, and through implication, become 'dirt' (1996: 38).

In this sense, the manner in which Kika's transformation eventually concludes
is perhaps of little surprise. In what marks the final scene of the film and with
all vestiges of the prudish evangelical protestant now having been consigned to
oblivion, a tracking shot reveals the now wild-looking woman striding through the
streets of the historic centre. Removing her wedding ring, she throws it decisively
into the gutter before making her way into a hairdressing salon. The camp male
hair stylist runs his hands through her hair before asking what she would like done,
to which Kika responds decisively that she wants him to 'Arranca tudo e pinta' [cut
it all off and dye it]. Predictably the colour of choice, we discover, is yellow. The
stylist suggests hopefully that maybe she is thinking of a rusty or clay-like yellow.
'Não, não,' she replies, clearly not in the mood for compromise, 'uma coisa mais
manga. Amarelo manga' [something a bit more mango. Mango yellow], at which
point we cut to the film's title and end credits.

The Limits of Transgression

Amidst this litany of seemingly transgressive behaviour (at points, as the sex scene
between Kika and Isaac demonstrates, of apparently queer proportions) *Amarelo
manga* might arguably subscribe to a distinctly carnivalesque discourse, which,
according to Stam and others has informed a whole tradition of Brazilian cinematic
culture (see, for example, Stam 1997). The spatial confusion which inflects the
film's centre of action and its subsequent dissolution and/or inversion of hierarchies,
for example, is synonymous with Da Matta's account of the carnival ritual. During
its enactment, he writes, it is as if society has managed finally to create 'um espaço
especial' [a special space] in which the space of the *rua* and the space of the *casa*
come together (1997b: 111). Here, all beings, types, personalities, categories and

groups may coexist, forming what he calls 'um campo social aberto, situado fora da hierarquia' [an open social field, beyond hierarchy] (1997b: 63).

The film's recourse to the grotesque, if read through a Bakhtinian lens, might also be regarded as indicative of a carnivalesque tendency. Originally the domain of pre-Renaissance folk cultures, Bakhtin writes that grotesque realism, which would later define the aesthetics of carnival celebration in the Middle Ages, was principally concerned with what he terms 'the material body principle', that is 'images of the human body with its food, drink, defecation and sexual life' which were always offered 'in an extremely exaggerated form' (1984: 18). Accordingly, in contrast to that of 'modern canons', the grotesque body was not closed off from the world, with an emphasis instead placed on those parts of the body — most notably the open mouth, the genital organs, the breasts, the nose and so on — 'where the world enters the body or emerges from it, or through which the body itself goes out to meet the world' (1984: 26).[11] In this respect the concepts of 'degradation and debasement' were fundamental, and are defined by Bakhtin as the 'lowering of all that is high, spiritual, ideal and abstract [...] a transfer to the material level, to the sphere of earth and body in their indissoluble unity' (1984: 20). And whilst, he notes, the implied processes of defecation and copulation endowed the concept of 'degradation' with negative connotations, those relating to conception, pregnancy and birth, with which the lower stratum of the body, in particular, has also been associated, simultaneously implied a regenerational aspect in which degradation 'digs a bodily grave for a new birth' (1984: 21).

Allusions to the 'material body principle' and the opening of bodily orifices to the world are indeed numerous in *Amarelo manga*, with Lígia's flaunting of her pubic hair, the cladding of Dona Aurora's vagina with an oxygen mask, Kika's severing of Dayse's earlobe and her subsequent penetration of Isaac's anus with a hairbrush serving as just a few examples. The way in which these instances are presented to us also clearly subscribes to this discourse of exaggeration. In the case of Lígia, for example, the character is framed performing the episode of self-exposure standing on a table, the incident thus clearly visible to the entire bar. Cutting to a close-up of the lower portion of her body, we then see her teasing her onlookers with the hem of her skirt which she slowly inches up towards her nether regions. Rather than cutting away modestly at this point, however, and reverting perhaps to a reverse shot of Isaac's facial expression, the camera lingers tantalizingly on her now bare crotch. Significantly, we see that her pubic hair, in keeping with the film's colour motif, is dyed a brash yellow blonde, eliciting rounds of rapturous applause from her appreciative audience. In this respect, whilst in his introduction to the film on its Global Initiative DVD release (2002) Richard Peña's discussion of the film's carnivalesque discourse somewhat problematically is articulated solely in the context of its melodramatic elements, a sense of what he describes as the 'grandiose', 'overblown' and the 'operatic' is certainly pervasive within *Amarelo manga*'s manner of corporal representation.

In spite of this, however, it is difficult, on closer examination of the film, to find anything that is utopian or transcendental about the world of *Amarelo manga*. For whilst, according to Donna Goldstein, Da Matta's account posits carnival as a 'moment *out* of time' (2003: 32), life in the forgotten centre of Recife is defined overwhelmingly, as previously touched upon, by its tedious circularity. This is embodied in the cyclical nature of the film, set over a period of twenty-four hours, to which Lígia's monologue marks both the beginning and the end. In this light, a naturalist reading of the film (see, for example, Alves Cunha 2003) would perhaps appear more fitting, with the dual settings of the Texas Hotel and Bar Avenida arguably recalling the collectivized spaces of the proletariat found in the seminal Brazilian novel *O Cortiço* by Aluísio de Azevedo (1890).[12] Here, argues Alves Cunha, as in Azevedo's rendering of nineteenth-century Rio de Janeiro, these spaces are envisaged as pertaining to a species of organism within which the proletariat grows and proliferates like a mass of seething worms eating away at the rotting meat of society from within (2003). Certainly the image of 'meat' itself in Assis's film is all-pervasive, with one of the film's opening scenes depicting Wellington, through a high-angled shot, stripping down a carcass at the abattoir where he is employed. In another scene, against the backdrop of extra-diegetic heavy metal music, the audience is then subjected to the image of a cow being slaughtered in the same location, a spike inserted into its neck, before its body is then hauled unceremoniously onto the concrete floor as a tide of blood gradually fills the screen. Kika, too, comes to be directly associated with the produce of the abattoir, and on returning from her evangelical church service is framed retrieving a slab of meat from the refrigerator before placing it in a ceramic dish and cutting it into pieces for dinner. Barely has she started, however, before she begins to retch, and dashes to the open back door to vomit, the family cat then appreciatively lapping up the results. Kika's repulsion, however, is replaced by positive attraction in the case of Dunga, who as we have seen enthusiastically requests that Wellington, as he makes his delivery from the abattoir, put his meat 'really near' him, before later on sniffing and then furtively performing fellatio on the meat cleaver.

As Goldstein writes, within Brazilian national popular culture as a whole, metaphors about food and eating are often used to express ideas about sexuality, with the verb *comer* meaning both 'to eat' and actively to consume somebody sexually (2003: 236). Masculinity, she argues, hinges on a man's ability to consume, whilst conventional or socially-sanctioned femininity is contingent on being able to *dar* [give oneself for consumption] (2003: 236). In this sense, although Wellington explains his nickname, Cannibal, as something he earned by killing another man, as Alves Cunha suggests, it perhaps more readily points to his sexually predatory nature, as somebody who 'devours' his women (Alves Cunha 2003). Kika, herself, seems to be constantly reminded of his status as 'devourer' by the local children, who at one point in the film shout 'Kika Cannibal' as she passes them on the steps leading up to her house. The incident is raised at dinner that evening, when Kika expresses her disgust at the new nickname, leading to the lecture on adultery. She implies that she knows he is 'eating' somebody else (Dayse), hence her earlier revulsion towards the meat which now lies steaming on the plates before them. Isaac, too, is also depicted as an 'eater' in his advances towards Lígia at the Bar Avenida. Following the exposure of her vagina, in a later scene as she walks past Isaac to serve another customer she is grabbed by him as he mutters ambiguously to her, 'your hair gives me ideas, pure ideas'. His advances towards her are repeated towards the end of the film when he arrives to collect his ID card. Staring coldly straight into her eyes, he demands: 'Eu quero minha identidade, e quero você — você todinha. E todas suas idéias' [I want my ID card and I want you — all of you. And all your ideas].

The significance of 'eating' metaphors in the film also informs a subtler set of distinctions between the sexes in the film, where, to use Parker's phraseology, '*homem* (man) and *mulher* (woman) are not defined only with reference to one another but a range of other figures embodying a complex array of both positive and negative male and [in particular] female possibilities' (2009: 49). Kika's vomiting incident, for example, points not only to her aversion to her husband's infidelity, but also underscores the absolute importance she attaches to 'non-consumption' (read sexual passivity and monogamy within marriage) in order to preserve her status as respectable housewife and bastion of a particular brand of evangelical modesty.[13] Yet this status is inevitably defined against the negative characteristics of sexually predatory women (*galinhas* [hens] or *piranhas* in Brazilian Portuguese) such as Dayse. Dayse's failure to adhere to the norms of female inferiority and submission endows her with the reputation of being a 'loose' woman, leading her to complain in one scene to Wellington: 'Ontem, meu pai, que nem consegue andar direito, olhou para mim e falou assim na cara, vagabunda! [...] Sabe porquê? Sabe né? Por tua causa' [Yesterday, my father, who can't even walk straight, looked me straight in the eye and called me a slut! [...] You know why? Because of you]. This can be regarded as symptomatic of the virgin/whore dichotomy which, as Julian Pitt-Rivers (1971) and others have noted, has supposedly been so prevalent in the structuring of femininity in Mediterranean and other 'Latin' societies. However, according to Parker (quoting Candido 1951 and Freyre 1964), the virgin/whore dichotomy in the Brazilian context has its own particular significance stemming from the country's colonial past and its legacy of slavery, in particular the structuring of life in the *engenho*. Here there existed a strict delineation between the legal, procreative functions of the Christian, monogamous family of the plantation owner, and the sexual and affectual realm constructed around a 'de facto set of polygamous relationships with any number of his female slaves' (Parker 2009: 37). This, in turn, resulted in coexisting but conflicting visions of the legal wife and mother on the one hand, and the concubine on the other (2009: 39).

Lígia, of course, would appear to be the exception to the rule, appearing as sexually liberated, financially independent and respected by the majority of the customers at the Bar Avenida, thus apparently resisting these dualistic strictures within which the other female characters are constructed and which points to what Parker terms the 'lingering vision of [colonial] patriarchal life' in contemporary Brazilian gender ideology (2009: 40). Yet soon after exposing her vagina to her clientele, we learn that such respect hinges, in actual fact, on her own carefully maintained chastity, with Rabecão warning the interested Isaac: 'Parece puta, mas ninguém aqui comeu ela [...] Se tu come essa daí eu te devolvo a parada e pode comer meu cú!' [She looks like a whore but nobody's had her [...] If you manage to screw her, I'll give you back your dough and you can even fuck me up the arse!].

In turn, Wellington's and Isaac's reputations as 'real men' or *machões* are similarly defined not just in relation to members of the opposite sex, but against the negative characteristics of the *viado* or *bicha* ('queer', 'faggot' or 'queen'), a figure that constitutes a contrasting vision of masculinity but one which nevertheless complements (albeit negatively) the figure of the *homem*. Again the nuances of language here are significant, with *viado* allegedly deriving from *veado*, the Portuguese word for 'deer', and *bicha* referring to a variety of intestinal pests whilst also constituting the feminine form of *bicho*, a type of 'unspecified animal' (insect, mammal or otherwise) (Parker 2009: 51). Thus collectively they refer not only to an 'animal-like femininity' but, having abandoned the true *homem*'s identity through the adoption of the passive sexual role, a pest-like inferiority due to the *viado* or *bicha*'s position 'betwixt and between the accepted categories of normal human life' (2009: 51).

In the case of *Amarelo manga*, the *viado* or *bicha* in question is Dunga, whose apparent identification with the female of the species on the level of social role, dress and mannerisms is rather tiresomely spelled out for us in our initial encounter with him. Beginning with an extreme close-up of the character's small feet and lower portion of his shaved legs, Dunga is revealed sweeping the reception hall of the Texas Hotel cheerily singing a song to ease the tedium of his 'female' domestic chores. The camera then pulls back to reveal a small, slightly-built young man squeezed into an impossibly tight pair of denim shorts — barely extending below the base of his buttocks — with a cropped, close-fitting vest covering his upper torso. After helping Seu Bianor to locate the missing key, the telephone then rings with a call from Rabecão for Isaac, the mobile camera tracking Dunga as he scampers effeminately upstairs to fetch him. Isaac, however, is asleep and on being rudely awoken responds angrily with a tirade of homophobic abuse. Little room for doubt is similarly left for the viewer with regards to Dunga's sexual passivity, as demonstrated by his obvious delight at Wellington's threat of a 'fuck' in a later scene (described above) and his subsequent performance of fellatio on the meat cleaver, suggesting a desire for both anal *and* oral penetration.

Dunga's status as a foil for the assertion of Wellington's and Isaac's masculinities is made apparent in the litany of homophobic verbal insults to which he is subjected, of which the above is just one example. These serve as a constant reminder to Dunga of his dual failings as a *viado*, that is, his inability to live up to the expected norms of masculinity, on the one hand, and the sheer impossibility of him fulfilling the requirements of biological femininity on the other, thus simultaneously underscoring the 'normality' of the other two men. Wellington's threat of penetration, too, is symptomatic of the way in which symbolically the male characters are able to (verbally) exercise their consuming male prerogative, whilst simultaneously feminizing those men to whom this is directed (in this case Dunga) and bolstering their own sense of masculinity, with no threat, of course, posed to their own 'heterosexuality'. As Parker notes, 'the threat of anal penetration whether symbolic or real [...] defines the underlying structure of masculine relationships' (2009: 53).

What is significant is the distinctly exaggerated and retrograde proportions this form of machismo reaches in the film. With regards to Wellington, this manifests itself in the latent misogyny which characterizes his (mis)treatment of Dayse, which apparently is deemed both inevitable and socially acceptable, due to her status as a 'loose woman'. Following the initial showdown described above, Dayse, still enraged by Wellington's attitude towards her, calls him at the abattoir and apparently hurls yet more abuse at him. Wellington replies: 'Tu es uma fodinha! Caralho Dayse! Não, não, não. E não fala comigo assim... olha! [pause] Tu não seria capaz, eu te encho de porrada, eu te encho de porrada, viu Dayse!' [You're a fucking pain! Fuck off Dayse! No, no, no. Don't talk to me like that! Look! No... no. [pause] You wouldn't dare. I'll beat the shit out of you! I'll beat the shit out of you! Understand Dayse?]. And although Wellington's boss apparently seems to express concern about his employee's violent misogynistic tendencies once the receiver has been slammed down to terminate the unfortunate exchange, we realise such suppositions are premature as the boss complains: 'Tu briga com tuas raparigas, e vem descontar no meu telefone, porra!' [You row with your tarts and then take it out on my fucking phone!].

In Isaac's case, most significant is the bizarre and rather disturbing turn his blatant homophobia takes. Following his telephone call with Rabecão, which we assume relates to some sort of clandestine business transaction, Isaac goes to meet him in the 'lugar de sempre' [the normal place] for delivery of the 'mercadorias' [the goods]. These, it transpires, come in the form of dead bodies, which he purchases from Rabecão in exchange for hashish. From the Defesa Social de Pernambuco insignia on the side of his Volkswagen van, we presume the latter to be a local government employee. Although the body is a bit 'perfurado' [perforated], Rabecão assures Isaac that today's delivery is nevertheless 'picolé' [as icy as a lolly]. The camera then cuts to a medium shot, from Isaac's point of view, revealing the blood-stained body of a naked, muscular young man, propped up in the corner of a make-shift shed. Retrieving a revolver from his pocket, Isaac then proceeds to take aim, his face framed through a series of reverse close-ups as he unloads a round of bullets into the lifeless corpse. On completing the perverse ritual, there is a cut to a lingering extreme close-up of him biting his bottom lip, an apparent expression of ecstasy now etched on his face. Masculine assertion in this case, therefore, corresponds to a literal but detached act of penetration via the bullet of a gun, a rather ambivalent form of necrophilia which also, it would appear, allows Isaac simultaneously to satisfy and deaden his own homosexual impulses.

In light of the above account, one might treat the suggestions that the world of *Amarelo manga* is characterized by 'patriarchal demise' with a degree of caution. However, as Goldstein notes, 'eating' metaphors are not only indicative of gendered sexual power relations but also of 'the intimate ways in which economic and sexual aspects of normative gender relations are intertwined' (2003: 237). This gives wider significance to Assis's claim that one of the film's central postulates relates to the idea of human beings constituting little more than 'estomago e sexo' [stomach and sex] (in Alves Cunha: 2003). In Brazil, a man's ability to *comer*, writes Goldstein, has become synonymous with virility and sexual prowess, but also with his potential, quite literally, to provide food, something she argues that is 'a key element in a woman's recognition of a partner's good qualities' (2003: 237.). This ties in with

Parker's account of the dual figures through which the Brazilian *homem* has been construed — that of the *pai* [father] on the one hand, and the *machão* [big macho] on the other. These complementary aspects of the *homem* can, he writes (quoting Freyre 1964), again be traced back to the colonial *engenho*, where the patriarch was characterized by his status as father and provider, but also by his absolute right to invoke violence (often of fatal proportions) not only towards the slave population under his control, but also towards his own offspring (Parker 2009: 50). In this sense, the apparent over-identification with the figure of the *machão* amongst the male characters in *Amarelo manga* can be read as being inversely symmetrical to their inability to exercise the prerogatives of the *pai*, resulting in a distinctly lop-sided and ultimately flawed version of Brazilian masculinity.

Nowhere is this more evident than in Isaac's interaction with Lígia. As previously discussed, he condescendingly asks Lígia whether she can afford to dye *all* her hair blonde, to which she lifts her skirt to show him that indeed she can. Unable to match Lígia economically, Isaac then embarks on consuming her sexually, though his attempts are continually rebuffed. Now rendered doubly impotent, Isaac's rage reaches fever pitch in the closing minutes of the film, when he eventually resorts to pulling a gun on Lígia. Superficially, this rather extreme act is posited as an attempt to retrieve his ID card, left there after their last altercation. However, the incident would also appear indicative of the absolute state of despair that Isaac has reached in light of his dwindling sense of masculinity, which, it would seem, can now only be exercised through recourse to a loaded firearm.

The extent to which this *machão* version of masculinity becomes internalized and ultimately replicated by the female (-identified) characters of *Amarelo manga*, such as Lígia, Kika and Dunga, is significant. In the case of Lígia, her subjection to constant incidents of sexual goading on the part of the exclusively male clientele of the Bar Avenida manifests itself in her eventual explosion and loss of all self-control. In the face of Isaac's predatory advances, she viciously cracks a beer bottle over his head before running hysterically around the bar screaming repeatedly, 'Não aguento mais esta merda!' [I can't take any more of this shit!]. The violent tendencies which

FIG. 4.4. Dunga plotting his conquest of Wellington in
Amarelo manga (Claúdio Assis, 2002: Global Film Initiative)

simmered beneath Wellington's now defunct relationship with Dayse, in turn, reappear in Kika's rampage following her personal transformation. Here, apparently driven to a similar state of dementia as Lígia, she not only succeeds in hospitalizing her husband's former lover by biting her ear but then decides to eschew foreplay in favour of a punch in the face, which she delivers to Isaac during her subsequent sexual domination and sodomization of the man.

Even Dunga's behaviour, at certain points in the film, seems to betray the very discourse of misogyny and homophobia to which we would assume he would be averse. In a scene following the meat delivery which Wellington makes to the Texas Hotel, framed by the serving hatch of the kitchen, we hear a monologue by Dunga in which he plots his conquest of Wellington, announcing defiantly: 'Eu vou dar uma rasteira nas duas, vai chover racha [...] Meu filho, bicha quer, bicha faz' [I'll finish with the two of them! Fucking women! [...] Whatever the queer wants, the queer gets]. Moving on to the subject of Dayse, he reflects: 'é só escrotice, rala coxa, mulher viciada em macho casado' [She's just a shit-bag, a slag. Addicted to married men]. After spitting on the floor in apparent disgust, he continues his verbal onslaught claiming: 'até sapoeira mamou naqueles peitos [...] safada do jeito que é, deve ser verdade mesmo' [they say she's even had dykes licking those tits! [...] and being the dyke that she is, it must be true]. Then grabbing the knife and brandishing it towards the camera, in exactly the same way that Wellington does to him several scenes before, he hisses: 'lésbica... mas eu arranjo as coisas [...] jogo verde para colher maduro. Tá de brincadeira mas porra!' [That lesbian... I'll get it sorted out all right [...] Plant today and harvest tomorrow. Be fucked if I'm playing around!].

The plan, of course, functions to an extent and Wellington duly arrives at the Texas Hotel seeking consolation from Dunga. Ironically, though, so distraught is Wellington at the dual disappearance of Kika and Dayse from his life that Dunga's 'real man' is subsequently reduced to a tearful and effeminized shadow of his former self, and on spotting Seu Bianor's dead body in the living room of the Texas Hotel he hastily beats a retreat. Exasperated, Dunga shouts after him: 'Tu é bunda mole mesmo, né cagão!' [You're so fucking soft you silly shit!], thus subjecting Wellington to the same iniquitous gender expectations which for the entire film have relegated him so firmly to the status of *viado*. Thus despite the allusions to a liminal space of 'sexual anarchy' discussed earlier in this chapter, the performance of gender and enactment of desire, like other facets of life in *Amarelo manga*, are ultimately driven by the same tedious circularity. Kika and Dunga, especially, might appear to commit 'transgressive' acts of sexual 'subversion' which are 'exceptions' to the norm, but they do this according to a simple inversion of an already firmly established hierarchy in which human beings are divided, to repeat Goldstein's phraseology, into 'eaters' and 'those who are eaten' (2003: 122).

Excluded Middle?

By way of conclusion, Recife's historic centre as it is (re)imagined in *Amarelo manga* is inscribed most definitely as the sort of highly ambivalent space of 'in-betweenness' discussed in the introduction to this chapter, not solely through the disjuncture inherent in its status as a social periphery physically located at the very heart of a major metropolitan centre, but also the manner in which this ambiguous position impacts upon the production of gender and sexuality and the physical and affective relationships shared between its characters. The metaphorical distance which separates the film's setting from the regulation of the 'centre' in this respect and its resultant 'loss of social co-ordinates' does, on one level, endow this space with a degree of liminality, allowing for 'moments of discontinuity in the social fabric [and] in social space' (Shields 1991: 83). But, if, as Shields goes on to state, liminality also 'represents a liberation from the regimes of normative practices and performance codes of mundane life' (1991: 83), then, as the previous section makes clear, any promise the world of *Amarelo manga* may offer in this respect ultimately remains unfulfilled. For as Alves Cunha (2003) and others have argued, the characters fail to translate their anomalous position in society into any form of political consciousness, reflecting one of the central paradoxes of such in-between spaces. These may indeed be sites where 'sexual subjects may be least stable and hegemonic sexualities most open to challenge', but as Phillips and Watt remind us, they may also be concurrently removed from the critical discourses and emancipatory movements also located at this 'centre', meaning 'they may be less able to speak for or defend themselves and/or participate in liberatory politics' (2000: 1–2). Thus whilst Dunga, Lígia and eventually Kika on one level all reject the societal expectations imposed upon their respective gender identities and sexualities, their search for alternative constructions of self is necessarily limited to the same ideological field. Here Dunga pursues his same-sex desires according to the conventional subjective mould of the *bicha*, Kika assumes the identity of the sexually-predatory *puta* or *piranha* she so resisted, and Lígia asserts her independence through the emulation of the very *machão* behaviour with which she herself is threatened. In this sense, one might argue that 'yellow', as an omnipresent, symbolic colour in the film, serves as a particularly Brazilian shade of the colour pink, indexing, alongside all the other elements of decay in the film, a breakdown of patriarchal heteronormativity in the film, but also the all-pervasive inertia that prevents this from translating into any form of feminist, lesbigay or queer consciousness on the part of the characters who are unable to assert positive emancipatory rights to non-discrimination. Amidst the endless 'work-a-day' existence the most oppressed characters in the film have to endure, 'freedom', it seems, is an entirely relative phenomenon, with the notion of 'liberation' itself appearing as a luxury on a laundry-list of other, more basic needs such as food, shelter and human connection.

The question necessarily poses itself then, does the setting of *Amarelo manga* constitute some sort of 'sexual hinterland' that lies on the margins of supposedly 'progressive' Brazil? Certainly the highly dichotomized framework within which gender is performed — its divisions between activity and passivity and the manner in which this is subsequently mapped on to constructions of sexuality — would *appear* symptomatic of those 'traditional' models discussed in Chapter 1 and which are supposedly still prevalent in rural areas and amongst the urban 'popular' classes. This, however, cannot function as an absolute certainty, for as previously noted, referring to Rebhun's study of gender relations in north-eastern Brazil, the highly exaggerated form of machismo exercised by certain male characters such as Isaac, Wellington and Rabecão, and their subsequent demands for female submission, far from being 'traditional' can be linked to the rather more modern phenomenon of increased feminine participation in both the formal and informal labour markets. As Rebhun argues:

> The economic opportunities now available to women seem like an attack on masculine roles, masculine prerogatives, and, in some ways, masculinity itself. With increasingly divergent interests, men and women find it even more difficult than it used to be to achieve the consonance of understanding and interests necessary for affectionate co-operation. (Rebhun 1999: 126)

These shifts, in turn, point to the way in which such inner-city neighbourhoods, often perceived, to borrow Shield's phraseology, as having been 'left behind in the modern race for progress' (1991: 83), have become increasingly imbricated in both national and global modes of production and consumption. In this respect, Sassen argues that the growth in demand for both formal and informal low-wage labour brought about by global economic restructuring has seen a *reassertion* of specifically localized spaces pertaining to the neighbourhood and the household as sites of increased economic activity (2004: 172). As the representations in *Amarelo manga* imply, in terms of gender relations and sexuality, they are, however, consequently rendered highly ambivalent sites in which the dividing line between transgression and oppression can be difficult to determine.

Notes to Chapter 4

1. Gilberto Freyre in *Casa Grande e Senzala* [*The Masters and the Slaves*] goes into further detail about the white daughters of plantation owners, noting: 'a small room or bedroom was reserved for her in the centre of the house, and she was surrounded on all four sides by her elders. It was more of a prison than the apartment of a free being. A kind of sick-room where everyone had to keep watch' (1964: 353).
2. The Brazilian *cinema novo* movement was partly born out of the collapse of the Vera Cruz studios in São Paulo in 1954 and partly out of frustration at the continued dominance of what Glauber Rocha (1938–1981) dubbed 'digestive' cinema with purely 'industrial aims', such as the home-grown musical comedy or *chanchada* and of course Hollywood movies, which constituted the lion's share of box office returns (Stam & Johnson 1995: 68). Directors such as Rocha, Nelson Pereira dos Santos (b.1928), Carlos Diegues (b. 1940), Joaquim Pedro de Andrade (1932–88) and Ruy Guerra (b. 1931) proposed instead a 'new, critical and modernist vision of the nation' and a new cinematic language (what Rocha dubbed an 'aesthetic of hunger') that better reflected Brazilian reality (Shaw & Dennison 2007: 82). Influenced by Italian neorealist directors such as Roberto Rosellini and Vittorio de Sica, an emphasis was placed on location shooting, the use of non-professional actors and the use of hand-held cameras. This 'aesthetic of hunger' is aptly embodied in the composite slogan, begun by Rocha's famous phrase 'uma idéia na cabeça e um câmera na mão' [an idea in your head and a camera in hand] added to by Pereira dos Santos with the words 'e o povo na frente' [and the people in front] and later qualified by Guerra with the phrase 'mas não em festa' [but not only in their festivities] (Stam & Johnson 1995: 49).

3. Panavision is an anamorphic format originally initiated by the CinemaScope anamorphic lens series used between 1953 and 1967 for shooting widescreen films. Panavision continues to be used today though it is often referred to as 'Scope' to indicate any 2.35:1 and 2.39:1 presentation.

4. *Cinema marginal* followed *cinema novo* and was defined amongst other things by its 'trashy' aesthetic and inquiry into themes of drug abuse, promiscuity and thwarting of traditional values, along with an empathy with traditionally marginalized groups such as blacks, homosexuals, indigenous populations and women (Shaw & Dennison 2007: 89). Robert Stam aptly distinguishes between *cinema novo* and *cinema marginal* in the following terms: 'just as *cinema novo* decided to reach out for a popular audience, the Underground [*cinema marginal*] opted to slap that audience it its face' (Stam & Johnson 1995: 311). The movement is cited by Fernão Ramos as dating from around 1968 to 1973 (quoted in Shaw and Dennison: 2007: 89).

5. The transfer of the colonial capital from Salvador to Rio de Janeiro in 1763 can be regarded as symptomatic of the North East's declining economic and political importance in favour of the South East.

6. 'Historic centre' in this discussion refers to the island *bairros* of Recife Antigo (Ilha de Recife), São José and Santo Antônio (Ilha de Antônio Vaz), and the *bairro* of Boa Vista, situated on a mainland peninsular where the majority of the city's downtown area can be found. The two islands were the first parts of the city to be founded by the Dutch in the seventeenth century, constituting the *Mauritzstadt*, or capital of Dutch Brazil (Lapa 1987: 21). Two bridges (Recife and Boa Vista) were soon constructed to connect these islands to the mainland and by the 1820s the original nucleus of the city represented by the *bairros* of Recife Antigo, São José and Santo Antônio respectively, begun to expand with the emergence of the *bairro* of Boa Vista, which fulfilled both commercial and residential functions (Assies 1991: 44; see also Lapa 1987: 17–21). In *Amarelo manga*, exterior establishing shots of the real-life Texas Hotel (the inspiration for the preceding short film known by the same name) located on Rua Rosário da Boa Vista near to the Largo de Santa Cruz, suggests the film's principal setting to be the *bairro* of Boa Vista. However, the inclusion of exterior shots of the Rua do Sol, located on the island neighbourhood of Santo Antônio, contradicts this somewhat, thus preventing us from locating its setting in one particular neighbourhood.

7. One might point, in this respect, to the use of the word *rueira* [woman of the street] as a negative way of referring to a woman with 'lax' sexual morals. Of course, it is worth noting that this is a Brazilian variant of a more general understanding of space and gender found both north and south of the equator in which traditionally the presence of women in public, masculine-coded spheres, such as that pertaining to the street, has often been demonized and understood in terms of sexual deviance. Indeed Judith Walkowitz, in her book *Prostitution and Victorian Society: Women, Class and the State* (1980), notes how the state itself has frequently been implicated in the production of this system of values. The British Contagious Diseases Acts and the opportunities they offered for intervention in the lives of registered prostitutes succeeded in producing a distinction between the unrespectable and respectable poor, she writes, 'forcing prostitutes to accept their status as public women [of the street] by destroying their private associations with poor working-class community' (1980: 192).

8. Umbanda (or Macumba) is an Afro-Brazilian syncretic religion that blends elements of European Spiritism (founded by Allan Kardec, 1804–69) and Catholicism with Afro-Brazilian and Amerindian religious beliefs. It is often practised to cure illnesses and solve personal problems and for this reason has been called 'a form of psychotherapy for the poor' (Shaw & Dennison 2005: 297).

9. In this respect Carvalho writes that 'amarelo-manga é a cor da tina que usa outra personagem, liberada em seus desejos, com os olhos faiscando ao final do filme, nos revelando assim a tríplice face, trágica, lúdica e revoltosa da alma nordestina' [Mango yellow is the colour assumed by an 'other' character, liberated in their desires, their eyes a flash in the film's denouement revealing the tragic, ludicrous and revolting face of the north-eastern soul] (2004).

10. Significantly, in previous scenes Kika keeps her makeup hidden down the side of her wardrobe, implying that she regards it as sinful, deviant and a symbol of sexual proclivity, as a consequence of her evangelical faith.

11. The 'modern canons' of the Renaissance period, Bakhtin continues, saw the body in quite a

different light than in the Middle Ages, representing it as a completed, finished product that was 'isolated, alone, fenced off from all other bodies'. Any manifestations of its incompleteness were eliminated, and 'its protuberances and off-shoots were removed, its convexities (signs of new sprouts and buds) smoothed out, its apertures closed' (1984: 29).

12. Naturalism can be described as a branch of Realism which originated in France during the mid-nineteenth century as a response to the excesses of Romanticism. In this respect, the collectivized spaces of the working classes featured as a reoccurring narrative backdrop, constructed through what Claude Hulet describes as a 'deterministic' view of the world in which 'man is moulded and conditioned by his environment' (1974: 2). Naturalist writers were particularly inspired by positivist ideology and Darwinist theories of evolution, and sought to apply a scientific method to their writing based on observation and 'field work' whereby the author assumed the position of the objective, neutral observer.

13. Evangelical Protestantism, as in other Latin American countries such as Mexico and Guatemala, has grown rapidly in popularity over the last few decades in Brazil, particularly in poor areas from where the Catholic Church has begun to retreat. Whilst there is a range of Protestant churches represented in Brazil — including the Baptist Church, the Assembly of God, the Foursquare Gospel Church — Shaw and Dennison write that it is the Universal Church of the Kingdom of God which, for many Brazilians, 'epitomises the new brand of Pentecostalism', with its televised 'services' (the church purchased its own television channel in 1990) and emphasis on securing financial contributions from its congregations (Shaw & Dennison 2005: 309).

CHAPTER 5

Rio de Janeiro: *Madame Satã*

Back to the Future: Sexual Identity, Queer Transcendence and the Carnivalesque in 1920s/30s Lapa

Reimagining the Interstices

Thus far, through the course of this book the term 'liberation' has appeared as one of particular ambivalence, affirming, it would seem, Foucault's argument that there is 'no single locus of great Refusal or law of the revolutionary' (1978: 95). The imbrication of non-heteronormative sexualities (both mainstream and dissi-dent) with capitalism as it appears in *Un año sin amor* and *La virgen de los sicarios*, in particular, attests to his idea, that although 'where there is power, there is resistance [...] consequently, this resistance is never in a position of exteriority in relation to power' (1978: 95–6). As my discussion of *Amarelo manga* demonstrated, even within interstitial, 'in-between' spaces at some distance from the power and reach of the legal, medical, religious and political institutions which discursively constitute and regulate gender ideology and sexualities, 'transgression' often may only occur as an inversion within these existing (hegemonic) discourses. These may frequently remain untouched by the transformative potential of critical emancipatory politics from which sexual subjects on the periphery may also remain excluded.[1]

And yet, arguably, 'exclusion' itself does not necessarily have to be construed as an entirely negative phenomenon. Filc, cited in Chapters 1 and 2 in relation to her discussion of the privatization of public space in Buenos Aires, goes on in the same article to consider how the interstitial space of 'dislocation' produced between the house and the city by the errant characters of the novel *Vivir afuera* by Argentine writer Rodolfo Fogwill (1999) might be reclaimed simultaneously as one of 'absoluta sujección y de la libertad' [absolute subjection and liberty] (Filc 2003: 196). Her argument hinges on Giorgio Agamben's assertion that juridical historiography has been characterized by longstanding tensions between 'those who conceive exile to be a punishment and those who instead understand it to be a right and a refuge' (1998: 110). This, he continues, stems from the highly ambiguous meaning of the word 'banned' in romance languages, a word which originally signified both 'at the mercy of' and 'out of free will, freely', both 'excluded, banned' and 'open to all, free' (1998: 110).

In *The Location of Culture* (2004), Homi K. Bhabha does not go as far as to suggest that those who 'live in the minority' (and there are multiple ways this might be experienced, from being an immigrant in a foreign country to publicly declaring and living one's sexuality in the open) always do so out of free choice. Yet he does suggest, like Filc, that the interstices, despite their exclusionary associations, might also constitute a space of productive possibility, '[a] terrain of elaborating strategies of selfhood — singular or communal — that initiate new signs of identity, and innovative sites of collaboration, and contestation, in the act of defining the idea of society itself' (2004: 2). This relies, however, on a rather more nuanced conception of the interstices that goes beyond the idea of the 'in-between' simply as an empty space or 'no-man's land' separating two diverse ambits, which Filc's distinction between the house and the city in her reading of *Vivir afuera* seems to imply. Rather, he defines the interstices as 'the overlap and displacement of domains of difference', highly fluid and porous 'border zones' whose limits are constantly being breached and redefined, prompting a cultural cross-fertilization which results in the production of new and ever increasingly complex identities: 'The interstitial passage from fixed identifications opens up the possibility of a cultural hybridity that entertains difference without an assumed or imposed hierarchy' (2004: 5). And it is the inhabitants of such zones, those excluded from these 'domains of difference' and forbidden to exist legitimately within them due to their nationality, gender, ethnicity, or otherwise, who frequently mediate this process. In this sense, it *is* possible, argues Bhabha, to 'signify from the periphery of authorized power and privilege', though he suggests the transcendental possibilities of the 'in-between' are bound up not with the persistence of tradition, but rather with the way in which traditions are *reinscribed* through the 'contingencies and contradictoriness which attend upon the lives of those who live in the minority' (2004: 3, my emphasis).

As Bruno Carvalho argues in his fascinating book *Porous City: A Cultural History of Rio de Janeiro* (2013), Brazil's most iconic city is defined, as the title suggests, by such porosity. And the metaphor of the palimpsest (a manuscript in which the text of the first writing has been scraped off so that the parchment or clay tablet may be written on again) is key to his understanding of this porosity. For whilst relatively young by Old World standards, as his layered history of the city reveals, there are few cities which have been more 'scraped off' during the last 200 years (2013: 1). As a nation eager to prove its modern, cosmopolitan credentials the former capital served, he writes, as a 'laboratory' for numerous architectural, city planning and urbanism typologies which gave shape to remarkable and diverse urban forms, social relationships and cultural expressions (2013: 1). The porosity of contemporary Rio lies, he argues, within the relationships between the various historical layers of this palimpsest landscape, relationships which are 'full of passageways, cumulative, marked by unfixed boundaries' and which have given rise to a metropolis defined by its 'fluid frontiers between order and disorder, popular and erudite, black and white, natural and urban, public and private, sacred and profane, centre and periphery' (2013: 10).

The idea of porosity, combined with Bhabha's (re)conceptualization of the 'in-between' are pertinent to the discussion that follows. This focuses on a more positive representation of the urban interstices than we see in *Amarelo manga,* in this case, as they are imagined in Karim Aïnouz's film *Madame Satã* (Brazil, 2002). The setting of this particular film, the *bairro* of Lapa, located on the immediate periphery of the city's central downtown area, has long been considered one of Rio de Janeiro's most exciting and bohemian neighbourhoods. My discussion considers how this particular space is imagined in the film as a porous and productive domain of 'overlap' between diverse urban social groups, and asks to what extent the 'in-between' is produced as a space of empowerment for the protagonist in light of his exclusion from the 'legitimate' culture of the mainstream. Can 'resistance' ever be achieved here in complete opposition to the circuits of power which sustain this culture? Or, as in the other cinematic cities discussed in this book, as well as being an 'adversary', does this resistance simultaneously fulfil the role, as Foucault puts it, of 'support or handle' in their production (1978: 95–96)?

Of course, from one perspective, the inclusion of *Madame Satã* in this book, particularly in its final chapter, might appear somewhat anomalous, its narrative unfolding not in the contemporary era, as in the case of the other films discussed, but rather in the Rio of the 1920s and 1930s. And yet this is a necessary and deliberate strategy since it allows for a retrospective questioning of some of the assumptions and certainties relating to the production of dissident sexualities and urban spaces in Latin America that the previous chapters have already been at pains to destabilize. As will be discussed below, the film is inflected with what might be perceived as a surprisingly 'modern' discourse which rigorously *decouples* gender and sexuality, in defiance of those 'traditional' constructions of male homosexuality which we might expect to shape the representations we see in the film, given its temporal setting. The latent eroticism which informs the protagonist's sexual encounters with other men, and in particular the film's celebration of the black body in these and other scenes, similarly defies the reification of the heterosexual, white European male understood to have been so prevalent within official Brazilian nationalist discourse at the time. And although my analysis eventually rejects a reading of *Madame Satã* as some sort of pre-Stonewall tale of 'gay liberation' in the tropics, I do identify the presence of an arguably more radical (and perhaps more contemporary) queer discourse in the film linked to its discourse of the carnivalesque. In this sense, as in Chapter 4, my analysis further challenges the notion of such inner-city neighbourhoods being 'left behind', as Shields puts it (1991: 3), whilst also disturbing the assumption that critical sexual discourses (however widely this concept needs to be conceived) necessarily flow either in a unidirectional fashion from minority to majority worlds, or via the metropolitan elites at the centre of these worlds, as Castells's account of the 'dual city' would imply (1989: 227–28).[2]

Madame Satã: Divine Inspiration

Madame Satã was Aïnouz's feature-length debut, and alongside films such as *Cidade de Deus* (Fernando Meirelles, 2002), *Central do Brasil* (Walter Salles, 1998) and *O Invasor* (Beto Brant, 2002) can be perhaps regarded as one of the most critically successful Brazilian films of the first decade of the century, picking up over twenty-one awards on the festival circuit, most notably the Gold Hugo for best film at the 38th Chicago Film Festival (2002) and the Audience Award at the Toronto Inside Out Lesbian and Gay Film and Video Festival (2003). Before progressing any further with this discussion, it is worth outlining the socio-historical context in which the narrative is couched (in particular, the significance of its protagonist) and considering briefly why the film inspired such positive responses from international lesbian and gay audiences.

As previously mentioned, the film is set in Rio de Janeiro in the 1920s and 1930s, and was inspired by the story of João Francisco dos Santos, a real-life figure who lived between 1900 and 1974. A contradictory personality, remembered simultaneously as one of Rio's most feared *malandros* (streetwise hustler and petty criminal), but also as a cabaret artist and carnival performer who was defiantly open about his sexuality, João Francisco has acquired an almost mythical status within *carioca* [Rio de Janeiro] cultural and historical memory. His childhood years and early adulthood reflected the experience of many Afro-Brazilians at the beginning of the twentieth century. Of all the countries in the Americas, the slave trade had been most active in Brazil, with over three and a half million Africans sequestered to the country in total (Sheriff 2001: 13). Pressured by abolitionists such as the statesman Joaquim Nabuco, it was also the last country in the Americas to abolish the trade, in 1888, just one year before the demise of Brazil's monarchy and the inauguration of the First Republic (1889–1930) (Davis 1999: 44). The immediate result was mass migration from rural plantations and interior mining areas to coastal areas, in particular to Rio de Janeiro, the then capital, which even before abolition already had one of the highest concentrations of black inhabitants in the country, peaking at over 300,000 by the early 1870s (Sheriff 2001: 13).

Although the director ultimately decided not to recount moments from João Francisco's childhood in the film, we know from his memoirs that having been sold by his mother as an apprentice to a horse-seller, he himself ran away to Rio aged eight from his native north-eastern state of Pernambuco with a lady known as Dona Felicidade to work in a *pensão* [small hostel or guesthouse] that she was establishing in the city (Paezzo 1972: 8–9).[3] In 1913, he then moved to the Lapa neighbourhood of the city, sleeping rough for most of his teenage years whilst undertaking odd jobs here and there, and later, working as a waiter/cook in various brothels, hotels and restaurants (1972: 9). This precarious existence on the fringes of society was symptomatic of the fact that the concept of 'freedom' in post-abolition Brazil remained largely rhetorical, with little actual practical meaning for the average Afro-Brazilian, whose existence was often still defined by the same, back-breaking daily work as before. In relation to his employment with Dona Felicidade, the real-life João Francisco recalls: 'não tinha folga. E não ganhava nada. E não tinha estudo e nem carinho. E era escravo do mesmo jeito' [I didn't have a day off. I didn't earn anything. I hadn't studied and I wasn't looked after. I was a slave all the same] (1972: 9).

It is perhaps no surprise, then, that the lifestyle of the neighbourhood's legendary *malandro* figures such as Saturninho, Beto-Batuqueiro, Gavião and Sete-Coroa, who subsequently took him under their wing, seemed like an attractive option to the young João Francisco (Durst 2005: 22). Rejecting continued 'enslavement' in the form of domestic work or manual labour, idleness and pleasure-seeking were instead, for these men, the order of the day, the *malandro's* 'toil', according to Shaw, revolving around an exploration of 'all the hedonistic avenues open to him' (Shaw 2007: 91).[4] Of course, from another perspective one might regard João Francisco as being in the fortunate minority of Afro-Brazilians who were actually given the opportunity to spurn such jobs, with many having been excluded from the labour market due to the policy of *embranquecimento* (whitening) favoured by successive post-abolition governments. Here, white European immigrants were encouraged to settle in Brazil (and favoured in the sphere of employment) not only because they were deemed to be better workers than Afro-Brazilians, but also because it was hoped that through miscegenation they would gradually 'lighten' the country's gene pool (Butler 1998: 36).[5] Illegal activities such as pimping, drug-dealing, gambling and protection racketeering became a popular means of many black men scraping together a living, and, in this sense, unsurprisingly are all activities which have been also associated with the *malandro* lifestyle.

This correlation between Brazil's 'continued aversion to blackness' (Davis 1999: 8) and the socially and economically marginalized status of its Afro-Brazilian population at the time is made explicit not least in the film's opening sequence. Here, the face of João Francisco (played by Lázaro Ramos) is framed in a close-up akin to a mug shot as he is incarcerated in prison, the desired effect, according to the director, being 'to strip the character of everything' (Aïnouz 2002a). A voiceover, taken from an original transcript of one of the many court cases in which he was a defendant, can be heard, informing us that:

> É pederasta passivo, usa as sobrancelhas raspadas e adota atitudes femininas até alterando sua própria voz. Não tem religião alguma. Fuma, joga, e é dado ao vício de embriaguez. Sua instrução é rudimentar. Exprime-se com dificuldade, intercale sua conversa com palavras da gíria do desambiente. É de pouca inteligência. Não gosta do convívio da sociedade por ver que esta o repele dado ao seus vícios. É visto sempre entre pederastas, prostitutas, proxenetas e outras pessoas do mais baixo nível social. Ufana-se de possuir economias mas como não aufere provendas e trabalho digno só podem ser essas economias produtos de atos repulsivos ou criminosos.

> [He is a passive pederast who shaves his eyebrows and imitates women even altering his own voice. He has no religion. He smokes, gambles and is an alcoholic. He has no education. He has difficulty expressing himself and uses the language of the gutter. He is of little intelligence. He hates society from which he is rejected because of his vices. He is to be found socializing amongst other pederasts, prostitutes, pimps and other dregs of society. He boasts of having money but because he has no regular job this can only come from criminal activity]

Spoken against the backdrop of his bruised and battered face, the statement that
João Francisco is a 'passive pederast', in particular, is symptomatic of the way in
which homosexuality became cross-hatched over the correlation that eugenics
made between dark-skinned people and criminal deviance. Referring to Leonídio
Ribeiro's 1938 study entitled *Homosexualismo e endocrinologia* [*Homosexuality and
Endocrinology*], Green argues, for example, that the latter's studies into the racial
makeup of homosexuals in 1930s Rio may have been subjected to a possible process
of '*de-whitening*' (my emphasis), that is, a conscious or unconscious distortion that
involved classifying men as coming from a mixed racial background when they
themselves may have identified as white (1999: 75).[6] Green also suggests that the
under-representation of white men amongst those classified as 'homosexual' might
also have been due to the fact that middle- and upper-class men could more
easily avoid arrest (due, presumably, to connections and/or their ability to buy
their way out of problematic situations), attesting to the role played by class in the
conceptualization and classification of homosexuality in Brazil at the time (1999: 74).
Certainly the director, in a self-authored piece on the film appearing in Brazilian
film journal *Cinemais* in 2003, was keen to underline how class, race and sexuality
were all mutually implicating in the film, arguing that 'em nenhum momento a
questão racial, sexual ou de classe é a questão central do filme' [at no moment in the
film does the question of race, sexuality or class emerge as being more important
than the other] (Aïnouz 2003: 181). The protagonist is in this respect, according to
Aïnouz, *triply* stigmatized: poor, black and homosexual (2003: 181).

In spite of this, however, the film vehemently refuses any discourse of victimization. Instead, as the narrative unfolds to recount the details leading up to his
incarceration in this opening sequence, we witness João Francisco consistently
'imploding' (Aïnouz 2003: 181) the stereotypes constructed through hegemonic
discourse used to relegate him to this position of inferiority alluded to by the
voiceover. As the director writes, 'como abordar este homem tripalmente estigma-
tizado? Desestigmatizando' [how do you tackle this triply stigmatized man? But
destigmatizing him] (2003: 181). At the level of class and race, fundamental here
would appear to be the protagonist's clear identification with the *malandro* figure
who, although somewhat narcissistic and self-interested, embodies a transgressive
edge that goes beyond simple hedonism. Shaw writes: 'The *malandro* is [...]
vehemently opposed to the exploitation of his social class. He challenges any form
of manipulation by the state and is thus worshipped by the rest of his community'
(2007: 8). João Francisco's adoption of a *malandro* identity is underscored not only by
his proud proclamation to his friend Laurita (played by Marcélia Cartaxo) that 'nasci
pra ter vida do malandro' [I was born to be a *malandro*] but also by the diegetic use
of the famous samba 'Se Você Jurar' ['If You Swear'] (Francisco Alves, Ismael Silva
and Nilton Bastos, 1931) at various points in the film, whose lyrics provide a defiant
endorsement of the *malandro* lifestyle. In one early scene João Francisco and Laurita
are framed in a medium close-up dancing to the tune as the cross-dressing Tabú
(Flávio Buaraqui) looks on from beside the bar. Their mutual repetition of the lyrics
'A mulher é um jogo, difícil de acertar, e o homem como um bobo, não se cansa
de jogar' [Women are a game, difficult to win, which men, like idiots, never tire

of playing], however, is clearly tongue-in-cheek, a fact to which João Francisco's subsequent pursuit of the handsome Renatinho (Felipe Marques) who enters the rear of the frame, indeed attests. Cutting to the toilets, we then witness João Francisco flirting with the young sailor before stealthily removing the latter's stash of cocaine from his pocket, suggestively licking a small pile off the back of his hand and then blowing the rest in his face. Unsurprisingly, Renatinho is unimpressed by this rather audacious form of seduction, and after a brief scuffle João Francisco is forced to return to the bar only to discover Laurita being dragged outside by a drunk, lecherous man demanding her services. Rushing to her assistance, João Francisco quickly restores order and brings the overweight man to the ground with the deft delivery of a spinning *capoeira* kick before turning to Renatinho and purring: 'Tu sabe que foi por você e não por mais ninguém que eu quebrei a cara daquele porco. Foi por esses olhos de madre pérola que eu dei aqueles golpes' [You know it was for you, and nobody else, that I broke that fat pig's face. For those mother-of-pearl eyes, those blows were for them].[7]

The way in which João Francisco, here, is somehow able to reclaim his sexuality, alongside poverty and blackness, as a source of pride, might appear somewhat surprising, especially given that he was a self-declared *bicha* [faggot or queer]. Green writes of the real-life João Francisco:

> Satã was proud of his ability to wield a knife and win a fight, two marks of a *malandro*'s bravery and virility. Yet he openly admitted that he liked to be anally penetrated, a sexual desire that was socially stigmatized and the antithesis of manliness represented by the penetrating knife blade [of the *malandro*]. (Green 1999: 91)

However, in this respect, João Francisco makes no apology, nor sees any contradiction between these two aspects of his personality, answering defiantly when challenged on the subject by a drunk bar patron in a later scene, 'eu sou bicha e não sou menos de um homem por causa disso não' [I'm a faggot and that doesn't make me any less of a man, no]. Given the long-standing conflation within dominant Brazilian gender ideology (discussed in relation to *Amarelo manga* in Chapter 4) of sexual passivity with effeminacy, and concurrently the conception of homosexuality as something contingent on sexual role as opposed to sexual object choice, João Francisco's admission here might be regarded as particularly transgressive in its decoupling of gender and sexuality. So too is the way in which he claims an identity from and takes pride in a term (*bicha*, but more commonly in his memoirs, *viado*) that continues to have pejorative connotations in Brazilian popular parlance. In this respect, it is easy to see why certain critics (see, for example, Green 1999) have drawn parallels between João Francisco's story and a discourse of gay liberation. The protagonist, as we learn in the film's epilogue, eventually transcends the social barriers in his path to realize his long-standing dream of becoming a recognized *artiste* by winning a prize in the 1942 Rio carnival procession as depicted in the cover image of this book. This, of course, renders *Madame Satã* a markedly different proposition from *Amarelo manga*, which was characterized by an overwhelming inability on the part of its protagonists to transcend the status quo and free themselves from the dichotomous straightjackets within which their respective performances of gender and enactments of desire were articulated. As the director informs us, in a statement which sheds light on the source of the film's transnational appeal (despite the specificity of the socio-historical context in which it is set):

> Ele é nada típico, porque sempre se fez respeitar. Além de exercitar a liberdade, encontrar prazer e realizar o seu sonho, apesar de todas as adversidades, ele sempre se afirmou como ser humano. E um testemunho bacana de resistência. É um exercício de liberdade não passivo. (Aïnouz 2003: 182)

> [He is not exactly typical in that he always made people respect him. Beyond exercising his freedom, finding pleasure and realizing his dreams, in spite of all the barriers he faced, he always affirmed himself as a human being. It is an amazing story of resistance. A non-passive show of liberty]

Lapa: The 'Montmartre of the Tropics'?

The question necessarily poses itself, however, as to why the specific period of the 1920s and 1930s should figure as a backdrop for such a story, a time when same-sex erotic activity was attracting increasing surveillance from the state (see, for example, Green 1999 or Higgs 1999) and blacks still struggled for inclusion in the 'Brazilian national family' despite the nascent discourse of 'racial democracy'. In answering this question, it is perhaps natural that our attention should first be directed to the film's setting, the neighbourhood of Lapa. Like the principal setting of *Amarelo manga*, Lapa can be regarded as a similarly 'in-between' space and one which, in the era in question, was also produced as a space of exclusion. Located on the immediate periphery of Rio's downtown area, its emergence as one of the city's main red-light districts was perhaps inevitable. Such edge-of-centre locations lend themselves well to prostitution due to a fruitful source of passing trade and cheap property rentals (Ribeiro 2002: 45). Lapa's narrow streets and absence of public lighting would have further limited surveillance by the authorities and naturally aided hustling and other illicit activities. It was no surprise, then, that it was here where many *malandros* such as João Francisco could be found. Not only frequently excluded from the workforce but subject also to anti-vagrancy laws which potentially could have had them arrested simply for being on the streets, many Afro-Brazilians were literally forced to 'retreat to the shadows' (Shaw 2007: 89).

Male same-sex prostitution, too, had always flourished in Lapa for the same reasons as its heterosexual counterpart. Furthermore, the neighbourhood's relative anonymity and abundance of guesthouses and pay-per-hour rooms aided the pursuit of more romantic same-sex (as well as heterosexual) relations which could not be accommodated within mainstream Brazilian life (Green 1999: 84). Men who had sex with men were also attracted to the area due to the employment opportunities as cooks and cleaners offered by its many brothels, whose owners deemed them less likely to interfere with the girls working inside than a heterosexual man (Green 1999: 86). In this sense, the neighbourhood's marginality was also inscribed by its status as the major centre of the city's homoerotic topography, in addition to those areas surrounding Praça Floriano Peixoto, the Passeio Público in Cinelândia and Praça Tiradentes.

With regards to the construction of space in the film and its establishment of Lapa as a space of exclusion, clear parallels can be drawn with *Amarelo manga*. Like the area of the city of Recife in which Assis's film is set, the neighbourhood is represented as being somehow 'apart' from the rest of the city, despite its relatively central location, with panoramic establishing shots of the city itself (notably those iconic Rio short-cuts such as Pão de Açúcar [Sugar Loaf Mountain] and Cristo Redentor [Christ the Redeemer Statue] on Corcovado Mountain) largely excluded from the film's cinematic landscape. This has the effect of preventing the viewer from situating the main space of action within the city's wider geography and, in turn, contributes to the impression of a separate, hermetically-sealed 'universe', as the director describes it on the DVD commentary: 'the Republic of Lapa [...] with its own laws, codes and rituals' (Aïnouz 2002a).

The dilapidated house and the alternative domestic setup we see established within it by João Francisco and his two friends, Laurita and the cross-dressing Tabú, both prostitutes, similarly recalls the marginal space of the Texas Hotel in the way that it straddles the *casa/rua* divide discussed by Da Matta (see Chapter 4). In *Madame Satã*, this has less to do with any physical, architectural fluidity established between these two spaces than with the metaphorical infiltration of the *rua* in those moments where the house serves as a site of prostitution. Despite this, however, the director firmly establishes the ensemble as a 'family', with João Francisco effectively fulfilling the roles of surrogate husband and father to Laurita and her illegitimate baby respectively, who also resides with them, and arguably also to Tabú, who is responsible for domestic chores in the house. This impression of domesticity is reinforced in two particular scenes when the characters are depicted on 'family' outings, firstly to the beach and then to the park, the hand-held camera and grainy footage in the case of the latter evoking the feeling that we are watching a 'home movie' (Shaw 2007: 91). Aïnouz states on the DVD commentary: 'it's a family of choice, not a blood family [...] it's important for people to understand that there are other ways to construct a family' (2002a). Yet this claim would appear to be undermined by the fact that João Francisco, in typical *malandro* style, also acts as a pimp to Laurita and Tabú, firmly inscribing their 'family home', like the Texas Hotel, as a space of enterprise, further undermining its status as *casa*.

As was argued in Chapter 4, if, as Shields suggests, a state of liminality is partly concerned with the production of 'discontinuity in the social fabric [and] in social space' (1991: 83–84), then as well as being a space of exclusion, Lapa would also appear to take on aspects of the liminal too. Indeed, the film's temporality and its visual composition all embody such a sensation of 'discontinuity'. The story, for example, is recounted through a series of vignettes depicting moments of the prot-agonist's life, as opposed to submitting to a standard linear narrative. The editing, in turn, tends to cut on many occasions between different locales in a way that eschews standard framing devices (exterior establishing shot, medium shot, interior shot). This has the result of further confusing those boundaries between centre/periphery, public/private, interior/exterior, which serve as 'ordering' elements within the spatial imagination.

However, traditionally the perception of Lapa as a liminal space has not merely been concerned with its status as a space of exclusion but, as previously mentioned, for being the centre of 'bohemian' Rio. The period between 1910 and the late 1930s, in particular, is often regarded as the neighbourhood's 'golden age', a time when, as Gasparino Damata writes, 'a Lapa tinha o sabor de um Montmartre caboclo, mistura de Paris requintada e Bahia afro-luso-brasileira' [Lapa had the flavour of a *caboclo* Montmartre, a mixture of Parisian refinement and Afro-Luso-Brazilian Bahia] (2007: 22). These words can be found in his volume, *Antologia da Lapa* [*Lapa Anthology*] which comprises a selection of poems, essays, short stories and memoirs relating to Lapa whose contributors include a range of cultural producers and commentators, such as the journalist Millôr Fernandes, artist Di Cavalcanti, writers Almeida Fischer and Carlos Drummond de Andrade and, of course, Damata himself. Collectively they reveal the extent to which Lapa has burnished itself into the *carioca* cultural and historical memory as a socially eclectic neighbourhood synonymous with music, dancing, drinking, gambling, drug-taking, prostitution and a whole gamut of other 'pleasure-seeking' (and illicit) activities. Di Cavalcanti's poem 'A mocidade com Jayme Ovalle' ['Youth and Jayme Ovalle'] (c. 1922), in particular, sums up well the spirit in which the neighbourhood was viewed at the time in which *Madame Satã* is set, aptly evoking this rather schizophrenic combination of high life and low life:

> Nosso tempo! Nosso tempo!
> As meninas eram tristes,
> As meninas e os rapazes
> Pertencíamos à boêmia artística
> E não compreendíamos os malefícios que nos cercavam.
>
> Noites cheias de flores mortas
> Envolvendo velhos espelhos
> Como borboletas de seda
> Almofadas de cetim
> Alcalóides
>
> Na Rua do Lavradio
> O bar cabaré Passatempo Internacional
> Lá se iam os homossexuais assustados
> Galgando as escadas intermináveis
> Dos grandes sobrados verdes
> E as palavras não podem definir
> A beleza de Iracema
> Cantando a Cumparcita
>
> Aqui na Lapa vive o mundo!
>
> Ó Lapa, o que tu és a grande ópera
> Pequim, Chicago e Macau
> A Lapa é também tu, Graziela
> Que és moça e bela
> E tens um riso de rapaz. (Damata 2007, 52–53)

[Our time! Our time! | The girls were sad | The girls and the boys | We belonged to artistic bohemia |And we didn't understand the evils that surr-

ounded us. | Nights full of dead flowers | Surround old mirrors | Like silk
butterflies | Satin cushions. | And alkaloids | On the Rua do Lavradio | The
cabaret bar Passatempo Internacional | Where the startled nancy-boys would
go | Bounding up the never-ending steps | Of old green houses | Words can-
not express | The beauty of Iracema | Singing the Cumparcita. | Here in Lapa
lives the world! | Oh Lapa, you are the grand opera | Peking, Chicago, Macau
| Lapa is also you, Graziela | Girlish and beautiful | And with a boyish smile]

The comparisons made in the final verse between Lapa and Peking, Chicago and
Macau, are particularly symptomatic of Rio's internationalist aspirations at the
time and the desire amongst the city's progressive classes to transform the city from
provincial backwater to global metropole. As Luiz Noronho writes:

> O deslumbramento geral criou uma onda ufanista segundo o qual acreditava-se
> que era possível construir uma Paris nos trópicos, um núcleo urbano moderno,
> civilizado, que mira o futuro [...] combinando todos os confortos da vida do
> século XX com uma paisagem única no mundo. (Noronho 2003: 58)

> [The general atmosphere of wonderment created a wave of civic pride and the
> belief that it was possible to construct a Paris in the tropics, a modern, civilized
> urban centre that looked to the future [...] combining all the comforts of the
> twentieth century with a landscape found nowhere else in the world]

This manifested itself in a rapid process of modernization which swept the city, and
which partly explains why Lapa was to become more than just another down-at-
heel, inner-city neighbourhood. The first of these urban reforms led by the city's
mayoral administration under Pereira Passos between 1903 and 1906, and which
were born under the slogan 'Rio civiliza-se' [Rio is civilizing itself], was the *bota-
abaixo* [knocking-down]. Here, large areas of downtown Rio were demolished and
rebuilt, with many of the city's poor forced to the periphery (Noronho 2003: 58). As
Luiz Noronho notes, the sanitation of urban space, the construction of wider, more
accessible streets, and the widespread introduction of electric lighting, encouraged
the development of the city's street-life and nocturnal entertainment (2003: 56).

Although the reforms left much of Lapa in a grave state of deterioration, there
is evidence to suggest that some parts of the neighbourhood were transformed,
particularly through the building of new roads in areas where previously there had
only existed slums, junk stores and brothels (Ribeiro 2002: 77). Alongside these and
the shadier entertainment venues which had always existed in Lapa, in turn opened
more refined establishments. Small business holders, businessmen and politicians,
in particular, were attracted to new casinos and cabarets such as the Assírio, the
Apollo, the Royal Pigalle and the Casino High-Life (see, for example, Durst 2005
and Damata 2007), the latter, incidentally, a feature of *Madame Satã*'s cinematic
landscape. Damata suggests in this respect, 'a Lapa teve, nessa época, papel de
grande importância na vida política nacional [...] o destino da nação palpitava no
coração da Lapa' [Lapa in this period assumed great importance in national political
life [...] the nation's destiny was beating in the heart of Lapa] (2007: 23). Thus at
the time, the terms of Lapa's interstitiality, when compared to those of Recife's
historic centre, were somewhat contrasting. For whilst Recife's historic centre has
traditionally been characterized by its neglect and relegation to the periphery of

social hierarchies of space in the city, quite the reverse was true in the case of Lapa, which began, in the first two decades of the twentieth century, to re-establish itself as an alternative centre of the city.

With the formalizing of prostitution in 1906 and the issuing of *carteiras de meretriz* or prostitution licences, which not only fiscalized the activities of prostitutes but required them to submit to periodic medical examinations (Ribeiro 2002: 78), many of these establishments also functioned as sites for the practice of 'closed' prostitution, consolidating Lapa's reputation as a domain of *'zona' meretrício* or 'mid-level' hustling, in contrast to the *'baixo' meretrício* or 'low-level' hustling of the less salubrious male and female trade found in the city's immediate downtown area (2002: 79). In turn, creative types, intellectuals and influential figures from *carioca* (Rio) high society soon added to the *geleia geral* or melting pot, attracted by the opening of 'ateliers' by some of the city's most influential artists from around 1910 (2002: 78).[8] Noronho writes:

> Na malha desordenada de cabarés, prostíbulos e antros de jogos, a Lapa desta época reunia os dois mundos de uma cidade que começava a se partir. Nas mesas das casas noturnas, já chamadas de cabarés, encontravam-se lado-a-lado intelectuais, artistas em ascensão, artistas em decadência, sambistas, desordeiros de variados graus, jornalistas, policiais, militares, funcionários públicos, comerciantes de variados tamanhos, burgueses, dandies, mocinhas espevitadas vindas dos bairros chiques em busca de aventuras, prostitutas, taxi-girls [...] garçonetes e a nata da malandragem. (Noronho 2003: 82)

> [Amidst the chaotic rabbit-warren of cabarets, brothels, gambling dens, Lapa in this period brought together two divergent sides of the city. At the tables of the nightclubs, which were now known as cabarets, a whole host of characters found themselves sitting side-by-side: intellectuals, artists, samba musicians, troublemakers of varying notoriety, the bourgeoisie, dandies, lively young ladies from upmarket neighbourhoods looking for adventure, prostitutes, taxi-girls [...] waitresses and the cream of *malandragem*]

These two divergent sides of the city are starkly reflected in the transition between the film's opening sequence and the scene which follows: cutting from his bruised and battered face, a close-up subsequently reveals the mesmerized João Francisco peeping through an opulent glass-beaded curtain as he mouths the lyrics of Josephine Baker's iconic song 'Nuit d'Alger' ['Night of Algiers'] (1936) being performed off-screen. A reverse shot then reveals the singer of the words, the white female cabaret performer, Vitória dos Anjos (Renata Sorrah), performing to an audience in the chic surroundings of the Cabaret Lux, where João Francisco works as her valet.[9] On a metaphorical level, the curtain, in particular, would appear to allude to the social distance that exists between the two characters, with João Francisco here literally on the outside looking in. At the same time, however, the porous nature of the curtain, which allows the latter not only to look through, but also to be seen and heard, makes nods to Lapa's status at the time, in contrast to Recife's historic centre in *Amarelo Mango*, as a space of potential social mobility, not simply with regards to the influx of a higher-status demographic into the area, but also to the empowerment of previously disenfranchised populations. And it is here wherein lies the other aspect of the neighbourhood's liminality and its potential to provide,

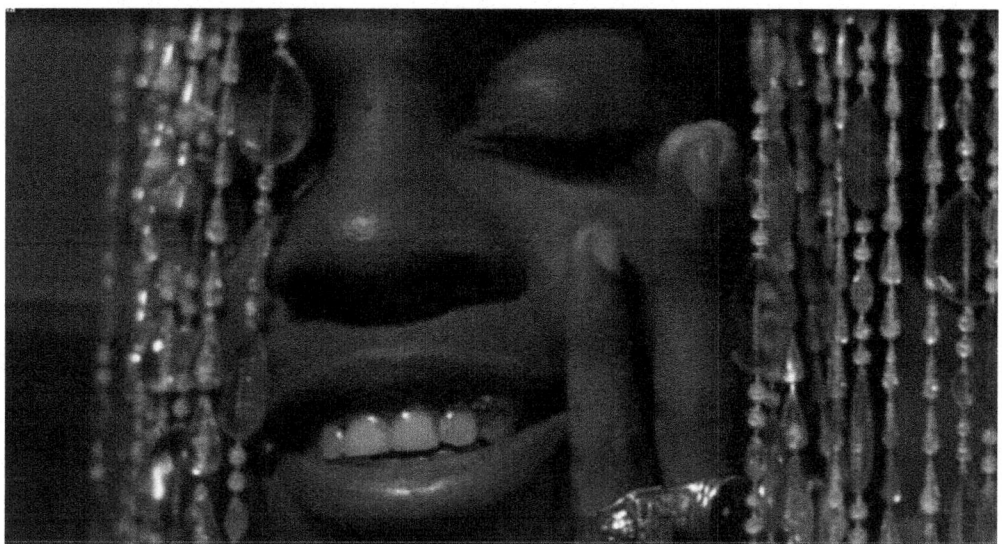

FIG. 5.1. Porous city: João Francisco admires Vitória at Cabaret Lux in
Madame Satã (Karim Aïnouz, 2002: Wellspring Media)

quoting Shields once again, 'liberation from the regimes of normative practices and
performance codes of mundane life' (1991: 83–84).[10]

Perhaps the most obvious manifestation of this 'mobility' was the increased
access black samba musicians were being given to the nascent music and radio-
broadcasting industries (Medreiros de Carvalho 1980: 25–26),[11] something which
this contact between the city's lower and upper echelons afforded within the social
microcosm of Lapa and other 'bohemian' neighbourhoods such as Vila Isabel,
appears to have facilitated. Bryan McCann writes:

> To a degree unimaginable in earlier decades, intellectuals and popular musicians
> began to move in the same circles. They did not necessarily see themselves as
> equals, but parties from each camp knew that they had something to say to each
> other, across the dividing lines of class and education. (McCann 2004: 8, but
> see also Vianna 1999: 77–92)

The musical partnership between Ismael Silva, a black musician-cum-*malandro* who
hailed from the Rio *bairro* of Estácio de Sá, and Francisco (Chico) Alves, one of the
most popular light-skinned singers of the era, was one such example, with Alves
recording virtually all of Silva's compositions until around 1935 (Shaw 1999: 46).
Both are documented as having been regular frequenters of Lapa's cafes and bars, as
Holanda's account of Rio's bohemian underworld in *Memórias do Café Nice* indeed
attests (1969: 152–74).[12] Medreiros de Carvalho goes as far as saying that Ismael Silva
was 'o próprio ser da *mobilidade*: seu comportamento revela uma tentativa de escapar às
qualificações desabonadoras sobre o negro' [the absolute embodiment of mobility: his
attitude reflected an attempt to escape the limits imposed on black people] (1980: 37).[13]

Interestingly, both Ismael Silva and Chico Alves are widely regarded as having
had a preference for men with regards to affairs of the heart, with the latter indeed
being a close friend of João Francisco, something the latter states in his interview

with *O Pasquim* (in Noronho 2003: 23). Whilst Silva's penchant for gay sex seems to have remained shrouded in secrecy, Alves, according to Green, seems to have been less discreet and 'didn't even bother to hide the fact that he had sexual escapades with men in public places', symptomatic of what he terms the 'lax social environment of Rio de Janeiro's bohemian quarter' (1999: 85).[14] This is hinted at in an early scene depicting João Francisco's brazen pursuit of Renatinho, which seems to raise few eyebrows amongst the onlookers in the Danúbio Azul bar. Similarly, a later scene relating to João Francisco's amateur cabaret performance (discussed below) reveals a pair of male extras comfortably showing affection towards each other in the background and the presence of two women dressed in 'gentlemen's attire', again implying a relative acceptance of homoerotic practices and behaviour which might depart from the dictates of hegemonic gender ideology in this particular social milieu.

In this respect, the particular song which João Francisco performs to in this scene, 'Mulato bamba' ['Cool Mulato'], written by Noel Rosa in 1931, is significant. Like 'Se você jurar', the thematics of the samba are again centred on the figure of the *malandro*, as the opening lines of the song suggest:

> Esse mulato forte é do Salgueiro
> Passear no tintureiro é o seu esporte
> Já nasceu com sorte e desde pirralho
> Vive às custas do baralho
> Nunca viu trabalho.

[The big mulato now turns tricks | And writes sambas for kicks | Since a kid he goes for the glitz | Never works | Lives on his wits.] (Translation from the DVD release)

However, as Shaw notes, the song is given an 'ironic twist' when we learn that 'as morenas do lugar vivem a se lamentar por saber que ele não quer se apaixonar por mulher' [All the girls, he makes them cry, because they know, he prefers the guys] (2007: 96). 'It seems like this song was written for João Francisco', notes the director in the DVD commentary (Aïnouz 2002a) and certainly Noel Rosa's biographers, João Máximo and Carlos Didier, suggest that he was a source of inspiration for Rosa in the writing of this song (quoted in Shaw 2007: 98). This is not to say, however, that João Francisco, in terms of his erotic same-sex preferences was in any way an anomaly amongst his fellow *malandros*. Journalist Sérgio Cabral, for example, was left positively stunned when the real-life character revealed to him that two of Rio's other well-known *malandros* at the time — Meia-Noite and Tinguá — were not only *bichas* but also long-term lovers (in Noronho 2003: 29).

Deconstructing the Myth: Karim Aïnouz's 'anti-Lapa'

Superficially, then, *Madame Satã*'s 'liberatory' narrative might appear to conform to Lapa's reputation at the time as a 'tropicalized Montmartre', which the film's title, with its simultaneous connotations of both Parisian chic and sub-equatorial sin, serves to illustrate. Yet, in reality, these allusions to Lapa as a sophisticated, 'anything-goes' space of opportunity characterized by some permanently euphoric state of social conviviality are, in fact, cursory and/or frequently debunked in the film.

As Carvalho points out in *Porous City*, 'porosity is often positive and desirable, but it is not necessarily so' (2013: 11). Its clearest expressions, he writes, can be seen in Rio's vibrant and multiracial music scene where people of different social classes have mingled and collaborated for years. But, quoting, Sérgio Buarque de Holanda's *Raízes do Brazil* [*Roots of Brazil*] (2012), this 'cordiality' speaks of 'an incapacity to comprehend the distinction between private and public domains, where those performing public functions are chosen according to personal trust, family ties, or friendship rather than their capacity' (in Carvalho 2013: 11). Beneath this 'veneer' of cordiality' lies a system that does not favour merit or change, and if we pursue this logic, he continues, then the city's cultural forms arguably only serve to sustain the vast distance that separates the material conditions of its social classes (2013: 11). Rio is therefore both the *cidade maravilhosa* [marvellous city] and also the *cidade partida* [split or broken city]: a divided city can be argued to presuppose a porous city and vice versa, he argues (2013: 12).

Central then to the film's narrative is the attempt not only to 'desmistificar o mito' [demystify the myth] behind Madame Satã, as the director puts it (Aïnouz 2003: 181) but also to demystify the space in which this myth evolved. For as Luis Martíns's reflections make clear, Lapa's 'bohemian' age existed as much as an imagined as a material reality:

> Eu não hesito em afirmar que o prestígio da Lapa na década de 1930 foi, um pouco, promoção nossa, os jovens escritores e artistas que a freqüentávamos. Nós escrevíamos sobre ela artigos, crônicas e reportagens; criávamos assim, a sua tradição, o seu mito e a sua lenda. (Martíns 2015: 100)

> [I have to admit that Lapa's prestige in the decade of the 1930s was something of our own creation, the young writers and artists who went there. We wrote articles, chronicles and reports about it; we created, in this sense, its tradition, its myth, its legend]

On an aesthetic level, cinematography, set design and lighting are all fundamental to this process of debunking, reflecting the director's concern that the film should feature not as a period drama, but rather as a 'genealogia' [genealogy] in which Lapa was transformed into a 'personagem' [character] in itself (Werneck 2002: 2).[15] As previously mentioned, panoramic establishing shots of the city itself and its most iconic landmarks are, with the notable exception of the Santa Teresa *bondinho* [tram], all excluded from the film's cinematic landscape, diminishing the viewer's ability to situate the main space of action within the city's wider geography. In their place, we see a predominance of medium shots and close-ups in the construction of cinematic space, itself largely corresponding to interior locations, most notably the Danúbio Azul bar and Cabaret Lux, but more often grubby, low-lit bedrooms, murky stairwells, ominous doorways, fetid bathrooms and other undesirable corners of the neighbourhood. Here, as Wilton García notes, the frequent exclusion of the laterals of set space from the image — left, right, front, back, ceiling and floor — has the effect of negating a sense of three-dimensionality and diminishing depth of field, often allowing the human body, he continues, to emerge as the principal feature of *mise-en-scène* (2004: 238–44).

At these points, the director's desire to transform Lapa into a character in itself would appear to be literally fulfilled: skin, hair, sweat and grime thrust into the viewer's face, transforming the neighbourhood from a static, purely architectural phenomenon into a living, breathing organism. This is reflected too in director of photography, Walter Carvalho's use of filters, a dirty yellow for scenes of daylight, as if one were 'de ressaca' [experiencing a hangover], and a 'suffocating' red for night-time scenes (Carvalho in Werneck 2002). The result is what Carvalho has termed an 'anti-Lapa' (2002) at odds with the rather more rosy image constructed by the likes of Martíns or Damata.

And it is an anti-Lapa which extends well beyond the aesthetic realm to inform a whole side of the film's narrative. For beneath its mythical façade of *boêmia desenfreada*, cultural intermingling and celebration of all things Afro-Brazilian, the film makes no hesitation in revealing racial discrimination and the segregation of blacks and whites to be just as prevalent in the Lapa of that particular era as it was in other parts of Rio. The court transcript which constitutes the voiceover in the film's opening sequence, for instance, relates to an incident which actually took place in the 1940s (and not 1932, as the film suggests) in which the real-life character was arrested for disorderly conduct after having been refused entry to the Cabaret Brasil due to being 'improperly dressed' (Green 1999: 90). The claim seems unlikely bearing in mind that *malandros* like João Francisco prided themselves on being impeccably turned out. As Moreira da Silva writes, the standard attire consisted of a silk shirt with rhinestone buttons, a white tie, Mexican-heeled shoes, a Panama hat and a fistful of rings, supposedly worn in parody of the middle classes and posing thus another affront to the established order (in Durst 2007: 13).

A more probable reason for his refused entry was the colour of his skin, the first line of the original report written by the police commissioner reading: 'He is a person of above average height, rather robust and black' (Green 1999: 90). Certainly this is the implication in the film, the incident transposed to an earlier period of

FIG. 5.2. Anti-Lapa: João Francisco and his friends are barred entry to Casino High-Life in *Madame Satã* (Karim Aïnouz, 2002: Wellspring Media)

his life against the backdrop of the Casino High-Life, which João Francisco decides to visit with Laurita and Tabú one evening. A tracking shot follows the smartly-dressed ensemble as they approach the entrance to the casino, before we cut to a high-angled shot framing their approach towards the reception area and the waiting doorman. Immediately they are told entry is not permitted, with the doorman stating unapologetically when pressed on the matter by João Francisco that it is 'porque aqui não entra nem puta nem vagabundo' [we don't admit prostitutes or bums here]. A fight then ensues (the latter again putting to use his *capoeira* skills) in which the three are unceremoniously ejected from the establishment onto the street. Significantly, of all the other guests who *do* enter the casino whilst the altercation is taking place, not a single one is black or mulatto, suggesting that João Francisco and Tabú are most definitely 'out of place' in what appears to be an exclusively white establishment.

Yet even before this episode occurs, the film has already firmly dismissed any idea of Lapa being a space of social mobility in which João Francisco's contact with the city's elite via his job at the Cabaret Lux might somehow afford him the prospect of respect, let alone career progression. In one scene, we encounter João Francisco in Vitória dos Anjos's dressing room, enrobed in one of her costumes and mimicking the performance she is concluding on stage. The stunt, however, proves to be a source of incensement rather than flattery and on arriving back at her dressing room, Vitória demands furiously: 'Tu acha que tu é quem? Chega atrasado, fica me imitando desse jeito, vestindo minha roupa. [...] Bem que me avisaram não confia nesse preto. É mais doido que cachorro raivoso' [Who do you think you are? You arrive late, sit there pretending to be me, dressing in my clothes [...] Don't trust that nigger they told me, he's crazier than a rabid dog]. João Francisco's response to the verbal attack again consists of a physical confrontation, slapping the now shrieking cabaret artiste and shouting at her: 'Nunca mais me trata desse jeito, tá ouvindo? Eu vou fazer uma avenida da tua cara' [Never treat me like that, do you hear? I'll smash your face in].

Although Vitória's initial question would appear to be prompted by João Francisco's furtive use of her outfit, the clearly racist overtones which inflect the rest of the tirade suggest that for Vitória the incident goes beyond simple interference with her personal property. For her, João Francisco, if only symbolically, has attempted to cross a line, a line which clearly separates her world from his, and whose transgression constitutes a threat to the privileges she feels she rightfully enjoys due to the colour of her skin. João Francisco, it seems, has neither the right to *aspire* to a better life nor to expect any rewards for his subservience, as the conclusion of the scene suggests. Here, storming out of Vitória's dressing room, the protagonist confronts the owner of the cabaret and demands his wages, which, it would appear, are long overdue. The owner pulls a gun on João Francisco and orders him out of the club, and it is only when the latter deftly produces a knife and holds it to the man's crotch that he is eventually paid the money he is owed.

Both incidents are symptomatic of the ambivalent relationship blacks shared with the Vargas regime's nationalizing project. Certainly the government's co-optation of elements of Afro-Brazilian culture, most notably samba but also *capoeira*,

Candomblé and Umbanda, created the illusion of black inclusion in the Brazilian 'national family' whilst garnering a new sense of Afro-Brazilian pride with regards to increased (but still limited) black participation in arenas such as music and football.[16] At the same time, however, it also glossed over the historical inequalities which had led to the pauperization and marginalization of Afro-Brazilians in the first place (Davis 1999: 92). In turn, the prevailing discourse of *brasilidade* ensured the maintenance of the status quo since any attempt to contest the asymmetrical power relations that continued to exist between blacks and whites could be dismissed as anti-nationalistic.[17] Significantly, by 1938, the Frente Negra Brasileira [Black Front of Brazil] had already been banned by the government (Stam 1997: 79), reflecting the more hardline nationalist stance taken by the regime during the *Estado Novo* [New State] between 1937 and 1945 (see Hentschke 2006: 11–19).

Amidst the film's rather candid and unfavourable representation of race relations in the Lapa of the 1920s and 1930s, claims that the neighbourhood might also have figured as some sort of enclave of tolerance vis-à-vis same-sex erotic practices are, simultaneously, seen to be rather tenuous. As Green suggests, despite its 'lax social environment', there was no guarantee that men who sexually desired other men would be immune from hostility or that they automatically felt comfortable in openly expressing their homoerotic preferences whilst circulating in the neighbourhood or its environs (1999: 84). Indeed, there seems to be evidence of only one bar that explicitly catered to Rio's queer population at the time — the Passatempo Internacional on Rua do Lavradio, as cited in Di Calvicanti's poem, 'A mocidade com Jayme Ovalle' (Damata 2007: 52–53). Discretion, it seems, appears to have been the order of the day, with Chico Alves's homoerotic escapades, for example, common knowledge amongst his particular social milieu but *not* amongst a wider audience (Green 1999: 85), whilst those pertaining to Ismael Silva were most definitely kept under wraps (Shaw 2007: 103).[18] The real-life João Francisco, of course, refused any such censorship of his behaviour, recalling in his memoirs:

> Mas o que devia fazer? Tornar-me um covarde só para satisfazer as pessoas deles? Deixar que fizessem comigo o que faziam com as outras bichas que viviam apanhando e eram presas todas as semanas só porque os policiais achavam que as bichas deviam apanhar e fazer a limpeza de todos os distritos? [...] Não, eu não podia me conformar com a situação vexatória que era aquela. (in Paezzo 1972: 142)

> [What was I supposed to do? Be a coward just to satisfy other people? Let them do what they did to other queers who were beaten up and arrested every week just because the police thought that they ought to clean up every district? [...] No, I could not conform to that demeaning situation]

His fierce repudiation of the abuse routinely meted out to the city's *bichas* is epitomized by his unremorseful shooting dead of a policeman who dared to pass judgement on his sexual orientation, which according to the interview in *O Pasquim*, earned him a prison sentence of twenty-six years and sealed his fate as one of the city's most renowned *malandros* (Noronho 2003: 18). And it is precisely this crime for which we see João Francisco being incarcerated in the opening sequence, the incident itself recounted in the film's denouement. Here, a medium shot frames

João Francisco relaxing after a cabaret performance at the Danúbio Azul, before being confronted by an inebriated man slumped at the bar. In reference to João Francisco's costume the latter enquires, 'Tu tá fantasiado de homem o de mulher?' [Are you dressed up as a man or a woman?]. João Francisco's lack of response prompts a vicious verbal onslaught from the man, who demands: 'Fala, fala? Viado, bicha, sola de merda [...] Tem mais merda na cara do que qualquer meretriz daqui da Lapa!' [So which is it? Speak up! You queer, you faggot, you nigger! [...] You've got more shit on your face than the dirtiest whore in Lapa!].

João Francisco's retort, 'Eu sou bicha porque eu quero. E não deixo de ser homem por causa disso não' [I'm queer by choice and it doesn't make me any less of a man!], is symptomatic of the fearless manner in which the real-life João Francisco defended his sexual orientation, in particular his refusal to let his preference for passive anal sex be used to question his virility. However, the ultimate outcome of this particular encounter (João Francisco's decision to return to his house, retrieve a loaded gun and shoot the man dead, which subsequently earns him three decades in jail) can hardly be regarded as particularly 'liberatory'.

Indeed, in a similar manner to the characters Dunga, Lígia and Kika in *Amarelo manga*, João Francisco ultimately seems to wind up internalizing the very attitudes he appears to react against. His treatment of Tabú is particularly telling in this respect. One moment he expresses what appears to be a warm, almost sibling-like affection for his transvestite friend, and the next, a deep-seated repulsion manifested in outbursts of physical or verbal abuse towards the latter. In one scene, in what appears to be a well-practiced scam, we see Tabú removing the wallet from the trousers of a man João Francisco has lured back to the house under the pretence of having sex. Just as proceedings move into full swing, however, the shrieking Tabú bursts into the room alerting them that a police raid is taking place. The man having fled (amidst the commotion, failing to notice, of course, that he has been pick-pocketed), the two characters reel back in fits of laughter, in apparent mutual appreciation of their ingenuity. The jovial atmosphere, however, is quickly cut short when João Francisco enquires how much money was in the wallet, to which Tabú answers one thousand reais. The former, however, appears not to be in the mood for charity and despite having been short-changed himself by Gregório at the Cabaret Lux, hands Tabú a paltry two hundred reais for his efforts, this now the second occasion on which the latter apparently fails to receive what (s)he is due. Tabú, somewhat understandably, begins to protest, prompting a drastic change of mood in João Francisco, who rasps: 'Essa tua voz miada está me dando um enfado, enjôo, se tu não está satisfeito com meu trato puto, evapora! Toma desenxabida' [Your whining voice makes me sick, if you're not happy with how you're treated then scram!]. Thus whilst João Francisco is apparently self-affirming about his *bicha* identity, his 'pride', it seems, can only be exercised (and, concomitantly, respect gained) via a consistent defiance of the principal characteristics associated with this identity — frailty and weakness — and a denigration of those who *do* conform to the stereotype. In the *Making of Madame Satã* documentary, the director explains the ambivalent relationship between the two characters in the following terms:

Ele tem uma admiração pela Tabú e tem uma abjeção pela Tabú. Porque Tabú é uma pessoa que tem uma coragem gigantesca [...] uma pessoa que tem corpo biológico de homem e que tem papel social de mulher. Ele admira mas também odeia ela porque ele se vê um pouco no espelho dele meio torto. Porque ela precisa ser tão frágil? Quer dizer ele admira nela a coragem, o que ele detesta nela é a fragilidade. (Aïnouz 2002b)

[He admires Tabú but also despises her. Because Tabú is a person with a huge heart [...] a person with the biological body of a man who assumes a woman's social role. He admires her but also hates her because he sees something of himself in her. Why does she have to be so fragile? What I'm trying to say is that he admires her heart but detests her fragility]

Subero takes up this issue in his analysis of the film, arguing that the director's insistent 'hypermasculinizing' of the protagonist (reinforced through the character's interplay with the film's other 'cross-dresser', Tabú) means his body really only disrupts the conventions of (heteronormativity) at the level of his sexual orientation rather than that of his gender identity (2014: 153). He argues this insistence as present even in within the film's representation of João Francisco's cabaret performances, whereby traces of inner femininity (alluded to through his costume) are subsequently erased through the camera's fixation on his muscular body. The film's disavowel of femininity in these scenes is symptomatic, he argues, of the director's desire to 'posit the male protagonist as part of a parodic discourse of ambigusexuality, rather than transgenderism' (2014: 153). I would hesitate to define the fictitious João Francisco as 'a woman trapped in the wrong biological gender' and therefore base my subsequent readings of his stage identities on Brazilian ideas about carnivalesque performativity as opposed to transgenderism (which is closer, I believe, to the director's own understanding of them). However, it must be acknowledged, as Subero cautions, that this hypermasculine image contradicts somewhat both the diegetic information provided about him and the historical facts surrounding the real character. There is no trace here, he reminds us, of the João Francisco who, beyond the cabaret stage, plucks his eyebrows or speaks in a high-pitched feminine voice as the voiceover suggests in the opening sequence, nor the *bicha* we encounter in Green's account who enjoys being anally penetrated, since we only ever see João Francisco fulfilling the active role in sexual proceedings.

'Black as Body'

Arguably these contradictions, in particular as they manifest themselves through João Francisco's projection of these disavowed aspects of himself onto Tabú, only serve to contribute to the polyvalent character whom the director wished to create, somebody who 'refuses to fall into the trap of being evil or a good guy' (Aïnouz 2002b). And although João Francisco's adoption of a 'macho *bicha*' identity in the film is to a large degree fuelled by the same (internalized) homophobic discourse that it would appear to resist, his decoupling of sexuality from an albeit still problematic gender identity can nevertheless be considered dissonant and transgressive. This resistance to conforming to the behavioural stereotypes of the *bicha* despite self-identifying as such, perhaps mirrors a more general trend seen in emerging sexual cultures, particularly during the 1970s in countries such as the USA and the UK. Here in a clear rebuttal to the stereotype of the effeminate 'nancy boy', campness went most definitely out of fashion in favour of a highly exaggerated form of masculinity whose valorization of stocky or muscular builds, facial hair and 'butch' attire (leather, construction boots, military-style clothing, lumber-jack shirts and so on) verged on the parodic.[19] And as Foster argues, this hypermasculinized body was celebrated through 'unbridled promiscuity of abundant sexual experience' which rejoiced in the erotic possibilities of male same-sex activities and, in clear difference to the past, their enjoyment in an open and guilt-free manner, a situation he contrasts with Fernando's sex life in *La virgen de sicarios*, defined, he argues, by 'a virtual retreat into asexuality' (2003: 71).

For Foster, the eroticization of the (queer) body is symptomatic of what he terms one of the 'clichés' that defined the sexual revolution that began in the 1960s: 'Eros or Death'. This implied that to live without Eros, that is the combination of love and sexuality understood to constitute a complete and fulfilling erotic life, was akin to death, if not literally then metaphorically through an 'emotional starvation' of the soul (2003: 71). And it is a formula, he continues, that is customarily attributed to Herbert Marcuse and his 1955 book *Eros and Civilization: A Philosophical Inquiry into Freud*, which itself echoes Freud's 1930 essay *Civilization and its Discontents*. Both essays regard the modernist project of civilization as one which has been intimately bound up with an inversely proportional process of de-eroticization with regards to human relations (2003: 71). Foster writes:

> For Freud it meant recognising that civilization was necessarily going to pro-
> duce malcontents, who in turn would then not have any reason to support the
> project of civilization, resulting in suffering for them and a problem for society.
> For Marcuse it meant being able to turn away from the stifling effects of civili-
> zation, to overcome the death threat inherent in civilization, and to reinvest in
> an erotic life that could allow one to live a fully human life, overcoming the
> deadly consequences of dehumanising civilization. (Foster 2003: 71)

The 'Eros or Death' formula can therefore be regarded as being of some relevance to *Madame Satã*, bearing in mind the modernizing fervour that was gripping Rio during the early twentieth century and which was attempting to design 'order' back into Rio's central zone which, as Higgs puts it, had traditionally been perceived as 'crowded, promiscuous and other' (1999: 147). The civilizing project, as previously mentioned, had only partially affected Lapa and a clear tension is established in the film between the gentrified but more regulated spaces pertaining to the Casino Highlife and the Cabaret Lux and the defiantly down-at-heal Danúbio Azul bar, where the protagonists often socialize. The latter is clearly presented as a sexualized space not just of prostitution (Laurita appears to use the place to find potential clients) but of more romantic intimate encounters. It is here, of course, where João Francisco first audaciously pursues Renatinho before inviting him back to the (relative) privacy of his apartment, which becomes the location of further trysts between the two characters as the film progresses. One of the remarkable features of *Madame Satã* is the latent eroticism which pervades the representation of these encounters, which in clear contrast to those which take place between Fernando and his lovers in *La virgen de los sicarios,* crackle with sexual energy, desire and, most importantly, enjoyment, a representation which defies shame or censure and is highly affirming of their same-sex erotic preferences. The fluid camera work, in particular, is reminiscent of that employed in *Un año sin amor* and embodies the sensuality of the encounters. The use of close-ups and extreme close-ups, in turn, visually embraces the contact of male body on male body, their interlocking mouths, in particular, often occupying the frame to clearly convey the sensation of intimacy between the two men. This can be juxtaposed with the relative discomfort and self-revulsion expressed by some of the partners in João Francisco's other liaisons, in one scene the protagonist farcically having to adopt the fictional persona of a black woman called 'Josefa' before the man in question yields to his advances.

To return to the sex scenes involving Renatinho and João Francisco, however, what is particularly significant here is the nuanced depiction of black skin. Carvalho's intimate style of cinematography not only conveys to the viewer a real sense of skin texture, but more importantly skin colour, with João Francisco's body positively glowing amidst the murky shadows of his dimly-lit room, despite the natural reflectivity of Renatinho's white skin. This representation of the protagonist's body was enhanced by the use of the bleach by-pass technique in the processing of the negative, allowing the tonal spectrum of the image to be broadened, thus revealing, according to Aïnouz, not only different shades of 'brownness' but also the 'goldenness of brownness' (2002a). In this sense not only does the film reclaim same-sex erotic practice as a gratifying expression of what is presented as a legitimate desire between two men, but also, in defiance of its traditional perception as being ugly, dirty and something to be avoided or hidden from view, it celebrates 'blackness' as something beautiful that might (as in Renatinho's case) be enjoyed from the other side of the racial divide.

FIG. 5.3. 'Black as body': João Francisco embracing Renatinho in
Madame Satã (Karim Aïnouz, 2002: Wellspring Media)

Indeed, the style of corporal representation adopted in these scenes is symptomatic of the privileged place the image of the 'black body' enjoys within the wider film text, with the conventional establishing and re-establishing shot, normally used to situate and resituate the body within space, frequently replaced with direct cuts to extreme close-ups of parts or surfaces of João Francisco's body. On these occasions the protagonist effectively *becomes* the landscaping or establishing shot, something epitomized in one scene depicting one of their 'family outings' to the beach, identifiable as Praia Vermelha in Urca. Here we cut from the water where they have been swimming to a close-up of João Francisco's upper torso which fills the screen, the outline of his shoulder and arm exactly matching that of the lower section of Sugar Loaf Mountain visible in the background. Beyond its establishment as an object of beauty, then, the black body is also quite literally foregrounded as an integral part of the *carioca* landscape, thus simultaneously reversing its traditional exclusion from official Brazilian national imagery, of which the prevalent policy at the time of *embranquecimento*, of course, was so representative.

Yet despite being reclaimed as a source of pride and self-expression in the film, the black body nevertheless remains a highly ambivalent site which can never quite disentangle itself from the prevailing ideologies which traditionally have relegated it to such a marginalized position. Certainly its looming presence in the film is symbolic, as the director explains, of it being 'a única coisa, objetivamente, que ele tem' [the only thing that he owns] (Aïnouz 2003: 181), and, in the absence of official, politicized, emancipatory discourses relating to gender, sexuality and race, his primary instrument of self-assertion. Thus, unsurprisingly, beyond the erotic realm where the sexual encounter of the black body with other (in particular, lighter-skinned) male bodies constitutes a potent act of sexual defiance, it also offers the protagonist his most effective means of resistance with regards to the societal discrimination and prejudice which surround him. And certainly those instances of physical resistance which we witness in the film would seem indicative of somebody who was 'sempre se afirmando e nunca se deixou abater' [somebody who always affirmed himself and never let himself be put down] (2003: 179). However, this (over)emphasis on João Francisco's physicality in the film is arguably problematic in so far as it necessarily subscribes to what Charles Johnson has termed the notion of 'black-as-body' that is, the way blacks, when subjected to the white person's gaze, are drained of a psychical interiority and instead are reduced to a solely bodily existence (1994: 123, 129). Here, he writes, the problem is not diminished by the customary strategies for escaping it, rather 'the black body [...] is still susceptible to whatever meanings the white gaze assigns to it' (1994: 132). Recalling his unease when entering a predominantly white bar in Manhattan, he elaborates in the following terms:

> I am *seen*. But, as a black, seen as stained body, as physicality, basically opaque to others [...] Their look, an intending beam focusing my way, suddenly realises something larval in me. My world is epidermalized, collapsed like a house of cards into the stained encasement of my skin. My subjectivity is turned inside out like a shirtcuff. (Johnson 1994: 122)

Johnson's account echoes that of Frantz Fanon, who in *Black Skin, White Masks* (originally published in 1952) wrote one of the most influential accounts of black subjectivity, mobilizing psychoanalytic theory to explain this heightened sense of physical self-awareness and/or inferiority engendered through the presence of the black body in a white world. For Fanon, 'the Negro symbolises the biological', with muscular strength and/or latent sexual potency cited by the white man as redeeming features in the face of his supposedly limited intellectual capacities. The black body, in this sense, is invoked as a space onto which the white man projects his own insecurities (physical frailty and a lack of sexual potency), symbolizing 'an irrational longing for unusual eras of sexual license [and] orgiastic excess' (1968: 167). And yet, as Fanon continues, the expression 'a handsome Negro' is simultaneously enveloped by 'the imaginary reek of rape and pillage' reflecting its concurrent status as a symbol of biological danger, 'a phobogenic object, a stimulus to anxiety' (1968: 151, 165). He writes: '*Negro* brought forth biology, penis, strong, athletic, potent, boxer, Joe Louis, Jesse Owens, Senegalese troops, savage, animal, devil, sin' (1968: 66).

The eventual outcomes of João Francisco's acts of resistance in the film, beyond the preservation of his personal honour, can only tenuously be cited as 'personal victories' over barriers of class, race or sexuality. The first act of defiance, for example, fails to secure either João Francisco or his friends' entry to the Casino High-Life, instead resulting in their rather humiliating ejection from the establishment. The second two, in turn, whilst they do indeed illicit some degree of temporary justice for João Francisco (at the Cabaret Lux he is able to extract the wages he is due, whilst the patron at the Danúbio Azul pays for his insolence with his life) are both ultimately punished by the authorities with lengthy jail sentences. Here, blackness and criminal deviance, it would seem, can be regarded as mutually fulfilling prophecies. Afflicted with the 'stain of blackness', the expression of physical and libidinal potency remains João Francisco's only means of self-affirmation, yet without a 'reasoning' mind to control such 'animal' instincts this expression necessarily requires greater regulation and control than that pertaining to a white person, with his eventual punishment, in turn, serving as convenient 'proof' of the 'inherent' nature of his degeneracy. As Fanon laments: 'it is not I who make a meaning for myself, but it is the meaning that was already there, pre-existing, waiting for me' (1968: 134).

Queer Transcendence and the Carnivalesque

The above discussion necessarily begs the question as to where the 'liberatory' force of the film's narrative really lies. The shackles of poverty, race and sexuality on many levels would appear to weigh as heavily on João Francisco's shoulders in 'bohemian' Lapa as anywhere else, the neighbourhood offering little protection from the punishing hand of the state. Similarly, whilst the director suggests that João Francisco's body is his 'fortaleza' [fortress] (Aïnouz 2003: 181), something clearly celebrated in the film's manner of corporal representation, it is a fortress in which ultimately he appears to be imprisoned. Blackness, as Fanon reminds us, is a 'fact' which exists in the world of the white man (1968: 134). Yet, João Francisco, of course, does indeed fulfil his dream of becoming a recognized artiste, with the film's epilogue, in this sense, offering the protagonist a final reprieve from the injustices suffered in the preceding narrative. Here, we see the exuberantly costumed João Francisco, framed in an out-of-focus shot (see front cover image) dancing frenetically on a carnival float against the backdrop of diegetic samba music, a postscript informing us:

> Em janeiro de 1942, após cumprir pena de dez anos, João Francisco dos Santos é posto em liberdade. No carnaval do mesmo ano, ganha o concurso do bloco caçadores de veados com a fantasia Madame Satã, inspirada no filme 'Madam Satan' de Cecil B. de Mille.

> [In January 1942, after ten years in prison, João Francisco dos Santos was released. In that year's carnival he won the fancy dress prize wearing a costume inspired by Cecil B. de Mille's film 'Madam Satan']

And it is precisely here, amidst this discourse of the carnivalesque, where the answer to the above question arguably can be found. Although the pre-Lenten Brazilian celebration of *carnaval* has had a long line of scholarly observers, Da Matta perhaps remains one of the most influential, himself greatly influenced by Bakhtin's account of carnival celebration in medieval Europe (previously discussed in relation to *Amarelo manga*'s 'grotesque' elements in Chapter 4). For Da Matta, *carnaval* is essentially a festival of the 'periphery', enacted by and for the destitute of society, a ritual of 'forgetting' in which everyday reality — with its hierarchies, restrictions and obligations — is inverted or dissolved to create a 'special' space *outside* the space of the *casa* and *above* the space of the *rua* (1997b: 111). Here the sufferings of the real world are banished and instead sexual transgression, tomfoolery, parody, the grotesque, the absurd, the high and the low all merge to project 'multiple visions of social reality' (1997b: 100). It is a moment *out of time*, the arduous passage of everyday life replaced by a 'cronologia cósmica' [cosmic chronology] in which the earth and not official institutions (government, army, church and so on) reigns supreme (1997b: 54). As Nancy Scheper-Hughes writes, for Da Matta, 'the ideology of *carnaval* hints at a brave new world, a world of pleasures and many different freedoms' (1992: 481). And whilst, as my previous discussion has underscored, João Francisco is, for the majority of the film, constantly *reminded* of his socially marginalized status, there are moments of 'rupture' in the film's narrative, where the *dia-a-dia* [day to day] implodes into a temporary space of carnivalesque liminality in which João Francisco is permitted to forget and, if only temporarily, construct his own reality, his own vision of this 'brave new world'.

His cabaret performances, which he organizes at the Danúbio Azul, are, in this respect, perhaps most significant. They arguably constitute a last-ditch attempt to salvage his dream and finally secure applause from his public, the possibility of career progression in Lapa's professional cabaret circuit having been effectively curtailed by his altercation at Cabaret Lux and resultant prison sentence. Perhaps the first remarkable feature of these performances is the way in which they are depicted on screen. Whilst the cinematic gaze in other scenes might be argued to have objectified, or to use Johnson's phraseology 'epidermalized', its subject, quite the opposite is true here. Through cross-cutting between successions of extreme close-ups revealing his mouth, eyes, shoulders, torso, arms, legs and so on, and reverse shots of the crowded bar's jostling clientele, the protagonist's body is effectively deconstructed and fragmented in cinematic space in these scenes, suggesting (temporary) reprieve from his corporal incarceration and the pursuit of alternative identities.

The first of these manifests itself in the form of Jamaci, 'a formosa feiticeira da floresta' [the beautiful enchantress of the forest] whose costume, in clear defiance of the boundaries erected between valet and star at Cabaret Lux, recalls the costume worn by Vitória in her Arabian Nights routine, a classic case of carnivalesque inversion one might argue. The name of the personality, and the song which he performs, endow this latest incarnation, however, with a distinctly Brazilian twist, symptomatic of his anthropophagous consumption of new ideas. The notion of hybridity is further reinforced by specific wardrobe decisions, with the director recalling that he chose to leave the actor's bare torso on show, so its toned, muscular contours contrast with the delicacy of the beads and fabric of which his costume is composed (Aïnouz 2002a). As Da Matta writes, the carnivalesque body is one which simultaneously exhibits male and female aspects, and is 'um corpo que "chama" o outro' [a body that 'calls out' to the other] (1997b: 140).

The performance, though, ultimately proves to be a rather sombre and nostalgic affair, a necessary process of 'looking back', a mourning not only of Renatinho's death but also of opportunities lost, for which Vitória's stage personality serves as such an emphatic reminder. João Francisco's subsequent metamorphosis into the 'Mulata de Balagoché' in his second stage appearance is an altogether contrasting proposition, eschewing this discourse of inversion for a distinctly upbeat, intra-subjective dialogue. In this respect, the combination of sequined head-dress, sarong-style skirt and frenetic, 'tribal' dancing in this performance seems clearly inspired, as Shaw notes, by Josephine Baker's 'mix of flapper girl and African tribal princess' (2007: 96) encountered in one scene by João Francisco's visit to the cinema to see *Princess Tam-Tam* (Edmond T. Gréville, 1935).[20] Here Baker plays Aouina, a Bedouin beggar girl, who is 'discovered' by French novelist Max de Mirecourt (played by Albert Préjean) on his travels through North Africa. Enchanted by the young girl, he decides to bring her back to the *métropole* to be 'tamed and civilized' (Jules-Rosette 2007: 102), introducing her to Parisian high society as Princess Parador. Aouina performs the role with admirable aplomb until one night, when 'instinct' gets the better of her and she breaks into a spontaneous performance of tribal dancing at a high-society soirée. The diegetic inclusion of this particular scene in *Madame Satã* is fleeting, yet the series of cross-cuts between Baker's frantic performance of the Charleston and the Conga and the image of João Francisco's mesmerized face are enough to cement clearly the latter's identification with the actress before him. Here, in what perhaps might be described, to borrow Judith Williams's terminology, as 'an intra-diasporic gaze of recognition' (2006: 8),[21] João Francisco's idealization of Vitória finally appears to melt away with the sight of this inspiring emblem of black mobility celebrating so unapologetically her African roots. Of course, this 'celebration', as Denean Sharpley-Whiting notes, was articulated often via a clear exploitation of French exoticist fantasies (1999:

107), which arguably did little to challenge colonial roles, resulting often in their reinforcement. Writing of *Princess Tam-Tam*, Bennetta Jules-Rosette remarks: 'It is a perfect example of Bhabha's notion of doubling [...] all stereotypes are intact, and order is imposed on the chaos of primal dreams and drives' (2007: 102).[22]

Yet this is something of which João Francisco seems perfectly aware, his second cabaret appearance, with its wildly overemphatic body movements, perilous oscillations between the high and low melodic octaves of Noel Rosa's song 'Mulato Bamba' and incorporation of spinning dance moves, evocative of the rituals of the Afro-Brazilian religion Candomblé, simultaneously parodying, domesticating and

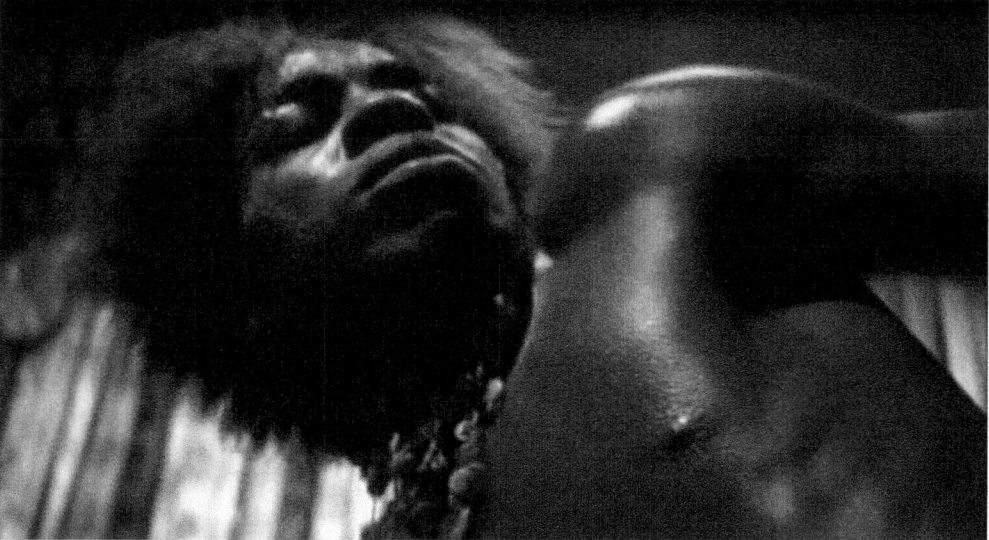

FIG. 5.4. João Francisco appearing as 'Jamaci' and the 'Mulata de Balagoché' at the Danúbio Azul bar (Karim Aïnouz, 2002: Wellspring Media)

queering Baker's performance of blackness.[23] As Bhabha argues (quoted in the opening section of this chapter):

> The 'right' to signify from the periphery of authorized power and privilege does not depend on the persistence of tradition; it is resourced by the power of tradition to be *reinscribed* through the conditions of contingency and contradictoriness that attend upon the lives of those who are 'in the minority'.
> (Bhabha 2004: 3, my emphasis)

And it is precisely the idea of 'contradictoriness' that I wish to argue is key here in João Francisco's passage of carnivalesque transcendence to 'um outro lugar' [another place] (Aïnouz 2003: 182) at these moments in the film. For whilst one might regard, as previously suggested, the diegetic inclusion of Noel Rosa's samba 'Mulato bamba' in this particular sequence as pointing to a *reconciliation* of João Francisco's *malandro* and *bicha* identities, the cinematic dismembering and subsequent reassembling of João Francisco's body in these scenes, in fact, alludes to hybridity not as the sum of fixed parts, but rather as a constant state of ephemerality produced through a continual slippage of competing and contrasting identities. As the director writes, one of his most fascinating characteristics is his constant capacity for 'self-reinvention' and the way in which he 'sempre criava curtos-circuitos nas definições' [created short-circuits in definitions]. The director continues: 'quando diziam que era preto aparecia como viado, quando diziam que era viado aparecia como pobre — era sempre outra coisa' [when he said he was black he was queer, when he said he was queer he was poor — he was always something else] (2003: 182). From this account, therefore, resistance in the case of João Francisco appears overwhelmingly as a strategy of discursive avoidance, *the inability* to be defined. And it is here, in this overtly queer discourse, where the dissonant force of *Madame Satã's* narrative can be found. For what is significant about João Francisco's deconstructive performances is how they reject the notion of the 'true self' as a singular unified force and, subsequently, any pretentions to a personal oppositional politics that attempts to replace supposedly false ideologies with non-normative truths. Here there is no 'single locus of great Refusal... or pure law of the Revolutionary', to borrow Foucault's phraseology (1978: 95–96). Rather, by mobilizing a performative strategy that operates outside the symbiotic dyads of oppression and supposed emancipation, João Francisco, if only temporarily, escapes the strategic field of power relations that shape, materially and discursively, our society.

Back to the Future

Like *Amarelo manga*, *Madame Satã* demonstrates, then, albeit in somewhat contrasting ways to the former film, the highly ambiguous nature of 'in-between' or interstitial spaces with regards to the production of non-heteronormative sexualities and the opportunities they may or may not afford for the construction of accompanying cultures and identities. As we have seen, the Lapa constructed in Aïnouz's film, on a superficial level, might appear broadly to conform to its mythical status at the time as 'The Montmartre of the tropics': a bohemian, 'anything-goes' space of liminality and potential empowerment in which João Francisco might be able to achieve social mobility whilst reconciling both with himself and those around him his multiple and often conflicting identities: *bicha,* father, artiste, *malandro* and so on. However, as my analysis demonstrates, amidst the anti-Lapa which subsequently emerges in the film, the obstacles in João Francisco's path appear almost as insurmountable here as in any other part of the city. In this respect, as argued above, it is within the film's carnivalesque elements and the subsequent emergence from these of an overtly queer discourse where the transgressive force of the film's narrative is to be found.

Superficially *Madame Satã* may not appear to share much with *Un año sin amor,* the film which began the main body of this book's discussion. And yet both arguably are transnational films par excellence, not just in terms of their production, distribution and reception but also in the way in which foreign cultural trends exert such influence on their respective protagonists. Like members of the outward-facing, internationalized S/M subculture we encounter in Berneri's film, the dialogue established between João Francisco and Josephine Baker and their shared 'intradiasporic gaze of recognition' underlines the fact that as Rio orientated itself towards Paris in its quest to join the 'civilized world', marginalized groups in Lapa, Harlem and Montmartre were establishing their own dialogues and disrupting and diverting supposedly unidirectional flows of modernizing ideologies and ideas from 'centre' to 'periphery'. In this sense, even before the postmodern era and the much discussed growth of supra-territorial space, *Madame Satã* shows that the notion of the 'metropolitan centre' was already somewhat precarious and significantly destabilized by the productive potential of such in-between spaces.

Certainly from the perspective of (homo)sexuality, the film would seem to endorse the opinion of some historians, sociologists and anthropologists that a homoerotic subculture of men who transcended the active/passive binary to enjoy multiple sexual experiences, whilst also being self-affirming about their sexual preferences, has been a longstanding phenomenon in Brazil and one which existed *prior* to the introduction of western European medical ideas of homosexuality in the late nineteenth century. Luiz Mott, for example, takes particular issue with the social constructionist perspective pursued by Foucault, and formulating the essentialist side of the debate argues that as far back as the sixteenth century, 'we can notice the emergence of a gay subculture in the New World' with colonial Brazil being no exception (2003: 168). Writing in the context of Pernambuco, he points, for example, to the existence of two types of homosexual existence in this period pertaining to the 'explicit' *fanchonos* and *tibiras,* and the 'closeted' sodomites. Both categories, he writes, 'behaved with a clear code of conduct, engaged in intra-group communication and used distinctive signs of external identification and specific strategies of social survival', which he regards as the necessary elements 'for the anthropological characterization of the concept of a subculture' (2003: 192). From this perspective, then, whilst the 'Global Gay' has often been understood as an entirely contemporary (and 'foreign') phenomenon issuing from North Atlantic domains, João Francisco's experience of homosexual identity and community might more readily be attributed to a specifically Brazilian history of sexuality. This seems to be the opinion of Green, who broadly concurring with Mott's perspective, suggests that the post-Stonewall cultural changes of the late 1960s and 1970s merely provided a social context for multiple representations to coexist and even to develop *new* space or values in what was, in fact, a *pre-existing* subculture (1999: 8).

Notes to Chapter 5

1. Parts of this chapter have been previously published as 'Representing and Performing Interracial Love in the Roles of Lázaro Ramos: The Black Body Reframed', in Shaw, Bergfelder & Vieira 2016.

2. Castells's 'dual city' refers to what he argues is a stark social division between two varieties of community. On the one hand, there are the elites whose advantaged position in society allows them to forge connections with the wider world. On the other, there are the poor and the marginalized who are excluded from these transnational networks and whose very survival depends on the production and maintenance of contrasting *internal* networks (1989: 227–28).

3. In the film's DVD commentary, Aïnouz remarks that 'there are things that were important to leave out [...] It was almost as if you can spend two hours of your life with this man — feel him, smell him, share his daily life — it's more valuable than knowing his life history' (2002a).

4. The samba composer, or *sambista*, Moreira da Silva, in his book *Último malandro* [*The Last Malandro*], writes in this respect, 'malandro é aquele que não pega no pesado. Malandro é o gato, que come peixe sem ir à praia' [a *malandro* is someone who doesn't stretch himself. He's the cat who eats fish without going to the beach] (in Durst 2005: 14). *Sambistas* were synonymous with the lifestyle of *malandragem* pursued by the *malandro* in the first decades of the twentieth century in Rio, and they often composed sambas around these themes.

5. This policy of *embranquecimento* reflected deeply entrenched Positivist attitudes of the eighteenth and nineteenth centuries and the belief that the greatest impediment to modernization was the 'barbarous paganism' of Brazil's black population (Butler 1998: 36–40). João Batista Lacerda, director of the National Museum, was one of the first members of the scientific community to endorse this strategy of 'constructive miscegenation', calculating in 1912 that by 2012 the black population would be reduced to zero, while mulattoes would make up merely three per cent of the total population (Butler 2001: 36). The debate would contribute to the growing popularity of the international eugenics movement in Brazil during the late 1910s with at least seventy-four major works on eugenics published between 1897 and 1933 in the country (1998: 36).

6. The presumption that darker-skinned people were somehow more 'naturally' predisposed to sexually deviant behaviour was widespread not just in the medical profession but in the legal profession too. Sueann Caulfield, for example, notes in her study of legal disputes in Brazil between young couples over cases of lost virginity which took place between 1918 and 1940 that, 'a white man had [...] a 20 per cent greater chance of escaping indictment for rape if the victim was black, or a 10 per cent greater chance if she was *parda* [mixed race], than if she was white' (2000: 179).

7. *Capoeira* is a mixture of dance and martial art developed by Angolan slaves on Brazil's colonial plantations in the eighteenth and nineteenth centuries, where it was performed as clandestine training for slave rebellion and self-defence, and which remains a popular sport/performance art in Brazil today (Shaw 1999: 188).

8. The diversity of artists and musicians attracted to Lapa during the 1920s is reflected well in Lúcio Rangel's essay 'A Lapa e a música popular' ['Lapa and Popular Music'] (Damata 2007: 80–81), in which he notes having encountered, amongst others, José Barbosa da Silva, Sinhô, Pixinguinha, Bexiguinha, João Mangabeira, Vírgilio Marício, Francisco Alves, Ismael Silva and Nilton Bastos in the district.

9. Speaking about this scene in the 'making of' documentary, Renata Sorrah notes: 'É aquela relação da diva e do camareiro, do fan. Ele acha tudo do universo dela maravilhoso, é o feminino, é a sensibilidade, é a fantasia, é a viagem, as coisas bonitas [...] ela canta em francês, ela tem perfume, ela tem joias [...] acho isso tudo no imaginário do João, é enlouquecedor' [It's that relationship between the diva and her valet. He thinks everything in her world is wonderful: the femininity, the sensibility, the fantasy, all the pretty things [...] the fact she sings in French, wears perfume and jewellery [...] it catches João's imagination] (in Aïnouz 2002b).

10. It should be noted that the Cabaret Lux is subsequently revealed in a later scene (in which the police attempt to arrest João Francisco for supposedly robbing the establishment) as being located in the area surrounding Praça Onze, and therefore outside the environs commonly understood as pertaining to Lapa. The inclusion of this detail is somewhat puzzling bearing in mind that previously, on the level of narrative and/or cinematography, no attempt is made to isolate the nightclub from the principal space of action. Furthermore, Praça Onze had been, for much of the 1920s, the centre of social life for Rio's poor black inhabitants (Shaw 1999: 4) and whilst the *bota abaixo* may have altered the area's demographic, the presence of an upscale club such as the Cabaret Lux might be argued as somewhat incongruous. With regards to the other 'glitzy' venue depicted in the film (the Casino High-Life), João Francisco, Tabú and Laurita's return home from the establishment by the *bondinho* (little tram) across the aquaduct-cum-tramway known as the Arcos da Lapa, might, in contrast, be regarded precisely *as* an attempt to create a certain distance between there and the characters' normal zone of residence. However, this is negated by the fact that the Casino High-Life is widely cited as being a landmark Lapa institution at the time, whilst it is the highly recognizable atrium of Democraticus, one of the area's most famous samba clubs of recent times, that is used in the preceding scene as the entrance to the fictitious Casino High-Life. This ambiguity perhaps reflects the fact that what does and does not constitute Lapa has always been both highly fluid and subjective, and as Luis Martín's admission implies, less a geographical reality than a state of mind. In this sense, I have chosen to interpret, along with the majority of critics who have written about the film, both the Cabaret Lux and the Casino High-Life as being Lapa institutions, which, bearing in mind my argument which follows, would seem to be a necessary clarification.

11. Holanda writes in *Memórias do Café Nice: subterrâneos da música popular e da vida boêmia do Rio de Janeiro* [*Memories of Cafe Nice: Underground Popular Music and Bohemia in Rio de Janeiro*] (1969), that: 'a Lapa como não podia deixar de ser, está ligada à música popular' [Lapa is intimately bound up with popular music, as it could never fail to be] (1969: 163).

12. Other 'white patrons' included Gilberto Freyre, who played an important role in exposing the talents of Sinhô (José Barbosa da Silva, 1888–1930) (Vianna 1999: 79), and Carmen Miranda, who spread many of the melodies and compositions of Assis Valente and Dorival Caymmi (Davis 1999: 140).

13. This period of Afro-Brazilian cultural effervescence must be placed within the context of President Vargas's nationalizing project (1930–45) which sought to forge economic, cultural, political and racial unity in the country under the rhetoric of *brasilidade* or 'Brazilianness', in particular the idea of a racially harmonious 'national family' (Davis 1999: 92). Whilst expressions of black culture had traditionally been repressed in Brazil, the co-opting of samba, Afro-Brazilian religions such as Candomblé and Umbanda, and *capoeira* into the national cultural repertoire was a powerful tool in Vargas's quest for national and racial integration. Of course, this move was not innocent: by transforming these from ethnically-marked practices to ones which were supposedly 'Brazilian' and symbolic of the whole nation he effectively removed what potentially could have been some of the major cultural foundations for the forging of ethnic separatism.

14. As Shaw notes, there is no mention of homosexuality whatsoever in Maria Theresa Mello Soares's biography of the famous samba composer (2007: 101). However, Ricardo Van Stein's film *Noel: poeta da Vila* (2007), set around the same time as *Madame Satã*, does make a veiled reference to his (homo)sexual preferences in one scene towards the end of the film. Here, Silva (played by Flávio Buaraquí, who plays Tabú in *Madame Satã*) challenges a man who is paying for sex with his sister, the former responding with a (mock?) attempt at seduction. Just as he leans in to kiss Silva, however, the latter shoots him in the crotch, thus bringing the scene to an ambiguous conclusion.

15. An example of a film with such a 'period drama' aesthetic might be the above mentioned film *Noel: poeta da Vila*. Here, a preoccupation with creating an 'authentic' image of the 1920s and 1930s Rio is reflected, for example, in the use of old motorcars, faithful reproduction of shop/business facades and the interiors of iconic Rio landmarks, as well as a meticulous attention to detail with regards to fashion and costume. Despite this, however, whether the film is as successful as *Madame Satã* in evoking the *spirit* of Rio in this period is, I would argue, debatable.

16. Candomblé is another Afro-Brazilian religion (for Umbanda see endnote 13 and Chapter 4) that originated amongst slaves taken from the Dahomey and Yoruba regions of West Africa. It is a syncretic belief system that combines elements of Catholicism and African religious practices, reflecting the associations made by slaves between their own religious figures and the Catholic God and saints in order to preserve their beliefs in the context of forced conversion to Christianity (Shaw & Dennison 2005: 295).

17. Robert Stam provides a particularly insightful observation into the mechanics behind the ideology of the *democracia racial* in Brazil, writing that: 'the apparent inclusionism of "racial democracy" masks fundamental exclusions from social power. Indeed the phrase "racial democracy" itself encodes a blame-the-victim strategy. If Brazil is democratic, then blacks have only themselves to blame if they do not succeed' (1997: 50).

18. In this respect Shaw writes that the biography of Silva, written by Maria Thereza Lacerda, makes no reference to his sexual orientation, 'concentrating instead on his encounter with his alleged illegitimate daughter' (2007: 103).

19. For cinematic accounts of gay life in the UK during the 1970s see Ron Peck's *Night Hawks* (1981) and his later documentary on the making of the film *Strip Jack Naked (Night Hawks 2)* released in 1991.

20. Apart from Vitória's rendition of Baker's 'Nuit d'Algers' in the scene immediately preceding the film's opening sequence, there are also several other references to Baker in the film. Renatinho, for instance, remarks on the presence of a poster depicting the star in João Francisco's bedroom asking if he is a 'fan'. In another scene the latter, whilst seducing the policeman in the wallet-robbing incident, asks if the man concerned has heard of Josephine Baker before leading his hand towards 'Josefa's' thighs, which, of course, are his own.

21. Williams uses this term in reference to Baker's stage-managed encounter with the Brazilian mixed-race *teatro de revista* star, Aracy Cortes, on her visit to Rio in 1929. This she situates within the context of Brazil's participation in the transnational flows of people and ideas that have characterized the shared culture of the 'Black Atlantic'.

22. It is easy to see why Baker would have served as such a powerful icon for João Francisco. One of the great symbols of the Harlem Renaissance, Baker (1906–75), like João Francisco, was similarly of African origin and from a humble background; she also began her career as a valet, tending to the costumes of the blues singer Clara Smith between 1920 and 1921 (Wintz & Finkleman 2004: 91). And although early career breaks came in the form of chorus line singing with vaudeville troops and Broadway appearances, it was really in Paris, where she emigrated in 1925, that she made her name. Her appearance in the *Dance sauvage* with Alex Joe, as part of the revue show *La Revue nègre* [*The Black Revue*] in particular, is widely regarded as her 'catapult' to fame (2004: 93). As well as her stage career, she also starred in a series of films in the 1920s and 1930s (though these did not garner as much critical recognition as her theatrical appearances), was a published novelist and, somewhat curiously, fought for the French Resistance during the Second World War, being rewarded for her efforts by General Charles de Gaulle with a Croix de Lorraine in 1945 (2004: 91). In addition, Baker dedicated much of her life to promoting social justice, racial equality and human rights, clinging tirelessly to a utopian ideal of a multicultural society, despite often being dubbed a 'political reactionary' (Jules-Rosette 2007: 92). In Brazil, she became a household name, first appearing on stage at the Teatro Cassino in 1929, and returning on numerous occasions, most notably in 1939 for her performance of 'O que é que a baiana tem?' (1939) at the Casino da Urca and appearing alongside the Afro-Brazilian comic performer Grande Otelo (Shaw 2011: 94).

23. In this respect, as well as Baker's style of dancing in *Princesse Tam-Tam,* a clear dialogue also exists between his performance and the ceremony which accompanies the ordination of religious leaders of Candomblé whereby existing priestesses dance frenetically to the sound of *atabuque* drums and chant in African languages until the new *pai / mãe de santo* falls into a trance (Shaw & Dennison 2005: 296).

POSTSCRIPT

Queer Afterthoughts

Reprojecting the City began as a response to the largely negative stereotypes projected onto Latin American cities and their sexual citizens mainly, but not exclusively, within the western geographical imagination. I use the words 'not exclusively' because the idea of Latin America as a 'cartographically dark' region also informs the imaginaries of its own cultural production. *Dependencia sexual*, which served as my point of departure, is a case in point. Juxtaposing a 'sinister' vision of urban Latin America with an (apparently) more civilized one pertaining to metropolitan USA, it aptly illustrated my point and seemed therefore like a fitting place to begin. And arguably the analysis of the subsequent four cinematic cities in the main body of my discussion would appear largely to concur with Bellott's pessimism. Yet this is not the whole story for power, particularly that vested in the capitalist apparatus, may unwittingly enable the very sexualities it seeks to supress. As we have seen, this frequently occurs in function to capitalism rendering 'liberation' a somewhat allusive goal. However, as the films suggest (*Un año sin amor* and *Madame Satã* in particular) there may be moments of discontinuity and rupture when these sexualities succeed in reappropriating and manipulating this power in surprising ways and according to their own needs. They may even succeed in redirecting it and creating alternative circuits able to bypass, if only temporarily, the regulation from the centre. These are indeed spaces of discrimination, exclusion and violence, but they are also spaces of hope, empowerment and productive possibility. Where there is power there is most definitely resistance.

The question necessarily poses itself, however, as to how far this perspective really takes us. Chapter 1 touched upon some of the perceived limits of queer theory and criticisms that its focus on the ephemeral, unstable and contingent nature of subjectivity, social relations, power and knowledge is accompanied by a distinct lack of clarity as to what kinds of politics and/or ethics it is attempting, if at all, to promote (Seidman in Sullivan 2003: 47). Altman, in this respect, argues that in its 'desire to deconstruct all fixed points in the interest of "destabilising" and "decentring" our preconceptions', queer theory winds up having little relevance 'to the vast majority of people whose lives it purports to describe' (1996). I would challenge this conjecture. Queer theory and politics emerged precisely as a response to the sense of dissatisfaction felt by 'real' people towards the unitary visions of gay liberation espoused from the late 1970s, constructed around a utopian (but hardly realistic) vision of 'liberated bodies and unrepressed psychic drives' (Reynolds

2002: 70), from which women, people of colour, the disabled and those living with HIV/AIDS, amongst others, were frequently excluded. As we have seen, the films examined in this book certainly resist subscribing to any such ideals but neither do they construct an entirely dystopian vision of the relationship between cities and dissident sexualities. Rather, the queer urban geographies which emerge are characterized simultaneously by pleasure and pain, empowerment and submission, fulfilment and disappointment, affection and violence, community and estrangement, and all the other ambiguous and contradictory experiences that constitute 'real life', not just as it is played out within cities, but within all domains.

In this respect, Altman is perhaps rather more forgiving, suggesting that 'queer' is 'an enormously useful term for aesthetic criticism' in that it may 'unsettle assumptions and preconceptions about sexuality and gender and their inter-relationship' (1996). And yet implicitly here, he seems to position representation and accompanying criticism *merely* as issues of aesthetics as opposed to politics or ethics. It is here where my discussion returns to one of the founding propositions made in Chapter 1, that the spatial imagination matters and has far-reaching effects. I argued that imagined geographies of sexuality have, in particular, often been conceived of through highly problematic distinctions between broad global regions. Whilst in the past, Latin America, Africa and Asia featured as 'porno-tropics for the European imagination' (McClintock 1995: 22), I suggested that more recently they have been drawn as 'cartographically dark continent[s]', to borrow Quiroga's phraseology (2000: 13), in need of 'liberation' from the international gay and lesbian lobby. I argued Scagliotti's *Dangerous Lives: Coming Out in the Developing World* to be, in this respect, a particularly patronizing documentary which simplistically reads events in the 'developing world' merely as developments of those occurring in the 'West' and which largely ignores the more discrete, elliptical, but no less effective, forms of *local* activism and politics occurring in the majority world. In this sense the film's insistence on the 'spread' of a universal globalized form of gay identity and culture only serves to reinforce, rather than challenge, oppositions between centre and periphery, us and them, rich and poor, modern and traditional, included and excluded, empowered and marginalized, the 'West' and the 'Rest'. My analysis of the films in question through the course of this book and the process of *re*projection in which it has engaged, shows that such oppositions are, and always have been, largely untenable. Without exception, urban dissident sexualities emerge in these films not as self-contained phenomena produced in isolation from each other and the world 'outside', but ones firmly imbricated into the trans-local and/or trans-national flows of capital, cultures and ideologies for which cities have always constituted primary disseminative nodes. Furthermore, my analysis draws attention to the fact that these flows have never issued solely from one domain and been unidirectional in nature.

With this in mind, the broader aim of the book outlined in the Introduction — that is to *re*project *global* (in addition to specifically local and urban) imagined geographies of sexuality — may now be revisited with more clarity. In this respect I suggested that the split screen so characteristic of *Dependencia sexual* embodied not only a 'fractured' vision of urban life in the region but also the dividing line between, to quote Parker, 'two discrete moral universes, north and south of the equator' (1999: 1). One of the twists in Bellott's tale is that Tyler, the supposed embodiment of the progressive form of heterosexual masculinity promoted by the RiGO BoSD advertising campaign, turns out to be sexually attracted to other men, though he is not open about this. Whilst other students such as Jeremiah live out their sexuality in the open, 'coming out of the closet' is a luxury which, bearing in mind his professional and extra-curricular pursuits (he is a college football player and model), Tyler feels he can ill afford. Homosexual experience, for him, is limited at best to swift, anonymous encounters around the university campus or, more frequently, furtive glances at other men through the steam of the locker room. He finds himself constantly torn between his sexual urges on the one hand, and the demands placed on his masculinity by his profession and the sport he so enjoys on the other. It is the latter which usually wins out, life reduced to a tiring performance in which the façade of heterosexuality must be maintained. And for all its pretence of inclusivity, campus LGBTQ activism is something from which Tyler feels wholly estranged, cutting short his one brief attendance at the 'sexuality workshop' led by Jeremiah, which he views from the back of the room. Here the politics of unproblematized visibility peddled by Jeremiah and his happy helpers with their simplistic calls to 'come out, come out, wherever you are' fail wholeheartedly to engage with Tyler's predicament, only serving to reinforce rather than to mitigate his sense of alienation. And so life continues for Tyler with his overwhelming day-to-day experience being one of repression in which feelings must be kept in check.

The consequences, as we discover in the film's harrowing final scene, ultimately are far-reaching. After an alcohol-fuelled night on the town, a group of young male students are seen walking home through a university car-park. On their way they meet Choco, a Bolivian exchange student, whose story forms the narrative bridge between the film's two respective settings. 'Who's this bitch?' we hear one of the men demanding. 'Do you want to dance with a white boy?' he continues, the only response from Choco coming in the form of his desperate panting as he attempts to walk away through the endless rows of parked cars. He is, however, eventually surrounded and quickly finds himself being unceremoniously slammed onto the bonnet of a nearby car. His trousers are then pulled down before he is systematically gang-raped by the men concerned, each taking turns in penetrating him. Significantly, one of his principle assailants turns out to be Tyler, the blond, blue-eyed demigod who appeared as the absolute antithesis of the transvestite-abusing young men encountered in the Bolivian section of the film but who here is rendered virtually indistinguishable from them. And so, as the two screens begin to cut between images of these events unfolding in the USA and those occurring back in Bolivia, the discriminatory violence so overt in Santa Cruz is revealed as being equally present within the confines of Ithaca College. Here, perhaps, it is better suppressed, its expression limited to the highly codified rituals of the American football game, yet the consequences of this suppression, as we see in this particular scene, are equally destructive.

Ultimately then, the dividing line between the two screens alludes not so much, as previously suggested, to contradictions, but, as the director states, to the '*dualities* inherent within contemporary social experience' (Bellott 2003, my emphasis). In

FIG. 6.1. Choco recomposes himself after being gang raped at Ithaca College, USA whilst in Santa Cruz, Bolivia, Sebastián celebrates losing his virginity outside a local brothel (*Dependencia sexual*, Rodrigo Bellott, 2003: Wellspring Media).

this respect, this book does indeed respond to Altman's call for queer theory and criticism to be more attuned to processes of 'economic and cultural globalization' with regards to the proliferation of gay identity and lifestyle (1996), though perhaps not in the way that he envisages. For whilst Altman seems to understand 'global queering' as an (imperialistic) process of homogenization issuing principally from North America, my analysis not only draws attention to the diversity of (urban) dissident sexual cultures as they are emerging in regions such as Latin America, but also, through this framing discussion of *Dependencia sexual*, in the 'core' countries in which (supposedly) they first began. Here, commercial gay culture and the politics of identity may serve as attractive propositions for many men and women, but others may wholly disidentify with them, feeling equally 'foreign' within a gay bar or an LGBTQ centre as a Bolivian, Colombian or any other Latin American national. As Green suggests, in order to avoid operating in a simplistic, bi-polar framework, we need to recognize 'the complexities and inconsistencies of an *overarching* model' (1999: 8, my emphasis). This highlights the value of the polycentric form of queer analysis embodied in this book, not only at the level of aesthetics, but also as a critical device capable of intervening in, and taking forward, explicitly political debates.

BIBLIOGRAPHY

AGAMBEN, GIORGIO. 1998. *Homo sacer: Sovereign Power and Bare Life* (Stanford, CA: Stanford University Press)

AGGLETON, PETER. 1999. *Men Who Sell Sex: International Perspectives on Male Prostitution and AIDS* (London: UCL Press)

AGUILAR, GONZALO. 2006. *Otros mundos: un ensayo sobre el nuevo cine argentino* (Buenos Aires: Santiago Arcos Editor)

AÏNOUZ, KARIM. 2003. 'Macabea com raiva', *Cinemais*, 33: 177–87

——2002A. *Madame Satã* [DVD Commentary] (New York: Wellspring Media)

——2002B. *The Making of Madame Satã* [DVD extra] (New York: Wellspring Media)

AITKEN, STUART. 2006. 'Imagining Geographies of Film', *Erdkunde*, 60:4: 326–36

ALENCAR, JOSÉ DE. 1895. *Iracema* (New York: Luso-Brazilian Books)

ALMAGUER, TOMÁS. 1998. 'Chicano Men: A Cartography of Homosexual Identity and Behaviour', in *Social Perspectives in Lesbian and Gay Studies: A Reader*, ed. by Peter Nardi and Beth Schneider (London: Routledge), pp. 537–52

ALMEIDA, HELÍO DE. 2001. 'Filme reconstitui Lapa da época de Madame Satã', *Jornal do Brasil,* Caderno B, 20 August

ALONSO, ANA MARIA, and MARIA KORECK. 1988. 'Silences: "Hispanics", AIDS and Sexual Practices', *Differences*, 1: 101–24

ALSAYYAD, NEZAR. 2006. *Cinematic Urbanism: A History of the Modern from Reel to Real* (London: Routledge)

ALTMAN, DENNIS. 1996. 'On Global Queering', in *Australian Humanities Review* (electronic journal), <http://www.australianhumanitiesreview.org/archive/Issue-July-1996/altman.html> [accessed 7 January 2009]

——1997. 'Global Gaze/Global Gays', *GLQ: A Journal of Lesbian and Gay Studies,* 3: 417–36

ALVES CUNHA, CILAINE. 2003. 'Trabalho, dominação e bestificação em *Amarelo Manga*', in *Trópico*, <http://p.php/uol/com.br/tropico?html?textos?2547,1.shl> [accessed 14 February 2007]

ALZATE VARGAS, CÉSAR. 2001. '*La virgen de los sicarios*, de Barbet Schroeder: consideraciones desde Medellín', *Kinescopio*, 56–57: 145–51

ASSIES, WILLEM. 1991. *To Get Out of the Mud: Neighborhood Associativism in Recife, 1964–1988* (Amsterdam: CEDLA)

AUGÉ, MARC. 1995. *Non-places: Introduction to an Anthropology of Supermodernity* translated by John Howe (London: Verso)

BAKHTIN, MIKHAIL. 1984. *Rabelais and His World* (Bloomington: Indiana University Press)

BAKEWELL, PETER JOHN. 1997. *A History of Latin America: Empires and Sequels 1450–1930* (Oxford: Blackwell)

BALDERSTON, DANIEL, and JOSÉ QUIROGA. 2003. 'A Beautiful, Sinister Fairyland: Gay Sunshine Press Does Latin America', *Social Text*, 21.3: 85–108

BARBERO, JESÚS MARTÍN. 2002. 'Communications: Decentring Modernity', in *Latin America Writes Back: Postmodernity in the Periphery*, ed. by Emil Volek (London & New York: Routledge), pp. 39–56

BAERLE, CASPAR. 1980. *História dos feitos recentemente practicados durante oito anos no Brasil* (Recife: Fundação de Cultura Cidade do Recife)

BATALLE, DIEGO. 2005. 'Conmovadora opera prima', *La Nación*, 24 March

BAUDET, HENRI. 1965. *Paradise on Earth: Some Thoughts on European Images of Non-European Man* (New Haven, CT, & London: Yale University Press)

BAZÁN, OSVALDO. 2006. *Historia de la homosexualidad en la Argentina* (Buenos Aires: Marea Editorial)

BEASLEY-MURRAY, JON. 2001. 'Translator's Introduction: In Argentina', in Beatriz Sarlo *Scenes from Postmodern Life*, (Minnesota: University of Minnesota Press), pp. vii–xviii

BECKEMANN, ANDREA. 2007. 'The "Bodily Practices" of Consensual "SM", Spirituality and "Transcendence"', in *Safe, Sane and Consensual: Contemporary Perspectives on Sadomasochism*, ed. by Darren Langbridge and Meg Barker (Basingstoke: Palgrave Macmillan), pp. 98–120

BELL, DAVID, and GILL VALENTINE (eds). 1995. *Mapping Desire: Geographies of Sexuality* (London: Routledge)

BELLOTT, RODRIGO. 2003. *Dependencia sexual Press Kit* (Toronto: Cinevault Releasing)

BEVINS, VINCENT. 2011. 'Brazilian Fashion: Taking on Dior', *Financial Times* (online), 22 June, <http://blogs.ft.com/beyond-brics/2011/06/22/brazilian-high-fashion-taking-on-dior/> [accessed 24 June 2011]

BHABHA, HOMI K. 2004. *The Location of Culture* (London: Routledge)

BINNIE, JOHN. 2004. *The Globalization of Sexuality* (London: SAGE)

BONFIL, CARLOS. 2007. 'El cielo dividido', *La Jornada*, 9 September, <www.jornada.unam.mx/2007/09/09/index.php?section=opinion&article=a10a1esp.htm> [accessed 20 October 2008]

BROWN, MICHAEL. 2000. *Closet Space: Geographies of Metaphor from the Body to the Globe* (London: Routledge)

BROWNE, KATH, and OTHERS (eds). 2007. *Geographies of Sexualities: Theory, Practices and Politics* (Farnham: Ashgate)

BRUNNER, JOSÉ JOAQUÍN. 2002. 'Traditionalism and Modernity in Latin American Culture', in *Latin America Writes Back: Postmodernity in the Periphery*, ed. by Emil Volek (London & New York: Routledge), pp. 3–31

BURNS, E. B. 1970. *A History of Brazil* (New York: Columbia University Press)

BURUCÚA, CONSTANZA. 2009. *Confronting the 'Dirty War' in Argentine Cinema, 1983–1993: Memory and Gender in Historical Representations* (Woodbridge, Suffolk: Tamesis)

BUTLER, JUDITH. 1990. *Gender Trouble: Feminism and the Subversion of Identity* (New York: Routledge)

BUTLER, KIM. 1998. *Freedoms Given, Freedoms Won: Afro-Brazilians in Post-Abolition São Paulo and Salvador* (New Brunswick, NJ: Rutgers University Press)

CABRAL, JOHN T., and ALEXANDRINA SOBREIRA DE MOURA. 1996. 'City Management, Local Power and Social Practice: Analysis of the 1991 Master Plan Process in Recife', *Latin American Perspectives*, 23: 54–70

CALDEIRA, TERESA P.R. 2000. *City of Walls: Crime, Segregation and Citizenship in São Paulo* (Berkeley: University of California Press)

CANDIDO, ANTONIO. 1951. 'The Brazilian Family', in *Brazil: Portrait of Half a Continent* ed. by Thomas Lynn Smith and Alexander Marchant (New York: Dryden Press), pp. 291–312

CANT, BOB. 1997. *Invented Identities? Lesbians and Gays Talk About Migration* (London: Cassell)

CARNEIRO CAMPOS, RENATO. 1980. *Tempo amarelo* (Recife: Editora Massangana)

CARRIER, JOSEPH. 1995. *De los otros: Intimacy and Homosexuality among Mexican Men* (New York: Columbia University Press)

CARVALHO, BRUNO. 2013. *Porous City: A Cultural History of Rio de Janeiro* (Liverpool: Liverpool University Press)

CASEY, MARK. 2007. 'The Queer Unwanted and Their Undesirable "Otherness"', in *Geographies of Sexualities: Theory, Practices and Politics*, ed. by Kath Browne and others (Farnham: Ashgate), pp. 125–35

CASTELLS, MANUEL. 1989. *The Informational City: Information Technology, Economic Restructuring and the Urban Regional Process* (Oxford: Blackwell)

——2000. *End of Millennium: The Information Ages: Economy, Society and Culture Vol 3* (Oxford: Blackwell)

——2010. *The Rise of the Network Society* (Chichester: Wiley-Blackwell)

CAULFIELD, SUEANN. 2000. *In Defense of Honor: Sexual Morality, Modernity and Nation in Early Twentieth-Century Brazil* (Durham, NC: Duke University Press)

CERTEAU, MICHEL DE. 1984. *The Practice of Everyday Life* (London & Berkley: University of California Press)

CHAMPAGNE, JOHN. 1999. 'Transnationally Queer?: A Prolegomenon', *Socialist Review*, 27, 1/2: 143–65

CLARKE, DAVID. 1997. *The Cinematic City* (London: Routledge)

COLACE, HUGO, and EZEQUIEL GARCÍA. 2005. 'La consistencia del camino: una charla con Lucio Bouelli por su trabajo en *Un año sin amor* de Anahí Berneri', *ADF*, Año 08: 16

CRESSWELL, TIM. 1996. *In Place/Out of Place: Geography, Ideology and Transgression* (Minneapolis: University of Minnesota Press)

DAMATA, GASPARINO (ed.). 2007. *Antologia da Lapa* (Rio de Janeiro: Desiderata)

DA MATTA, ROBERTO. 1997A. *A casa e a rua: espaço, cidadania, mulher e morte no Brasil*, 5th edn (Rio de Janeiro: Editora Rocco)

——1997B. *Carnavais, malandros e heróis: para uma sociologia do dilema brasileiro*, 6th edn (Rio de Janeiro: Editora Rocco)

DAVIS, DARIÉN. 1999. *Avoiding the Dark: Race and the Forging of National Culture in Modern Brazil* (Aldershot: Ashgate)

D'EMILIO, JOHN. 1983. 'Capitalism and Gay Identity', in *Powers of Desire: The Politics of Sexuality*, ed. by Ann Snitow and others (New York: Monthly Review Press), pp. 100–13

DENNISON, STEPHANIE, and SONG HWEE LIM (eds). 2006. *Remapping World Cinema: Identity, Culture and Politics in Film* (London: Wallflower)

DONALD, JAMES. 2010. 'Imagining the Modern City: Light in Dark Spaces', in *The Blackwell City Reader*, ed. by Gary Bridge and Sophie Watson (Oxford: Wiley-Blackwell), pp. 322–29

DUGGAN, LISA. 2002. 'The New Homonormativity: The Sexual Politics of Neoliberalism', in *Materializing Democracy: Toward a Revitalized Cultural Politics*, ed. by Russ Castronovo and Dana D. Nelson (Durham, NC: Duke University Press), pp. 175–94

DUJVONE ORTIZ, ALICIA. 'Buenos Aires [An Excerpt]', translated by Caren Caplan, *Discourse* 8: 73

DURST, ROGÉRIO. 2005. *Madame Satã: com o diabo no corpo* (São Paulo: Brasiliense)

FALICOV, TAMARA. 2007. *The Cinematic Tango: Contemporary Argentine Film* (London: Wallflower)

FANON, FRANTZ. 1968. *Black Skin, White Masks* (St Albans: Paladin)

FIELD, NICOLA. 1995. *Over the Rainbow: Money, Class and Homophobia* (London: Pluto Press)

FILC, JUDITH. 2003. 'Textos e fronteras urbanas: palabra e identidad en la Buenos Aires contemporánea', *Revista Iberoamericana*, I.XIX:202 (January-March), 183–97

FOGWILL, RODOLFO. 1998. *Vivir afuera* (Buenos Aires: Sudamericana)

FONTANA, JUAN CARLOS. 2005. 'Un año sin amor va hacia Berlín', *La Prensa*, 7 February

FOSTER, DAVID WILLIAM. 1998. *Buenos Aires: Perspectives on the City and Cultural Production* (Gainsville: University of Florida Press)

——2003. *Queer Issues in Latin American Cinema* (Austin: University of Texas Press)

FOSTER, KEN. 2001. 'Barbet Schroeder', *Bomb Magazine*, 77, <http://www.bombsite.com/schroeder/schroder.html> [accessed 15 January 2007]

FOUCAULT, MICHEL. 1967. *Madness and Civilization: A History of Insanity in the Age of Reason*, trans. by Richard Howard (London: Vintage)

——1978. *The History of Sexuality, Volume 1*, trans. by Robert Hurley (London: Allen Lane)

FREYRE, GILBERTO. 1964. *The Masters and the Slaves: A Study in the Development of Brazilian Civilisation*, trans. by Samual Putnam (New York: Alfred A. Knopf)

FRY, PETER. 1982. *Para inglês ver: identidade e política na cultura brasileira* (Rio de Janeiro: Zahar)

GARCÍA, WILTON. 2004. *Homoerotismo e imagem no Brasil* (São Paulo: U.N. Nojosa)

GARCÍA CANCLINI, NESTOR. 1995. *Hybrid Cultures: Strategies for Entering and Leaving Modernity*, translated by Christopher L. Chiappari and Silvia L. López (Minneapolis: University of Minnesota Press)

——1997. *Imaginarios urbanos* (Buenos Aires: Ediciones Eudeba)

GIBSON-GRAHAM, J. K. 1996. *The End of Capitalism as We Knew It: A Feminist Critique of Political Economy* (Oxford: Blackwell)

GOLDSTEIN, DONNA. 2003. *Laughter Out of Place: Race, Class, Violence and Sexuality in a Rio Shantytown* (Berkeley: University of California Press)

GORBATO, VIVIANA, and SUSANA FINKEL. 1995. *Amor y sexo en la Argentina: la vida erótica en los 90* (Buenos Aires: Planeta)

GORBATO, VIVIANA. 1999. *Fruta prohibida: un recorrido por lugares, costumbres, estilo, historias, testimonios y anécdotas de una sexualidad diferente: la cara oculta de la Argentina gay* (Buenos Aires: Atlantida)

GREEN, JAMES. 1999. *Beyond Carnival: Male Homosexuality in Twentieth Century Brazil* (Chicago: Chicago University Press)

GREGORY, DEREK, and others (eds). 2000. *The Dictionary of Human Geography* (Oxford: Blackwell)

GUASCH, ÒSCAR. 2000. *La crisis de la heterosexualidad* (Barcelona: Editorial Laertes)

GUGLER, JOSEF. 2004. *World Cities Beyond the West: Globalization, Development and Inequality* (Cambridge: Cambridge University Press)

HALPERIN, DAVID. 1995. *Saint Foucault: Towards a Gay Hagiography* (Oxford: Oxford University Press)

HARAWAY, DONNA. 1991. *Simians, Cyborgs, and Women: The Reinvention of Nature* (New York: Routledge)

HARVEY, DAVID. 1990. *The Condition of Postmodernity: An Enquiry into the Origins of Cultural Change* (Cambridge: Blackwell)

HAVER, WILLIAM WENDELL. 1996. *The Body of this Death: Historicity and Sociality in the Time of AIDS* (Stanford, CA: Stanford University Press)

HEISE, TATIANA. 2012. *Remaking Brazil: Contested National Identities in Contemporary Brazilian Cinema* (Cardiff: University of Wales Press)

HENTSCHKE, JENS R. (ed.). 2006. *Vargas and Brazil: New Perspectives* (New York: Palgrave Macmillan)

HERSHBERG, ERIC, and FRED ROSEN (eds). 2006. *Latin America after Neoliberalism: Turning the Tide in the 21st Century?* (New York & London: New Press)

HIGGS, DAVID. 1999. 'Rio de Janeiro', in *Queer Sites: Gay Urban Histories since 1600*, ed. by David Higgs (London: Routledge), pp. 138–63

——2003. 'Tales of Two Carmelites: Inquisitorial Narratives from Portugal and Brazil', in *Infamous Desire: Male Homosexuality in Colonial Latin America*, ed. by Pete Sigal (Chicago: Chicago University Press), pp. 152–68

HILL, W. JOHN, and PAMELA CHURCH GIBSON. 2000. *American Cinema and Hollywood: Critical Approaches* (Oxford: Oxford University Press)

HOFF, BENEDICT. 2008. '(Re) Traçando o armário de celulóide: espaço, homoerotismo e identidade no cinema latino-americano contemporâneo', *Contracampo: Revista do Programa de Pós-Graduação em Comunicação*, 19: 22–39

——2009. 'Uma experiência com a linguagem do cinema: objectivos, efeitos e consequências (*Dependencia sexual* de Rodrigo Bellot, 2003)', in *Geografias do corpo: ensaios de geografia cultural*, ed. by Ana Francisca de Azevedo, José Ramiro Pimento and João Sarmento (Porto: Figuerinhas), pp. 123–44

——2016. 'Representing and Performing Interracial Love in the Roles of Lázaro Ramos: The Black Body Reframed', in *Stars and Stardom in Brazilian Cinema*, ed. by Lisa Shaw, Tim Bergfelder and João Luiz Vieira (London: Berghahn)

HOLANDA, NESTOR DE. 1969. *Memórias do Café Nice: subterrâneos da música popular e da vida boêmia do Rio de Janeiro* (Rio de Janeiro: Conquista)

HOPKINS, JEFF. 1994. 'Mapping of Cinematic Places: Icons, Ideology and the Power of (Mis) Representation', in *Place, Power, Situation and Spectacle: A Geography of Film*, ed. by Stuart Aikten and Leo Zonn (Lanham: Rowman and Littlefield), pp. 47–65

HOWE, DESSON. 2001. 'Our Lady of the Assassins', *The Washington Post*, 27 September, <http://www.washingtonpost.com/ac2/wp-dyn?pagename=article&contentId=A3554 6–2001Sep27&notFound=true> [accessed 1 July 2008]

HULET, CLAUDE L. 1974. *Brazilian Literature: 1880–1920: Naturalism, Realism-Parnassianism, Symbolism* (Georgetown: Georgetown University Press)

HYLTON, FORREST. 2007. '"Extreme Makeover": Medellín in the New Millenium', in *Evil Paradises: Dreamworlds of Neo-Liberalism*, ed. by Mike Davis and Daniel Bertrand Monk (New York: New Press), pp. 153–63

JÁUREGUI, CARLOS. 1987. *La homosexualidad en la Argentina* (Buenos Aires: Ediciones Tarso)

JÁUREGUI, CARLOS, and JUANA SUÁREZ. 2002. 'Profilaxis, traducción y ética: la humanidad "desechable" en *Rodrigo D, no futuro, La vendedora de rosas* y *La virgen de los sicarios*', *Revista Iberoamericana*, 68:199 (April-June): 367–92

JOHNSON, CHARLES. 1994. 'A Phenomenology of the Black Body', in *The Male Body: Features, Destinies, Exposures*, ed. by Laurence Goldstein (Ann Arbor: University of Michigan Press), pp. 121–35

JULES-ROSETTE, BENNETTA. 2007. *Josephine Baker in Art and Life: The Icon and the Image* (Urbana and Chicago: University of Illinois Press)

JURADO, JUAN CARLOS. 2003. 'Socialización familiar urbana en Medellín: problemas y tendencias contemporáneas', *Historia Crítica*, 25 (December): 165–87

KANTARIS, GEOFFREY. 2002. 'Violent Visions: Representations of Violence in Contemporary Latin American Urban Cinema', in *Cambridge International Studies Association Conference on Popular Culture and the Political Discourse of Violence*, 18 May 2002, University of Cambridge

KNOPP, LARRY. 1990. 'Exploiting the Rent-gap: The Theoretical Significance of Using Illegal Appraisal Schemes to Encourage Gentrification in New Orleans', *Urban Geography*, 11 (1): 48–64

——1992. 'Sexuality and the Spatial Dynamics of Capitalism', *Society and Space*, 10 (6): 651–69

——1995. 'Sexuality and Urban Space: A Framework for Analysis', in *Mapping Desire*, ed. by David Bell and Gill Valentine (London: Routledge), pp. 149–64

KOONINGS, KEES, and DIRK KRUJIT (eds). 2007. *Fractured Cities: Social Exclusion, Urban Violence and Contested Spaces in Latin America* (London: Zed Books)

KORNBLIT, ANALIA. 1997. *Y la SIDA es entre nosotros: un estudio sobre actitudes, creencias y conductas de grupos golpeados por la enfermedad* (Buenos Aires: Corregidor)

KREISLER, HARRY. 2001. 'Conversation with Manuel Castells', *Globetrotter Berkeley*, <http://globetrotter.berkeley.edu/people/Castells/castells-cono.html> [accessed 1 July 2009]

LACEY, E. A. 1991. 'Latin America: Myths and Realities', in *Gay Roots: Twenty Years of Gay Sunshine: An Anthology of Gay History, Sex, Politics and Culture Vol 1*, ed. by Winston Leyland (San Francisco: Gay Sunshine Press), pp. 481–502

LANCASTER, ROGER N. 1992. *Life is Hard: Machismo, Danger and the Intimacy of Power in Nicaragua* (Berkeley: University of California Press)

LANGBRIDGE, DARREN, and MEG BARKER (eds). 2007. *Safe, Sane and Consensual: Contemporary Perspectives on Sadomasochism* (Basingstoke: Palgrave Macmillan)

LAPA, TOMÁS DE ALBUQUERQUE. 1987. *O Recife de frente e de perfil: estudo de uma paisagem urbana* (Recife: Inojosa)

LARVIE, PATRICK. 1999. 'Natural Born Targets: Male Hustlers and AIDS Prevention in Urban Brazil', in *Men Who Sell Sex: International Perspectives on Male Prostitution and AIDS*, ed. by Peter Aggleton (London: UCL Press), pp. 159–76

LEFEBVRE, HENRI. 1991. *The Production of Space* (Oxford: Blackwell)

LERER, DIEGO. 2005. 'Cuero cien por ciento argentine', *Clarín*, 24 March, <http://edant. clarin.com/diario/2005/03/24/espectaculos/c-00701.htm> [accessed 17 Feb 2015].

LEYLAND, WINSTON (ed.). 1979. *Now the Volcano: Anthology of Latin America Gay Literature* (San Francisco: Gay Sunshine Press)

—— 1983. *My Deep Dark Pain is Love: A Collection of Latin American Gay Fiction* (San Francisco: Gay Sunshine Press)

LUKINBEAL, CHRIS. 2005. 'Cinematic Landscapes', *Journal of Cultural Geography*, 23 (1): 3–22

LYOTARD, JEAN-FRANÇOIS. 1984. *The Postmodern Condition: A Report on Knowledge*, trans. by Geoff Bennington and Brian Massumi (Manchester: Manchester University Press)

MARTIN, EMILY. 1994. *Flexible Bodies: Tracking Immunity in American Culture from the Days of Polio to the Age of AIDS* (Boston: Beacon Press)

MARTIN, MICHAEL. 1997. *The New Latin American Cinema* (Detroit, MI: Wayne State University Press)

MARTINS, LUIS. 2015. *Noturno da Lapa* (Rio de Janeiro: Editora José Olympio)

MARTIN-JONES, DAVID 2006. *Deleuze, Cinema and National Identity: Narrative Time in National Contexts* (Edinburgh: Edinburgh University Press)

MASSEY, DOREEN. 2005. *For Space* (London: SAGE)

—— 2007. 'What Does This Place Stand For?', seminar given at the University of Liverpool, 23 February

McCANN, BRYAN. 2004. *Hello, Hello Brazil: Popular Music in the Making of Modern Brazil* (Durham, NC: Duke University Press)

McCLINTOCK, ANNE. 1995. *Imperial Leather: Race, Gender, and Sexuality in the Colonial Conquest* (New York: Routledge)

McDOWELL, LINDA, and JOANNE SHARP. 1999. *A Feminist Glossary of Human Geography* (London: Routledge)

MECCIA, ERNESTO. 2006. *La cuestión gay: un enfoque sociológico* (Buenos Aires: Gran Aldea Editores)

MEDEIROS DE CARVALHO, LUIZ FERNANDO. 1980. *Ismael Silva: samba e resistência* (Rio de Janeiro: José Olympio)

MENDONÇA FILHO, KLEBER. 2003A. 'Realismo Faux', in *Cinemascopio*, <http://cf.uol.com. br/cinemascopio/critica.cfm?CodCritica=874> [accessed 14 February 2007]

—— 2003B. 'O povão faz figuração, filme dá choque no sistema', in *Cinemascopio*, <http:// cf.uol.com.br/cinemascopio/critica.cfm?CodCritica=930> [accessed 14 February 2007]

MONTEAGUDO, LUCIANO. 2005. 'Anahí Berneri habla de *Un ano sin amor*', *Cultura e Espectáculos*, 2 February

MONTOYA, PABLO. 2001. '*La virgen de los sicarios*: una película en cinco movimentos', *Kinetiscopio*, 55: 89–105

MOTT, LUIZ. 2000. *Violação dos direitos humanos e assassinatos de homossexuais no Brasil* (Salvador: Editora Grupo Gay de Bahia)

——2003. 'Crypto-Sodomites in Colonial Brazil', in *Infamous Desire: Male Homosexuality in Colonial Brazil*, ed. by Pete Sigal (Chicago: University of Chicago Press), pp. 168–96

MURRAY, STEPHEN O. 1995. *Latino Male Homosexualities* (Albuquerque: University of New Mexico Press)

NAGIB, LÚCIA. 2006. 'Towards a Positive Definition of World Cinema', in *Remapping World Cinema: Identity, Culture and Politics in Film*, ed. by Stephanie Dennison and Song Hwee Lim (London: Wallflower), pp. 30–37

——2007. *Brazil On Screen: Cinema Novo, New Cinema, Utopia* (London: I. B. Tauris)

NAZZARI, MURIEL. 1991. *Disappearance of the Dowry: Women, Families and Social Change in São Paulo, Brazil, 1600–1900* (Stanford, CA: Stanford University Press)

NORONHO, LUIZ. 2003. *Malandros: notícias de um submundo distante* (Rio de Janeiro: Relume Dumará)

NORTH, PETER, and ULLI HUBER. 2004. 'Alternative Spaces of the "Argentinazo"', *Antipode*, 36/5: 963–84

NOWELL-SMITH, GEOFFREY (ed.). 1996. *The Oxford History of World Cinema* (Oxford: Oxford University Press)

NOYES, JOHN K. 1997. *Mastery of Submission: Inventions of Masochism* (Ithaca, NY: Cornell University Press)

ONG, AIHWA. 1999. *Flexible Citizenship: The Cultural Logics of Transnationality* (Durham, NC: Duke University Press)

ORELLA, OSA, and RAQUEL ORELLA. 1994. *Guía erótica de Buenos Aires* (Buenos Aires: Ediciones Temas de Hoy)

PAEZZO, SYLVAN. 1972. *Memórias de Madame Satã* (Rio de Janeiro: Lidador)

PAGE, JOANNA. 2009. *Crisis and Capitalism in Contemporary Argentine Cinema* (Durham, NC: Duke University Press)

PARKER, RICHARD. 1999. *Beneath the Equator: Cultures of Desire, Male Homosexuality and Emerging Gay Communities in Brazil* (New York: Routledge)

——2009. *Bodies, Pleasures and Passions: Sexual Culture in Contemporary Brazil* (Nashville, TN: Vanderbilt University Press)

PARRY, BENITA. 1987. 'Current Problems in the Study of Colonial Discourse', *Oxford Literary Review*, 9.1/2: 27–58

PASOLINI, PIER PAOLO. 1975. 'L'abiura dalla trilogia della vita', in *Trilogia della vita: Decameron, I racconti di Canterbury, Il fiore delle mille e una notte* (Bologna: Cappelli), pp. 11–13

—— 1988. *Una vita violenta* (Milan: Garzanti)

PAULSON, SUSAN. 2006. 'Connecting Queer Studies of Men Who Desire Men with Feminist Analysis of Unmarried Women in Bolivia', *Lasa Forum*, XXXVI:3: 12–15

PEÑA, RICHARD. 2005. *The Film in Context* [DVD Extra] (New York: First Run Features)

PHILLIPS, RICHARD, and DIANE WATT. 2000. 'Introduction', in *Decentring Sexualities: Politics and Representations Beyond the Metropolis* ed. by Richard Phillips, Diane Watt and David Shuttleton (London & New York: Routledge), pp. 1–16

PHILLIPS, RICHARD. 2006. *Sex, Politics and Empire: A Postcolonial Geography* (Manchester: Manchester University Press)

PICK, ZUZANA. 1993. *The New Latin American Cinema: A Continental Project* (Austin: University of Texas Press)

PILE, STEVE. 1996. *The Body and the City: Psychoanalysis, Space and Subjectivity* (London: Routledge)

POLHEMUS, TED, and HOUSK RANDALL. 1994. *Rituals of Love: Sexual Experiments, Erotic Possibilities* (London: Routledge)

PITT-RIVERS, JULIAN A. 1971. *Los hombres de la sierra: ensayo sociológico sobre un pueblo andaluz* (Barcelona: Ediciones Grijalbo)

QUIROGA, JOSÉ. 2000. *Tropics of Desire: Interventions from Queer Latino America* (New York & London: New York University Press)

REBHUN, LINDA-ANNE. 1999. *The Heart is Unknown Country: Love in the Changing Economy of Northeast Brazil* (Stanford, CA: Stanford University Press)

REYNOLDS, ROBERT. 2002. *From Camp to Queer: Re-making the Australian Homosexual* (Melbourne: Melbourne University Press)

RIAÑO-ALCALÁ, PILAR. 2006. *Dwellers of Memory: Youth and Violence in Medellín, Colombia* (London & New Brunswick, NJ: Transaction Publishers)

RIBEIRO, MIGUEL ANGELO. 2002. *Território e prostituição na metrópole carioca* (Rio de Janeiro: Ecomusen Fluminense)

ROLDÁN, MARY. 1999. 'Colombia: Cocaine and the 'Miracle' of Modernity in Medellín', in *Cocaine: Global Histories*, ed. by Paul Gootenberg (Abingdon: Routledge), pp. 165–82

SÁ, LÚCIA. 2007. *Life in the Megalopolis: Mexico City and São Paulo* (London: Routledge)

SABORIDO, JORGE, and LUCIANO DE PRIVITELLIO. 2006. *Breve historia de la Argentina* (Madrid: Alianza Editorial)

SAFFORD, FRANK, and MARCO PALACIOS. 2002. *Colombia: Fragmented Land, Divided Society* (New York & Oxford: Oxford University Press)

SALAZAR, ALONSO. 1992. *Born to Die in Medellín*, trans. by Nick Caistor (London: Latin American Bureau)

SALESSI, JORGE. 1995A. 'The Argentine Dissemination of Homosexuality, 1890–1914', in *Entiendes? Queer Readings, Hispanic Writings*, ed. by Emilie Bergman and Paul J. Smith (Durham, NC: Duke University Press), pp. 40–91

—— 1995B. *Médicos, maleantes y maricas: higiene, criminología y homosexualidad en la construcción de la nación Argentina, Buenos Aires, 1871–1914* (Buenos Aires: B. Viterbo Editora)

SÁNCHEZ-EPPLER, BENIGNO, and CINDY PATTON. 2000. *Queer Diasporas* (Durham, NC: Duke University Press)

SARABIA, DIANA LUCÍA. 2007. 'El carnaval en la representación del sicario y el intelectual en *La virgen de los sicarios*', *Revista de Estudios Colombianos*, 31: 30–44

SARLO, BEATRIZ. 2001. *Scenes from Postmodern Life*, translated by Jon Beasley-Murray (Minneapolis: University of Minnesota Press)

SASSEN, SASKIA. 2001. *The Global City: New York, London, Tokyo* (Princeton, NJ: Princeton University Press)

—— 2004. 'The Global City', in *A Companion to the Anthropology of Politics*, ed. by David Nugent and Joan Vincent (Oxford: Blackwell), pp. 168–77

SCHEPER-HUGHES, NANCY. 1992. *Death Without Weeping: The Violence of Everyday Life in Brazil* (London: University of California Press)

SCHIFTER, JACOBO. 1998. *Lila's House: Male Prostitution in Latin America* (New York: Hayworth)

SEIDMAN, STEVEN. 1995. 'Deconstructing Queer Theory or the Under-theorization of the Social and the Ethical', in *Social Postmodernism: Beyond Identity Politics*, ed. by Linda Nicholson and S. Seidman (Cambridge: Cambridge University Press), pp. 116–41

SHARPLEY-WHITING, T. DENEAN. 1999. *Black Venus: Sexualised Savages, Primal Fears and Primitive Narratives* (Durham, NC: Duke University Press)

SHAW, LISA. 1999. *The Social History of the Brazilian Samba* (Aldershot: Ashgate)

—— 2007. 'Afro-Brazilian Identity: Malandragem and Homosexuality in Madame Satã', in *Contemporary Latin American Cinema: Breaking into the Global Market*, ed. by Deborah Shaw (Lanham, MD, & Plymouth: Rowman and Littlefield), pp. 87–104

SHAW, LISA, and STEPHANIE DENNISON. 2005. *Pop Culture in Latin America! Media, Arts and Lifestyle* (Santa Barbara, CA: ABC-Clio)

—— 2007. *Brazilian National Cinema* (London & New York: Routledge)

—— (eds). 2005. *Latin American Cinema: Essays on Modernity, Gender and National Identity* (Jefferson, NC, & London: McFarland)

SHAW, LISA. 2011. '"What does the 'baiana' have?" Josephine Baker and the Performance of

Afro-Brazilian Female Subjectivity on Stage', *English Language Notes*, 49(1), 91-106

SHERIFF, ROBIN E. 2001. *Dreaming Equality: Color, Race and Racism in Urban Brazil* (New Brunswick, NJ: Rutgers University Press)

SHIEL, MARK, and TONY FITZMAURICE. 2001. *Cinema and the City: Film and Urban Societies in Global Context* (Oxford: Blackwell)

SHIELDS, ROB. 1991. *Places on the Margin: Alternative Geographies of Modernity* (London: Routledge)

SHOHAT, ELLA, and ROBERT STAM. 1994. *Unthinking Eurocentrism: Multiculturalism and the Media* (London: Routledge)

SIGAL, PETE. 2003. *Infamous Desire: Male Homosexuality in Colonial Latin America* (Chicago: University of Chicago Press)

SIMMEL, GEORG. 2010. 'The Metropolis and Mental Life', in *The Blackwell City Reader*, ed. by Gary Bridge and Sophie Watson (Oxford: Wiley-Blackwell), pp. 103–10

SIMONS, GEOFFREY LESLIE. 2004. *Colombia: A Brutal History* (London: Saqi Books)

SIMPSON, MARK. 1999. *It's a Queer World: Deviant Adventures in Pop Culture* (New York: Harrington Park Press)

SINFIELD, ALAN. 1998. *The Gay and After* (London: Serpent's Tail)

——2000. 'The Production of Gay and the Return to Power', in *Decentring Sexualities: Politics and Representations Beyond the Metropolis*, ed. by Richard Phillips and others (London & New York: Routledge), pp. 21–36

SÍVORI, HORACIO FEDERICO. 2005. *Locas, chongos y gays: sociabilidad homosexual masculina durante la década de 1990* (Buenos Aires: Editorial Antropofagia)

SOJA, EDWARD W. 1980. 'The Socio-spatial Dialectic', *Annals of the Association of American Geographers* 70.2: 207–25

SONTAG, SUSAN. 1991. *Under the Sign of Saturn* (New York: Anchor Books)

SOUSA SANTOS, BOAVENTURA DE. 1992. 'Law, State and Urban Struggles in Recife', *Social Legal Studies*, 1: 235–55

SOTHERN, MATTHEW. 2007. 'HIV + Bodyspace: AIDS and the Queer Politics of Future Negation in Aotearoa / New Zealand', in *Geographies of Sexualities: Theory, Practices and Politics*, ed. by Kath Browne and others (Farnham: Ashgate), pp. 181–94

SPIVAK, GAYATRI CHAKRAVORTY. 1988. 'Can the Subaltern Speak?', in *Marxism and the Interpretation of Culture*, ed. by Cary Nelson and Lawrence Grossberg (London: Macmillan), pp. 271–315

STAM, ROBERT. 1997. *Tropical Multiculturalism: A Comparative History of Race in Brazilian Cinema and Culture* (Durham, NC: Duke University Press)

STAM, ROBERT, and RANDAL JOHNSON. 1995. *Brazilian Cinema* (New York: Columbia University Press)

STAVANS, ILÁN. 1996. 'The Latin Phallus', in *Muy Macho: Latino Men Confront Their Manhood*, ed. by Ray González (Toronto: Anchor Books), pp. 143–64

SUARÉZ, JUANA. 2012. *Critical Essays on Colombian Cinema and Culture: Cinembargo Colombia* (London: Palgrave Macmillan)

SUBERO, GUSTAVO. 2014A. *Queer Masculinities in Latin American Cinema: Male Bodies and Narrative Representations* (London: I. B. Taurus)

——2014B. *Representations of HIV/AIDS in Contemporary Hispano-American and Caribbean Culture: Cuerpos suiSIDAs* (Farnham: Ashgate)

SULLIVAN, NIKKI. 2003. *A Critical Introduction to Queer Theory* (Edinburgh: Edinburgh University Press)

TAYLOR, GARY, and JANE USHER. 2001. 'Making Sense of S/M: A Discourse Analytic Account', *Sexualities*, 4:3: 293–314

TREXLER, RICHARD C. 1995. *Sex and Conquest: Gendered Violence, Political Order, and the European Conquest of the Americas* (Ithaca, NY: Cornell Univesity Press)

——2003. 'Gender Subordination and Political Hierarchy in Pre-Hispanic America' in

Infamous Desire: Male Homosexuality in Colonial Latin American ed. by Pete Sigal (Chicago: University of Chicago Press) pp.70–101

TURNER, VICTOR. 1974. *Dramas, Fields, and Metaphors: Symbolic Action in Human Society* (Ithaca, NY: Cornell University Press)

WINDDANCE TWINE, FRANCE. 1998. *Racism in a Racial Democracy: The Maintenance of White Supremacy in Brazil* (New Brunswick, NJ: Rutgers University Press)

URREA GIRALDO, FERNANDO, and OTHERS. 2006. 'Tensiones en la construcción de identidades de jóvenes negros homosexuals en Cali', *Race and Sexuality in Latin America Symposium*, 9–10 December 2006, University of Manchester

VIANNA, HERMANO. 1999. *The Mystery of Samba: Popular Music & National Identity in Brazil* (Chapel Hill: University of North Carolina Press)

WALKOWITZ, JUDITH R. 1980. *Prostitution and Victorian Society: Women, Class and the State* (Cambridge: Cambridge University Press)

WERNECK, A. 2002. 'A anti-Lapa de Karim Aïnouz: bairro surge recriado pelo fotografia', *Jornal do Brasil*, Caderno B, 17 December

WILLIAMS, JUDITH MICHELLE. 2006. 'Uma Mulata, Sim!: Araci Cortes, "the mulatta" of the Teatro de Revista', *Women & Performance: A Journal of Feminist Theory*, 16 (1): 7–26

WILLIAMS, LINDA. 1989. *Hardcore: Power, Pleasure and the 'Frenzy of the Invisible'* (Berkeley: University of California Press, 1989)

WINTZ, CARY D., and PAUL FINKLEMAN (eds). 2004. *Encyclopedia of the Harlem Renaissance* (New York: Routledge)

WOLF, SERGIO. 1993. 'Cuestión de poeticas: los otros cines argentinos', *Film*, 3: 265–79

ZANCHETI, S. M. 2005. 'Development Versus Urban Conservation in Recife: A Problem of Governance and Public Management', *City & Time*, 1, 3:2: 15–27

ZARETSKI, ELI. 1976. *Capitalism, the Family and Personal Life* (London: Pluto Press)

FILMOGRAPHY

21 Grams (Alejandro González Iñárritu, USA, 2003)
Alias Gardelito (Lautaro Murúa, Argentina, 1961)
Amarelo manga (Cláudio Assis, Brazil, 2002)
Amores perros (Alejandro González Iñárritu, Mexico, 2000)
Un año sin amor (Anahí Berneri, Argentina, 2005)
Baile perfumado (Paulo Caldas, Brazil, 1997)
Below the Equator (Fox Film Corporation, USA, 1927)
Bombón el perro (Carlos Sorin, Argentina/Spain, 2004)
O beijo da mulher aranha (Hector Babenco, Brazil/USA, 1985)
Capitães da Areia (Cecilia Amado, Brazil, 2011)
Carandiru (Hector Babenco, Brazil/Argentina/Italy, 2003)
Cenizas del paraíso (Marcelo Piñeyro, Argentina, 1997)
Central do Brasil (Walter Salles, Brazil/France, 1998)
Cidade Baixa (Sérgio Machado, Brazil, 2005)
Cidade de Deus (Fernando Meirelles, Brazil/France, 2002)
Cinco vezes favela (Miguel Borges & Joaquim Pedro de Andrade, Brazil, 1962)
Cinema, aspirinas e urubus (Marcelo Gomes, Brazil, 2005)
El cielo dividido (Julián Hernández, Mexico, 2006)
Le clan (Gaël Morel, France, 2004)
Comodines (Jorge Nisco & Daneil Barone, Argentina, 1997)
Crónica de un niño solo (Leonardo Favio, Argentina, 1964)
Cruising (William Friedkin, USA/West Germany, 1980)
Dangerous Lives: Coming Out in the Developing World (John Scagllioti, USA, 2003)
Dependencia sexual (Rodrigo Bellott, Bolivia/USA, 2003)
Dibu: la película (Carlos Olivieri & Alejandro Stoessel, Argentina, 1997)
Doña Herlinda y su hijo (Jaime Humberto, Mexico, 1985)
En el paraíso no existe el dolor (Víctor Saca, Mexico, 1995)
Fresa y chocolate (Tomás Gutiérrez Alea & Juan Carlos Tabío, Cuba/Mexico/Spain/USA
    1994)
La furia (Juan Bautista Stagnaro, Argentina, 1997)
Os fuzis (Ruy Guerra, Brazil, 1964)
La historia oficial (Luis Puenzo, Argentina, 1985)
Homme au bain (Christophe Honoré, France, 2010)
O Invasor (Beto Brant, Brazil, 2002)
Irréversible (Gaspar Noé, France, 2002)
La león (Santiago Otheguy, Argentina/France, 2007)
El lugar sin límites (Arturo Ripstein, Mexico, 1978)
Madame Satã (Karim Aïnouz, Brazil/France, 2002)
Memento (Christopher Nolan, USA, 2000)
Moonraker (Lewis Gilbert, UK/France, 1979)
Mundo grua (Pablo Trapero, Argentina, 1999)
Mulheres do Brasil (Malu de Martino, Brazil, 2006)

Noel: Poeta da vila (Ricardo Van Steen, Brazil, 2006)
Night Hawks (Ron Peck, UK, 1981)
No se lo digas a nadie (Francisco José Lombardi, Peru/Spain)
Nueve reinas (Fabián Bielinsky, Argentina, 2000)
Los olvidados (Luís Buñuel, Mexico, 1950)
Pizza, birra, faso (Adrián Caetano & Bruno Stagnaro, Argentina,1998)
Princesse Tam-Tam (Edmond T. Gréville, France, 1935)
Rio (Carlos Saldanha, USA, 2011)
Rio, 40 Graus (Nelson Pereira dos Santos, Brazil, 1955)
Rio, Zona Norte (Nelson Pereira dos Santos, Brazil, 1957)
Ronda nocturna (Edgardo Cozarinsky, Argentina/France, 2005)
Run Lola Run (Tom Twyker, Germany, 1998)
La sortie des usines (Louis Lumière, France, 1895)
Strip Jack Naked (Night Hawks 2) (Ron Peck, UK, 1991)
Tan de repente (Diego Lerman, Argentina/Netherlands, 2002)
Texas Hotel (Cláudio Assis, Brazil, 1999)
Tiempo de revancha (Adolfo Aristarain, Argentina, 1981)
Vagón fumador (Verónica Chen, Argentina, 2001)
Viajo porque preciso, volto porque te amo (Karim Aïnouz & Marcelo Gomes, Brazil, 2009)
Vidas secas (Nelson Pereira dos Santos, Brazil, 1964)
La virgen de los sicarios (Barbet Schroeder, Colombia/France/Spain, 2000)
XXY (Lucía Puenzo, Argentina/Spain/France, 2005)

Television Series

Cartas de amor en cassette (Claudio Ferrari & Gabriel Fullone, Argentina, 1993)
Como pan caliente (Jorge Maestro & Gastón Pesacq, Argentina, 1996)
Queer As Folk (Sarah Harding & Charles McDougall, UK, 1999–2000)
Verdad/Consecuencia (Daniel Barone, Argentina, 1996)
Zona de riesgo 2: atendida por sus propios dueños (Alberto Ure & Guillermo Íbalo, Argentina, 1992)

INDEX

Lightning Source UK Ltd.
Milton Keynes UK
UKOW07n1850120317
296435UK00008B/48/P